Praise for *Our Sec*

MW00809308

This book treats a difficult but crucial topic for the Christian life in a way that is both true to Scripture and pastorally sensitive. Written for a wide audience, not only pastors and teachers but other interested persons will find reading it edifying as well as instructive.

— **Richard B. Gaffin Jr.,** Westminster Theological Seminary

God's people often wrestle with family and friends who turn away from following the Lord. Robert Peterson gives wise, biblical, and pastoral insight into the problem of apostasy and the promises of God's preservation. Not only does he treat literally scores of biblical texts on these issues, but carefully collates these into a clear theological statement shaped by a pastoral heart. This is not only a book to read, but also one to share.

— **Sean Michael Lucas,** First Presbyterian Church

Vintage Peterson! Fresh, crisp, clear, honest, insightful, and edifying, this work is arguably the most helpful resource on the subject written for pastors, teachers, small group leaders, and interested church members.

— **Christopher W. Morgan,** California Baptist University

Our Secure Salvation offers a well-informed and warm pastoral exposition of the biblical teaching regarding preservation, perseverance, assurance, and apostasy. Readers will find strength and encouragement from both the biblical and theological themes so capably explained by Robert Peterson. I am confident that the careful and irenic presentation found in this volume will be helpful for Calvinists and non-Calvinists alike. It is a joy to recommend this book.

— **David S. Dockery,** Union Unviersity

Praise for the Explorations in Biblical Theology Series

Under the trusty captaincy of Professor Robert Peterson, a crew of seasoned Reformed sailors has set out to encompass a new Treasure Island—an up-to-the-minute, mid-range, pastorally focused collection of Explorations in Biblical Theology, covering the main themes of the Reformed faith and the main biblical books that set them forth. These are books to look out for, and to collect as they see the light of day. It is already clear that they will demonstrate afresh the truth, life, light, and power that the old Reformed faith can still bring to a befuddled and benighted world.

—**J. I. Packer,** Regent College

Explorations in Biblical Theology is a gift to God's people. Biblical theology was never meant to be reserved for academics. When the verities of the Reformed faith are taken from the "ivy halls" of academia and placed in the hearts and minds of the covenant people of God, reformation and revival are the inevitable result. I believe God will use this series as a mighty tool for the Kingdom.

—**Steve Brown,** Reformed Theological Seminary

There are many misconceptions today about systematic, biblical, and applicatory theology. One sometimes gets the impression that these are opposed to one another, and that the first two, at least, are so obscure that ordinary people should avoid them like the plague. The series Explorations in Biblical Theology seeks to correct these misunderstandings, to bring these disciplines together in a winsome, clear unity, edifying to non-specialists. The authors are first-rate, and they write to build up our faith, by pointing us to Christ. That's what biblical and systematic theology at their best have always done, and the best application of Scripture has always shown us in practical ways how to draw on the rich blessings of Jesus' salvation. I hope that many will read these books and take them to heart.

—**John Frame,** Reformed Theological Seminary

Explorations in Biblical Theology is a valuable new series of books on doctrinal themes that run through Scripture. The contributors are competent scholars who love to serve the church and have special expertise in the Bible and its theology. Following a thematic approach, each volume explores a distinctive doctrine as it is taught in Scripture, or else introduces the various doctrines taught in a particular book of the Bible. The result is a fresh and unique contribution to our understanding of the Bible's own theology.

—**Philip Ryken,** Tenth Presbyterian Church, Philadelphia

The message of a God who loved us before he formed the earth, called us his own before we could respond to him, died for us while we were dead in our transgressions and sins, made us alive when we were incapable of serving him, unites us to himself so that we can be forever holy, and now loves us more than we love ourselves—sparked a Reformation of hope and joy that transformed the world of faith. Re-declaring that hope and reclaiming that joy is the ambition and delight of this series of Explorations in Biblical Theology. Able and godly scholars trace the golden thread of grace that unites all Scripture to make the wonders of our God's redeeming love shine and win hearts anew. The writing is warm, winsome and respectful of those who differ. The motives are clearly to reveal truth and expose error by glorifying the message and manner of the Savior.

—**Bryan Chapell,** Covenant Theological Seminary

Neither superficial nor highly technical, this new series of volumes on important Christian doctrines is projected to teach Reformed theology as it is most helpfully taught, with clear grounding in Scripture, mature understanding of theology, gracious interaction with others who disagree, and useful application to life. I expect that these volumes will strengthen the faith and biblical maturity of all who read them, and I am happy to recommend them highly.

—**Wayne Grudem,** Phoenix Seminary

This is a series that the church needs more than ever, as we forge fresh links between the world of biblical studies and our

Reformed theology. The contributors remind us again that the Bible is a book about God and his purposes and encourages us to preach and teach the message of salvation which it contains. It will be an inspiration to many and give us new insight into the faith once delivered to the saints.

—**Gerald Bray,** Beeson Divinity School

The aim of these volumes is clear: as regards God's Word, rigor; as regards other scholars, respect; as regards current issues, relevance; as regards the Lord himself, reverence. Effective witness and ministry currently require more than simply extra effort and better methods: the call is heard from churches across the board for renewal in our grasp of Christian truth. Each author in this series contributes admirably to that urgent need.

—**Robert W. Yarbrough,** Trinity Evangelical Divinity School

The church of Jesus Christ faces massive cultural challenges today. More and more people in the western world are ignorant of or hostile to the Christian faith. The moral fabric of our society is unraveling, and as a result of postmodernism many are adopting a relativistic worldview. Some Christians have responded by trying to simplify and dumb-down the gospel. Others have tried to catch the cultural mood of the day in order to gain more converts, but they have often been co-opted by the culture instead of transforming it for Christ. What we truly need is to dig down deep into biblical foundations, so that our theology is robustly biblical. Only a worldview that is informed by both biblical and systematic theology can withstand the intellectual challenges that face us today. The series Explorations in Biblical Theology is designed to meet this very need. I commend these volumes enthusiastically, for they explain what the Scriptures teach from the standpoint of biblical theology. What we desperately need to hear and learn today is the whole counsel of God. This series advances that very agenda for the edification of the church and to the glory of God.

—**Thomas R. Schreiner,** The Southern Baptist
Theological Seminary

Our Secure Salvation

Explorations in Biblical Theology

*Election and Free Will: God's Gracious Choice
and Our Responsibility*

*Anointed with the Spirit and Power:
The Holy Spirit's Empowering Presence*

The Nearness of God: His Presence with His People

Our Secure Salvation: Preservation and Apostasy

The Elder: Today's Ministry Rooted in All of Scripture

Robert A. Peterson, series editor

Our Secure Salvation

Preservation and Apostasy

Robert A. Peterson

P&R PUBLISHING
P.O. BOX 817 • PHILLIPSBURG • NEW JERSEY 08865-0817

© 2009 by Robert A. Peterson

All rights reserved. No part of this book may be reproduced, stored in a retrieval system, or transmitted in any form or by any means—electronic, mechanical, photocopy, recording, or otherwise—except for brief quotations for the purpose of review or comment, without the prior permission of the publisher, P&R Publishing Company, P.O. Box 817, Phillipsburg, New Jersey 08865–0817.

Unless otherwise indicated, Scripture quotations are from The Holy Bible, English Standard Version, copyright © 2001 by Crossway Bibles, a division of Good News Publishers. Used by permission. All rights reserved.

Scripture quotations marked (NIV) are from the HOLY BIBLE, NEW INTERNATIONAL VERSION®. NIV®. Copyright © 1973, 1978, 1984 by International Bible Society. Used by permission of Zondervan Publishing House. All rights reserved.

Italics within Scripture quotations indicate emphasis added.

Printed in the United States of America

Library of Congress Cataloging-in-Publication Data

Peterson, Robert A., 1948–
  Our secure salvation : preservation and apostasy / Robert A. Peterson.
    p. cm. — (Explorations in biblical theology)
  Includes bibliographical references and indexes.
  ISBN 978-1-59638-043-1 (pbk.)
  1. Salvation—Biblical teaching. 2. Salvation—Christianity. 3. Perseverance (Theology) 4. Assurance (Theology) 5. Apostasy—Christianity. I. Title.
  BS680.S25P48 2009
  234—dc22
                                   2009031077

I fondly dedicate this book to my faithful and loving wife, Mary Pat, whose support and encouragement over thirty-six years of marriage I have too often taken for granted.

Contents

Series Introduction   ix

Acknowledgments   xi

1. Setting the Stage   1
2. Preservation and Apostasy in the Old Testament   11
3. Preservation in the Gospels   27
4. Preservation in Paul, Part 1   51
5. Preservation in Paul, Part 2   69
6. Preservation in the General Epistles   85
7. Warnings in the Gospels and Acts   101
8. Warnings in Paul, Part 1   119
9. Warnings in Paul, Part 2   137
10. Warnings in Hebrews   157
11. Warnings in the Other General Epistles and Revelation   179
12. Connecting the Dots   195

Questions for Study and Reflection   209
Select Resources on Preservation and Apostasy   217
Index of Scripture   219
Index of Subjects and Names

Series Introduction

BELIEVERS TODAY need quality literature that attracts them to good theology and builds them up in their faith. Currently, readers may find several sets of lengthy—and rather technical—books on Reformed theology, as well as some that are helpful and semipopular. Explorations in Biblical Theology takes a more mid-range approach, seeking to offer readers the substantial content of the more lengthy books, on the one hand, while striving for the readability of the semipopular books, on the other.

The series includes two types of books: (1) some treating biblical themes and (2) others treating the theology of specific biblical books. The volumes dealing with biblical themes seek to cover the whole range of Christian theology, from the doctrine of God to last things. Representative early offerings in the series focus on the empowering of the Holy Spirit, justification, the presence of God, preservation and apostasy, and substitutionary atonement. Examples of works dealing with the theology of specific biblical books include volumes on the theology of 1 and 2 Samuel, the Psalms, and Isaiah in the Old Testament, and books on the theology of Mark, Romans, and James in the New Testament.

Explorations in Biblical Theology is written for college seniors, seminarians, pastors, and thoughtful lay readers. These volumes are intended to be accessible and not obscured by excessive references to Hebrew, Greek, or theological jargon.

Each book seeks to be solidly Reformed in orientation, because the writers love the Reformed faith. The various theological themes and biblical books are treated from the perspective of biblical theology. Writers either trace doctrines through the Bible or open up the theology of the specific book they treat. Writers desire not merely to dispense the Bible's good information, but also to apply that information to real needs today.

Explorations in Biblical Theology is committed to being warm and winsome, with a focus on applying God's truth to life. Authors aim to treat those with whom they disagree as they themselves would want to be treated. The motives for the rejection of error are not to fight, hurt, or wound, but to protect, help, and heal. The authors of this series will be godly, capable scholars with a commitment to Reformed theology and a burden to minister that theology clearly to God's people.

ROBERT A. PETERSON
Series Editor

Acknowledgments

I THANK colleagues and friends who read the manuscript and shared comments: Jack Collins, Steve Lentz, Mary Pat Peterson, Mark Ryan, Ray Van Neste, Bob Vannoy, and Steve Wellum.

Thanks also to:

Marvin Padgett of P&R Publishing, for fellowship, cooperation, and aid.

Logan Almy, Dan Barber, and Jeremy Ruch, my TAs, for making suggestions.

Wes Vander Lugt, my former TA, for doing research for chapter 2.

Covenant Seminary's librarians James Pakala and Steve Jamieson, for gracious and expert help.

Chris Morgan, my writing partner, for offering much wise theological counsel in the planning and writing of this book.

Rick Matt, for expertly editing the whole manuscript.

Nick and Ellen Pappas, for kindly inviting me to their "farmhouse" in Bismarck, Missouri, where I spent pleasant days working on the book.

Setting the Stage

IRONICALLY, Slade Thompson found stability in his dangerous job, but in his faith it was a different story. Slade was a roofer whose specialty was the slate roofs on old houses in southeastern Pennsylvania.

"Are you comfortable up there?" I asked him as he climbed up on my roof in Souderton, Pennsylvania, to make repairs.

"Yes, I'm careful, but I know that the Lord will take care of me," came the reply. "He has for twenty years."

"Have you ever fallen?" I asked.

"Twice, and the Lord was with me each time. I was high up and would've been hurt bad if I'd hit the ground. Both times I landed in some bushes that broke my fall."

Though Slade had confidence on the rooftops, it was not the same when it came to the assurance of his salvation. When he had come to Christ, he felt a wonderful sense of forgiveness. Now, a year later, he was unsure if he was saved. He was grateful to the people who had led him to Christ. But now he was troubled about the messages he heard in church. This made him feel guilty because Pastor Atkins was a dedicated man of God who preached the Bible.

Most confusing to Slade was the church's practice of having altar calls every Sunday, during which some of the same people kept going forward. At first Slade thought that these people were rededicating their lives to Christ, but that was not how Pastor

Atkins described it. He explained that they were coming to Christ again for salvation.

"But why do you need to become a Christian over and over?" Slade mused. Because he loved his church, he questioned the "once saved, always saved" view he had heard from other friends, and over time he came to doubt his own salvation. For weeks this bothered him until one day he talked to Pastor Atkins.

"Yes," the pastor explained, "the people coming forward each week are getting saved again. They had come to Christ, but backslid and lost their salvation, just like the book of Hebrews warns. They are getting right with God again."

"But what about me, pastor? Do I lose my salvation each time I doubt?"

Slade was not satisfied with his pastor's answer to that question. He knew Pastor Atkins wanted to help him, but he was not able to assure Slade that he was safe in Christ. The pastor's view that Christians could lose their salvation prevented Slade from resting in Christ.

Frustrated, Slade turned to more earnest prayer and Bible study. Jesus' words spoke to his heart: "I give them eternal life, and they will never perish, and no one will snatch them out of my hand" (John 10:28). But then there were those threatening warning passages in Hebrews 6 and 10. Slade's frustration increased as he thought that maybe the Bible contradicted itself.

Slade is not the only Christian to be troubled by these issues. His story raises important questions for believers of all traditions. These questions especially concern two topics related to the assurance of salvation. The first is *preservation*, often called eternal security, which means that God keeps believers for final salvation. The second topic is *apostasy*, which is denial of the Christian faith formerly professed. Why give attention to preservation and apostasy? Here I offer four answers.

- God Uses Preservation to Assure His Children.
- God Teaches His Children the Need to Persevere to the End.

2

- God Warns His Children of the Danger of Apostasy.
- The Bible Often Speaks of Preservation and Apostasy.

God Uses Preservation to Assure His Children

Sincere Christians are sometimes confused about how two of the Bible's teachings fit together. On the one hand, Scripture says that God wants us to be assured of salvation: "I write these things to you who believe in the name of the Son of God that you may know that you have eternal life" (1 John 5:13). It comforts: "For I am sure that neither death nor life . . . nor anything else in all creation, will be able to separate us from the love of God in Christ Jesus our Lord" (Rom. 8:38–39).

But, on the other hand, the Bible also says, "Examine yourselves, to see whether you are in the faith. Test yourselves. Or do you not realize this about yourselves, that Jesus Christ is in you?—unless indeed you fail to meet the test!" (2 Cor. 13:5). Does God want us to have assurance or not?

Listen as Julie tells her touching story:

A few years ago a good friend of mine tragically took his own life. We had been working together in ministry for two years prior to this. I and many others were devastated. He had fallen into a deep depression and even lost assurance of his faith. When he died he didn't believe that he was saved. I know that I can't have assurance for someone else, but the Bible's teaching of preservation gives me cause to hope that he is with the Lord. We saw the fruit of ministry and the work of the Holy Spirit in his character.

As I grieved the death of my friend, I fell into a deep dread as I wondered if God for some reason simply abandoned him at the end. And what if God did the same to me? I clung to passages like John 6:39, where Jesus says he will lose nothing God has given him but will raise us up on the last day—and he says this more than once!

3

As I studied what Scripture said about preservation I became more deeply convinced of God's power, will, and love to keep his own. He does not hold us by the scruff of the neck that he might let go at any moment (the image that kept returning to my mind as I thought about my friend). God is deeply loving—he loved his own before the beginning of time. No one can snatch us from his hand (John 10:28). How much less would he ever drop us from his hand! I am amazed at his fatherly compassion as he guards and carries us. He will not walk away, turn his back, let us go—he cannot deny himself and his covenant to save those who believe. What comfort!

Julie and her friends passed through deep waters after their friend's suicide. It is normal for them to have doubted their own faith in the light of such a tragedy. But ultimately God used evil for good. Julie came out of her struggle stronger in her faith—which had been tested and proved—as she sought God in his Word. She became "rooted and built up in him and established in the faith" (Col. 2:7). Today she testifies that the Lord used that terrible experience to strengthen her and to prepare her to help others. God does want his children to have assurance of salvation. But sometimes he wants them to test that assurance in order to do something greater in and through them.

I do not want to give the false impression that I have all the answers to the difficult questions people ask concerning assurance. I do not. But I have learned many answers from God's Word and seek to whet your appetite for them here and to explore them more thoroughly in the pages to come.

God Teaches His Children the Need to Persevere to the End

Scripture not only teaches that God will not let his children fall away from salvation—it also teaches that those who profess Christ must persevere to the end to be saved: "[God will present you holy and blameless] if indeed you continue in the faith, stable and steadfast, not shifting from the hope of the gospel that you heard" (Col. 1:23). "Strive for peace with everyone, and for the holiness without which no one will see the Lord" (Heb. 12:14). Only those who continue to believe the gospel will be saved, Paul teaches in Colossians. And the writer to the Hebrews insists that without holiness no person will see the Lord in final glory. For people to profess faith in Christ, therefore, is not enough. We will discuss the Bible's extensive presentation of inadequate faith. A man or woman must truly believe to be saved. We are saved by faith alone, but the faith that saves is never alone; it is evidenced by a changed life.

Unfortunately, it is possible for professing Christians to take advantage of God's grace and to claim that they are saved while living in open sin. Such was the case years ago with a friend whom I will call Craig. Craig left his wife and two small children and moved in with another woman. When the pastor and an elder from his church came to rebuke him for his sin, Craig had a ready answer: "God wants me to be happy, and I am very happy. Sure, what I am doing is wrong, but you and I both know that I am saved." Craig's defiant words buffaloed the young pastor and elder. They *did* believe that he was saved. He had walked with the Lord for years and had given every indication of believing in Christ. His current behavior was entirely inconsistent with his previous life.

When a seminarian heard about the aborted pastoral visit to Craig, he was unhappy: "I too think that Craig is a Christian, but one thing is certain: He is not now living the way a Christian should live. And while he persists in such flagrant sin, he has no right to claim that he is a Christian. He may well be saved, but if that's the case, he will renounce his sin and return to his family. In the meantime, Craig's empty words remind me of Paul's words to the Ephesians:

> For you may be sure of this, that everyone who is sexually immoral or impure, or who is covetous (that is, an idolater), has no inheritance in the kingdom of Christ and God. Let no one deceive you with empty words, for because of these

things the wrath of God comes upon the sons of disobedience. (Eph. 5:5–6)"

Armed with the Word of God and a renewed determination to help Craig, the pastor and elder visited him again. This time they were not easily rebuffed by his brashly claiming to belong to Christ while living in sin. They lovingly but firmly told him, "Craig, we think that you are a Christian man. But this is plain: You are not living as a Christian man should." After sharing Paul's words quoted above, they said, "You have no right to say that you love Jesus while your life says that you love that which he hates. As long as you live in adultery, you have no right to the assurance of salvation. You may try to fool yourself, but you are no longer fooling us. As long as you live like this, in your heart of hearts you do not have assurance."

This tough love was exactly what Craig needed. The Word of God, shared prayerfully and boldly by men who cared for him, broke him. The Holy Spirit worked through the Word, and Craig repented, turned from his sinful lifestyle, and asked to be restored to his family. When Craig benefited from pastoral counsel, his patient wife took him back. As far as I know, they have lived happily together for the past thirty years.

God Warns His Children of the Danger of Apostasy

Many of us know people who have fallen away from the faith. Sincere believers disagree as to whether or not this can happen to saved persons and as a result ask many hard questions. Later I will attempt to address some of these questions. For now I will cite the most famous warning against apostasy:

> For it is impossible, in the case of those who have once been enlightened, who have tasted the heavenly gift, and have shared in the Holy Spirit, and have tasted the goodness of the word of God and the powers of the age to come, and then have fallen away, to restore them again to repentance, since they are cruci-

fying once again the Son of God to their own harm and holding him up to contempt. (Heb. 6:4–6)

This passage is so important that I will devote a chapter to it and to another equally tough warning passage in Hebrews 10:26–29. Here I will tell two true stories.

Almost thirty years ago a student of mine named Paul heard that I was beginning to study perseverance and apostasy.

"I am so glad to hear that," he said, "because the hardest thing I have ever dealt with was when a Christian friend walked away from the gospel."

I asked him to explain.

"Harry and I were close in the Lord. We ministered together, worshiped together, witnessed together. The day he turned away from Christ was the hardest day of my life."

"Did you try to help Harry?" I asked.

"Try?" Paul retorted, in a raised voice. "I tried everything. I begged him; I prayed for him; I rebuked him. Nothing worked. He just deserted Christ and his family."

"How long ago was this?" I wanted to know.

"Five years," he replied.

"What did Harry say when you asked him why he committed apostasy?" I asked.

"He said that he just got tired of fighting against sin," Paul explained.

Harry's answer seems telling. That is because on one level you and I can identify with Harry. We have all had really bad days, weeks, and maybe months. At our lowest ebb, we too might have felt like walking away from the faith. But I don't know how to explain it except to say that we couldn't. We just *couldn't*. Many people have told me stories similar to Paul's, and their stories have kept me interested in this subject for years.

In God's mercy, Paul had another story to tell, a remarkable one with a happy ending. It too involved apostasy. At a good church Paul had been attending while going to seminary, a dreadful thing occurred. An elder and another elder's wife had been having a secret affair and one day abandoned their spouses and children and left the church for parts unknown. They had thought things through carefully and had all of their ducks in a row. This included mailing letters of resignation to the church.

The departing couple had planned their escape well. But they seriously underestimated two things: the church's love for the Lord and for them. Paul told me that he had never seen anything like what happened. The Sunday that the announcement was made to the congregation, the people responded with sackcloth and ashes. During a time of prayer people wept openly over the sin of the couple and the losses felt by their devastated families. What really astonished Paul was the way God used the couple's sin for good. Believers, including leaders, openly confessed adulteries in their hearts. The church rallied around the two wounded families. Paul explains, "It was like a scene in the book of Acts, when a holy fear of God fell upon the early believers. It was awesome."

But the church's greatest response was to vow not to give up on the erring couple. The church made contact with them and assured them that the congregation would never stop praying for them. At first the couple hoped that these statements were pious but idle words, but time proved the church's love for them to be genuine. Many prayer meetings were held at various times of the day and night. After months of concerted prayer for the couple and many gentle but persistent contacts, God broke through.

There was cheering in the congregation the day the pastor announced that the couple had repented and wanted to return. But, he said, both parties were too ashamed to face their families or other members of the congregation. After weeks of pastoral counseling, the families were put back together and the elder—no longer in office, of course—and the other elder's wife returned to Sunday worship. Their fellow believers welcomed the repentant man and woman with open arms and tears of joy.

I was happy to hear Paul say that the joy he experienced that day exceeded the sorrow that he felt when his friend Harry had apostatized. I commended Paul for persevering after Harry's defection and praised God with him for his grace shown to Paul in allowing him to experience such a noteworthy demonstration in the church's dealings with the two defectors.

Once again I confess that I cannot answer all the hard questions about apostasy. But five chapters devoted to Scripture's warning passages will provide many answers that, Lord willing, will help us to serve God and help others who are dealing with these issues.

The Bible Often Speaks of Preservation and Apostasy

Preservation and apostasy are significant biblical themes. I count at least seventeen passages that teach that God will not allow his people to fall away from grace but will keep them for final salvation: Luke 22:31–34; John 6:35, 37–40, 44; 10:25–30; 17:9–12, 15, 24; Romans 5:9–10; 8:1–4, 28–39; 1 Corinthians 1:4, 8–9; 11:27–32; Ephesians 1:13–14; 4:30; Philippians 1:6; 1 Thessalonians 5:23–24; Hebrews 6:17–20; 7:23–25; 1 Peter 1:3–5; 1 John 2:18–19; 5:18.

I count even more warning passages: Matthew 7:21–23; 10:33; 24:24; Luke 8:5–15; John 15:1–8; Acts 5:5, 10; 8:13, 20–24; Romans 8:13; 11:20–22; 1 Corinthians 9:27; Colossians 1:21–23; 1 Timothy 1:18–20; 4:1; 5:8, 11–12; 2 Timothy 2:11–13, 17–19; Hebrews 5:11–6:12; 10:19–39; James 5:19–20; 2 Peter 2:20–22; 1 John 5:16–17; Revelation 3:5; 22:18–19.

Surely, these numerous passages deserve our attention. To ignore them is to close our ears to vital messages from God's Word. The rest of this book will seek to bring those messages to light. Chapter 2 treats the Old Testament background for the New Testament's teachings on God's preservation and human beings' apostasy. Chapters 3 through 6 explore the teaching of Jesus and his apostles on preservation. Chapters 7 through 11 deal with the most prominent warnings in Scripture, including those that deal with apostasy. Chapter 12 attempts to pull things together and underscore ways in which these teachings can help us live for Christ.

Preservation and Apostasy
in the Old Testament

BECAUSE PRESERVATION AND APOSTASY come to full flower in the New Testament, this book focuses on that Testament. These themes, however, have their roots earlier in the biblical story, and thus to ignore the Old Testament is unwise. But it is also unwise to try to force the Old Testament text to answer New Testament questions. Accordingly, we will try to deal with the Old Testament on its own terms. Here we treat the themes of preservation and apostasy with regard first to Israel and then representative individual Israelites. Those themes are:

- Corporate Preservation in the Old Testament.
- Corporate Apostasy in the Old Testament.
- Individual Preservation in the Old Testament.
- Individual Apostasy in the Old Testament.

Corporate Preservation in the Old Testament

The Old Testament's story deals with many individuals, but chiefly these individuals belong to the nation of Israel. The following oversimplification contains truth: The Old Testament story essentially speaks of God's historical preservation of Israel in spite

Thanks are due Wesley Vander Lugt, my former teaching assistant, for help in researching this chapter.

of its unfaithfulness and rebellion (apostasy). Let us examine God's keeping his rebellious people as a nation.

The Basis of God's Preservation of Israel

God's preservation of Israel in Old Testament times does not primarily concern eternal life, but the nation's ongoing identity and success as God's people. This preservation is based on God's covenant with, choice of, and love for Israel.

God's Preservation of Israel Is Based on His Covenant with Abraham, Isaac, and Jacob (Israel). The very reason for Israel's existence is God's covenant with Abraham. After initiating the covenant (in Gen. 12) and ratifying it (in Gen. 15), God provides more details in Genesis 17:

> Behold, my covenant is with you, and you shall be the father of a multitude of nations. . . . I will make you exceedingly fruitful, and I will make you into nations, and kings shall come from you. And I will establish my covenant between me and you and your offspring after you throughout their generations for an everlasting covenant, to be God to you and to your offspring after you. And I will give to you and to your offspring after you the land of your sojournings, all the land of Canaan, for an everlasting possession, and I will be their God. (vv. 4, 6–8)

God promises to make Abraham, who was as incapable of fathering children as his wife Sarah was of bearing them, "exceedingly fruitful," the father of many nations (Gen. 17:5–6)! The covenant that God establishes with Abraham and his descendants is "an everlasting covenant" (Gen. 17:7). God pledges to be God to them and to give them the land of Canaan. This last promise was fulfilled more than five hundred years later when Joshua conquered the Promised Land; it will be ultimately fulfilled in the new earth. God's covenant with Abraham, his son Isaac, and his grandson Jacob is the basis of God's preserving the nation of Israel.

God's Preservation of Israel Is Based on His Choice of the Nation. When he commands the Israelites to drive the pagan nations out of Canaan, God declares:

> The LORD your God has chosen you to be a people for his treasured possession, out of all the peoples who are on the face of the earth. It was not because you were more in number than any other people that the LORD set his love on you and chose you, for you were the fewest of all peoples, but it is because the LORD loves you and is keeping the oath that he swore to your fathers, that the LORD has brought you out with a mighty hand and redeemed you from the house of slavery, from the hand of Pharaoh king of Egypt. (Deut. 7:6–8)

Remarkably, God chooses Israel, out of all of the nations on earth, to belong to him as his treasure. His choice of Israel is not based on its great size—for it was tiny—but is rather due to his love and commitment to his covenant. Because of his commitment to and choice of Israel, God delivers it from Egyptian bondage. Israel's preservation is based on God's sovereign and gracious election.

God's Preservation of Israel Is Based on His Love for the Wayward Nation. God expresses this at many times, in many ways, and in many places in the Old Testament. In the quotation above (from Deut. 7:6–8), his love shines through: "the LORD set his love on you and chose you . . . the LORD loves you."

After Moses' bold request to see God's glory, the Lord permits him to glimpse it.

> The LORD passed before him and proclaimed, "The LORD, the LORD, a God merciful and gracious, slow to anger, and abounding in steadfast love and faithfulness, keeping steadfast love for thousands, forgiving iniquity and transgression and sin, but who will by no means clear the guilty, visiting the iniquity of the fathers on the children and the children's children, to the third and the fourth generation." (Ex. 34:6–7)

13

The revelation of God's glory ends with a reminder that he is just and punishes human sin. The Israelites, with hearts prone to wander, need to hear that message. But the message they need to hear first is one of God's mercy, grace, slowness to anger, abounding and steadfast love, and forgiveness. And that is exactly what God gives them.

David extols God's unmerited love for Israel: "He does not deal with us according to our sins, nor repay us according to our iniquities. For as high as the heavens are above the earth, so great is his steadfast love toward those who fear him" (Ps. 103:10–11).

Perhaps the most poignant expression of God's love for his people is seen in Hosea the prophet's marriage to unfaithful Gomer, serving as an object lesson of God's unrelenting love for his unfaithful people. Hosea represents God who loves the unlovely; his wife, a prostitute, stands for wayward Israel. God's tender words toward his stubborn and stiff–necked people are stunning: "Therefore, behold, I will allure her . . . and speak tenderly to her" (Hos. 2:14). God, in amazing love for his idolatrous nation, pledges, "And I will betroth you to me forever. I will betroth you to me in righteousness and in justice, in steadfast love and in mercy. I will betroth you to me in faithfulness. And you shall know the LORD" (Hos. 2:19–20).

The Result of God's Preservation of Israel

Plainly, God's words through Jeremiah to errant Israel are fitting: "I have loved you with an everlasting love; therefore I have continued my faithfulness to you" (Jer. 31:3). Because of God's covenant, election, and love for Israel, "the LORD will not forsake his people, for his great name's sake" (1 Sam. 12:22). Therefore, even in times of national apostasy, God keeps a remnant for himself. The theme of a faithful remnant among an unfaithful people plays a vital role in the Old Testament as the following two examples attest.

In the Time of Elijah. Elijah, exhausted after fleeing from murderous Jezebel, is despondent: "I have been very jealous for the LORD, the God of hosts. For the people of Israel have forsaken your covenant, thrown down your altars, and killed your prophets with the sword, and I, even I only, am left, and they seek my life, to take it away" (1 Kings 19:10). The dejected prophet, believing that he alone serves Yahweh, is ready to die. But because of God's love and faithfulness Elijah is not alone, as God reminds him: "Yet I will leave seven thousand in Israel, all the knees that have not bowed to Baal, and every mouth that has not kissed him" (1 Kings 19:18). Despite appearances, God keeps a people for himself.

After the Babylonian Captivity. At the end of the Old Testament again there is reason for despair. After God delivers the Israelites from Babylonian and Persian captivity, after he reestablishes them in the Promised Land, after he inspires the rebuilding of the temple and Jerusalem's walls, the people again forsake him. Malachi records abuses involving Israel's worship, priestly service, marriages, and social justice. Just when it seems again that no true Israelites are left we learn:

> Then those who feared the LORD spoke with one another. The LORD paid attention and heard them, and a book of remembrance was written before him of those who feared the LORD and esteemed his name. "They shall be mine, says the LORD of hosts, in the day when I make up my treasured possession, and I will spare them as a man spares his son who serves him." (Mal. 3:16–17)

God's choice of and love for his people and his covenant faithfulness move him to preserve them, even during times of national apostasy!

Corporate Apostasy in the Old Testament

Against the backdrop of God's persevering love for Israel, its repeated apostasy stands in bold relief. Two examples, out of many, stand out: Israel's rebellion in the wilderness and its rejection of the Lord that resulted in the two captivities.

Israel's Apostasy in the Wilderness

After delivering the people from Egyptian bondage, God leads them into the wilderness. Instead of responding with devotion, they repeatedly turn away from their Redeemer and Lord, as Numbers 11–14, 16, 20, 25 records. Psalm 78 eloquently testifies to this:

> In spite of all this, they still sinned;
>> despite his wonders, they did not believe.
> . . . .
> But they flattered him with their mouths;
>> they lied to him with their tongues.
> Their heart was not steadfast toward him;
>> they were not faithful to his covenant.
> . . . .
> How often they rebelled against him in the wilderness
>> and grieved him in the desert! (Ps. 78:32, 36–37, 40)

Despite Israel's apostasy, God does not utterly forsake them, and the children of the unbelieving wilderness generation enter the Promised Land. Why? Psalm 78 answers:

> Yet he, being compassionate,
>> atoned for their iniquity
>> and did not destroy them;
> . . . .
> And he brought them to his holy land,
> . . . .
> He drove out nations before them;
>> he apportioned them for a possession
>> and settled the tribes of Israel in their tents.
> . . . .
> but he chose the tribe of Judah,
>> Mount Zion, which he loves.
> . . . .

16

> He chose David his servant
> and took him from the sheepfolds. (vv. 38, 54–55, 68, 70)

Because of the Lord's love he does not destroy the people but gives them Canaan. Years later, in justice he rejects the northern kingdom, driving it into Assyrian captivity, but he preserves the southern kingdom of Judah.

Israel's Apostasy Leading to Captivity

Alongside the classic example of the wilderness apostasy are the two captivities of God's people. In Deuteronomy, the Lord promises blessings to the nation of Israel for obedience and warns of curses for disobedience. Among the latter is: "You shall father sons and daughters, but they shall not be yours, for they shall go into captivity" (Deut. 28:41). Centuries before the first captivity, God warns his people not to turn away from him lest they be taken away from their land.

Because Israel refuses to listen to repeated warnings from the prophets, including Amos, Jonah, and Hosea, it reaps curses instead of blessings. In 722 BC, the Assyrians capture the northern kingdom of Israel: "In the days of Pekah king of Israel, Tiglath-pileser king of Assyria came and captured Ijon, Abel-beth-maacah, Janoah, Kedesh, Hazor, Gilead, and Galilee, all the land of Naphtali, and he carried the people captive to Assyria" (2 Kings 15:29).

Although the southern kingdom lasts longer, it too shares the same fate. It rejects the calls to repentance from God's prophets— Micah, Isaiah, Nahum, Zephaniah, Habakkuk, and Jeremiah among them—and its people are taken into captivity by Babylon, which destroys Jerusalem in 586 BC.

> He [Nebuchadnezzar] carried away all Jerusalem and all the officials and all the mighty men of valor, 10,000 captives, and all the craftsmen and the smiths. None remained, except the poorest people of the land. And he carried away Jehoiachin to Babylon. The king's mother, the king's wives, his officials, and

the chief men of the land he took into captivity from Jerusalem to Babylon. (2 Kings 24:14–15)

In spite of Israel's repeated apostasy, God does not abandon the people forever. After the Assyrian captivity of Israel, God continues to warn Judah, until it too is taken captive—by Babylon. But even this does not signal God's rejection of his people. He sends prophets to them, including Daniel and Ezekiel, and after forty years of captivity brings a faithful remnant back to the land (Ezra 2:1–2). This is only due to God's preservation of them in exile, his working in Darius, king of Persia, to allow the people to return to Jerusalem, and his protecting them from enemies as they rebuild the temple, walls, and city. Bruce Waltke's words pertaining to Genesis apply to the whole Old Testament story: "Nevertheless, I AM faithfully preserves a remnant who participate in God's eternal covenant and merit the right to rule the earth as the true seed of Abraham (Mic. 4–5)."[1]

Individual Preservation in the Old Testament

The Old Testament's main message concerns Israel. But this corporate emphasis stands alongside God's keen interest in the faithfulness or unfaithfulness of individual Israelites. "Zion shall be redeemed by justice, and those in her who repent, by righteousness. But rebels and sinners shall be broken together, and those who forsake the Lord shall be consumed" (Isa. 1:27–28).[2] Indeed, within the Old Testament's large story are many smaller ones, some of which give insight into preservation and apostasy.

Promises of Individual Preservation

Before we hear stories of God's preserving individuals, we will hear God's promises to keep his own. One of the psalms of

1. Bruce K. Waltke with Charles Yu, *An Old Testament Theology* (Grand Rapids: Zondervan, 2007), 299.
2. See also Num. 14:21–24. I owe this insight to my colleague Jack Collins.

ascent, sung by the people on their way to the temple for the feasts of Israel, includes these comforting words: "Those who trust in the Lord are like Mount Zion, which cannot be moved, but abides forever. As the mountains surround Jerusalem, so the Lord surrounds his people, from this time forth and forevermore" (Ps. 125:1–2). Mountains are used twice in vivid comparisons. Believing Israelites are "like Mount Zion, which cannot be moved, but abides forever" (v. 1). In ancient Israel there is nothing as stable as a mountain. God's people too abide forever on account of his love. And the Lord is compared to mountains: as mountains encircle Jerusalem, so he will encircle them "from this time forth and forevermore" (v. 2) with his faithfulness.

After words of woe to idolaters, Isaiah reassures every faithful Israelite, "But Israel is saved by the Lord with everlasting salvation; you shall not be put to shame or confounded to all eternity" (Isa. 45:17). Of course, not all Israel is Israel (cf. Rom. 2:28–29; 9:6). Descendants of Abraham can break covenant with God and reap curses instead of blessings. But for faithful Israelite families these words bring great consolation.

The harrowing experiences of David and other psalmists are seed from which God causes beautiful plants to grow, such as this: "Who rises up for me against the wicked? Who stands up for me against evildoers? If the Lord had not been my help, my soul would soon have lived in the land of silence. When I thought, 'My foot slips,' your steadfast love, O Lord, held me up" (Ps. 94:16–18). These strong words have comforted many Christians, and rightly so, for the God of David is our God in Christ.

Many other passages speak of God's preservation of his people,[3] but here is one more from Isaiah: "'For the mountains may depart and the hills be removed, but my steadfast love shall not depart from you, and my covenant of peace shall not be removed,' says the Lord, who has compassion on you" (Isa. 54:10).

3. See G. C. Berkouwer, *Faith and Perseverance* (Grand Rapids: Eerdmans, 1958), 93–94.

Examples of Individual Preservation

Alongside God's promises of keeping believing Israelites, the Old Testament provides examples of his relentless love in individual lives. These include the case of a very flawed person—Jacob—and a great saint who sinned grievously—David.

Jacob. The son of Isaac and grandson of Abraham, Jacob is an unlikely candidate to serve as an example of a man of God. His sins are openly displayed: he was an unethical cheat (Gen. 25:31–33), deceitful (Gen. 27:19, 24, 35; 31:20), and cowardly (Gen. 26:7; 31:31; 33:3, 8). Paul House's evaluation is right on target: "God's grace selects this terribly imperfect man and not because of merit on his part."[4] God's grace keeps this terribly imperfect man too. Though God committed himself to Jacob more than twenty years before (Gen. 28:15), it is not until Jacob returns to Bethel (Gen. 35:9–15) that he commits himself to God. God's persevering grace does not give up on Jacob. As a result, Jacob makes the honor roll of faith in Hebrews 11: "By faith, Jacob, when dying, blessed each of the sons of Joseph, bowing in worship over the head of his staff" (v. 21).

David. Not a scoundrel like Jacob, David is to the contrary a man after God's own heart (1 Sam. 13:14), a mighty warrior, the exemplary king, the sweet psalmist of Israel, an ancestor and forerunner of Christ. He also is an example of a great person of God who falls terribly but is kept saved and restored to service by God's persistent grace.

The great sins of his life are adultery with Bathsheba and murdering her husband Uriah by sending him to the front lines of battle to be killed (2 Sam. 11; 12:9). For a year David refuses to confess his sins to the Lord. Finally God uses the prophet Nathan to confront David with his sin, who breaks down and repents: "I have sinned against the LORD" (2 Sam. 12:13).

4. Paul R. House, *Old Testament Theology* (Downers Grove, IL: InterVarsity Press, 1998), 78.

20

Justly famous is David's prayer of confession and forgiveness in Psalm 51. The superscription reads: "A psalm of David, when Nathan the prophet went to him, after he had gone in to Bathsheba." David pours out his heart to God: "Against you, you only, have I sinned and done what is evil in your sight" (v. 4). David does not seek forgiveness based on his righteousness but on God's love and mercy: "Have mercy on me, O God, according to your steadfast love; according to your abundant mercy blot out my transgressions" (v. 1). As the apostle Paul wrote many years later: "David also speaks of the blessing of the one to whom God counts righteousness apart from works" (Rom. 4:6, before quoting Ps. 32:1–2). David speaks of and knows that blessing.

Has David lost his salvation so that he must ask God to save him again? No; rather, he asks God to restore the joy of his salvation: "Restore to me the joy of your salvation, and uphold me with a willing spirit" (Ps. 51:12). David is indeed one of the great saints of God; he belongs among the heroes and heroines of faith in Hebrews 11: "And what more shall I say? For time would fail me to tell of . . . David and Samuel and the prophets" (v. 32). Nevertheless, David's life reminds us that even strong believers can commit terrible sins. Above all, David's life teaches us that he was kept by God's "steadfast love" and "abundant mercy" (Ps. 51:1)! So are we.

Jacob's and David's lives differ in many ways, but they have this in common: They were saved and kept by God's preserving love.

Individual Apostasy in the Old Testament

The Old Testament also warns God's people of the danger of turning away from him. In addition, it bears witness to individuals who denied the faith by their actions. Sadly, many figures come to mind. We will look at two: Esau, Jacob's brother, and Saul, Israel's first king. But first we will survey some of the many Old Testament warnings.

Warnings of Individual Apostasy

Perhaps the most famous warnings are the curses of Deuteronomy 28. Moses sets before the people both blessings that will come from obeying the Lord and curses that will come from disobeying him. Though the blessings and curses have to do with corporate Israel, they also have to do with individual Israelites: "And your dead body shall be food for all birds of the air and for the beasts of the earth. . . . You shall betroth a wife, but another man shall ravish her. You shall build a house, but you shall not dwell in it" (vv. 26, 30).

Joshua's last words to his fellow Israelites are another famous warning against apostasy. Once more, the nation is addressed, but Joshua intends his words for every individual and family as his speaking of himself and his family demonstrates:

> Now therefore fear the LORD and serve him in sincerity and in faithfulness. Put away the gods that your fathers served beyond the River and in Egypt, and serve the LORD. And . . . , choose this day whom you will serve, whether the gods your fathers served in the region beyond the River, or the gods of the Amorites in whose land you dwell. But as for me and my house, we will serve the LORD. (Josh. 24:14–15)

Examples of Individual Apostasy

Although Esau and Saul are different, they share this: they are both examples of apostates, of those who turned away from the Lord.

Esau. Isaac has two sons, Jacob and Esau. As we have seen, Jacob is a very flawed individual who is sought and kept by God's grace. By contrast, Esau is a person who takes much for granted, who despises his father's blessing and birthright, and who ends up as an example of an ungodly person.

In answer to her husband Isaac's prayer, Rebekah conceives and bears twins: Esau, the firstborn, and Isaac (Gen. 25:21–26).

Once when Esau comes in from hunting, famished, he accepts Jacob's offer of stew in exchange for his birthright. By thus swearing to Jacob, "Esau despised his birthright" (Gen. 25:34). Later, through Rebekah's scheming, Jacob steals Esau's blessing by deceiving his old and nearly blind father Isaac into thinking that he is Esau (Gen. 27). Esau responds by hating Jacob for stealing his blessing and threatening to kill him (Gen. 27:41).

The New Testament's evaluation of Esau's spiritual condition is not pretty. Although he is mentioned in faith's honor roll, it is not as a believer, but as the recipient of a lesser blessing of his father: "By faith Isaac invoked future blessings on Jacob and Esau" (Heb. 11:20; cf. Gen. 27:30–40). Sadly, when Esau's character is described in the next chapter of Hebrews, it is not as a model believer or even as a struggling one like his brother Jacob. Instead, it is as an example of an "unholy" person, one devoid of faith:

> See to it that no one fails to obtain the grace of God . . . that no one is sexually immoral or unholy like Esau, who sold his birthright for a single meal. For you know that afterward, when he desired to inherit the blessing, he was rejected, for he found no chance to repent, though he sought it with tears. (Heb. 12:15–17)

Esau is an apostate because although he is born into the people of God, he repudiates his birthright by despising the things of God. Hebrews uses him as an example of someone who "fails to obtain the grace of God," that is, who comes short of salvation (Heb. 12:15). When all is said and done, Esau is "unholy" (Heb. 12:16).

Saul. Outwardly, Saul has much going for him. This is how he first appears in the biblical record:

> There was a man of Benjamin whose name was Kish, the son of Abiel, son of Zeror, son of Becorath, son of Aphiah, a Benjaminite, a man of wealth. And he had a son whose name

23

> was Saul, a handsome young man. There was not a man among the people of Israel more handsome than he. From his shoulders upward he was taller than any of the people. (1 Sam. 9:1–2)

Saul is from a wealthy family with unmistakable physical gifts of attractiveness and height. He makes a good beginning, as the Lord instructs Samuel to anoint him Israel's first king (1 Sam. 9:15–17; 10:1; 11:15), he defeats the Ammonites (1 Sam. 11), and he fights the Philistines (1 Sam. 13:1–7).

But before long Saul stumbles. Impatient for Samuel to arrive at the appointed time to offer sacrifices, Saul offers them himself, lies to Samuel, and incurs the prophet's wrath: "You have done foolishly. . . . now your kingdom shall not continue. . . . because you have not kept what the LORD commanded you" (1 Sam. 13:13–14). So begins a downward spiral in Saul's life. The Lord rejects him as king, and Samuel anoints David instead (1 Sam. 15–16). After young David defeats the Philistine giant Goliath, Saul is angry and jealous. At their source, Saul's problems are spiritual: "Saul was afraid of David because the LORD was with him but had departed from Saul" (1 Sam. 18:12).

Sadly, though David never does him any wrong, "Saul was David's enemy continually" (1 Sam. 18:29). Texts such as this, along with Saul's later murderous intentions toward David, lead some Old Testament scholars to conclude that Saul was not a man of faith.[5]

But does not 1 Samuel 16:14 mean that Saul was saved and later lost his salvation when it says, "The Spirit of the LORD departed from Saul"? No; when the text speaks of the Holy Spirit coming on Saul (10:6, 10; 11:6; 19:23) or David (16:13), it does not speak of salvation but of divine enablement for various tasks as king. Therefore, when it speaks of the Spirit departing from Saul (16:14), this does not entail a loss of salvation but God's taking away the enablement to

---

5. An example is Waltke, *An Old Testament Theology*, 638, 639, 640, 645, 652, 653.

perform certain functions in keeping with God's rejecting Saul as king.[6]

Despite a few snapshots that could be interpreted in Saul's favor, the motion picture of his life is indicative of an unsaved person. He had Doeg, the Edomite, kill eighty-five of God's priests (1 Sam. 22:18). Repeatedly he tried to kill David (1 Sam. 18:11, 17, 21, 25; 19:1, 10, 11, 15; 20:31, 33; 23:15, 25–26; 24:2, 11; 26:2, 21), though David twice spared Saul (1 Sam. 24:3–15; 26:7–12). Saul stoops to consult a witch, an action forbidden by God, because God's prophets would not answer him (1 Sam. 28).

It is no surprise that Saul's name does not appear in the honor roll of faith in Hebrews 11 because it does not belong there. But it is surprising that his name never appears in the New Testament. The first king of Israel was a forgotten man.

Connecting the Dots

The Old Testament records the dynamic interplay between God's corporate preservation of Israel amidst his people's continuous rebellion and apostasy.[7] At the same time, God gives wonderful promises of individual preservation and warnings against the dangers of individual apostasy. Finally, there are examples of individual preservation—including Jacob and David—and apostasy—including Esau and Saul. All of this sets the stage for Christ's coming and ratifying the New Testament by his death and resurrection.

---

6. I owe this insight to J. Robert Vannoy, professor emeritus of Old Testament, Biblical Theological Seminary, Hatfield, Pennsylvania. See his *1–2 Samuel*, Cornerstone Biblical Commentary (Wheaton, IL: Tyndale House, 2009).

7. I. Howard Marshall capably treats the Old Testament texts, though he reaches different conclusions than I, in *Kept by the Power of God: A Study of Perseverance and Falling Away* (1969; reprint, Minneapolis: Bethany Fellowship, 1974), 29–38.

Preservation in the Gospels

"LONG AGO, at many times and in many ways, God spoke to our fathers by the prophets, but *in these last days he has spoken to us by his Son*, whom he appointed heir of all things, through whom also he created the world" (Heb. 1:1–2, italics added). As the great prophet of God, Jesus taught his disciples many important truths, among them God's preservation of his saints. The key texts are these:

- Luke 22:31–34
- John 6:35, 37–40, 44
- John 10:25–30
- John 17: 9–12, 15, 24.

Luke 22:31–34

> "Simon, Simon, behold, Satan demanded to have you, that he might sift you like wheat, but I have prayed for you that your faith may not fail. And when you have turned again, strengthen your brothers." Peter said to him, "Lord, I am ready to go with you both to prison and to death." Jesus said, "I tell you, Peter, the rooster will not crow this day, until you deny three times that you know me."

Satan's Request

After giving his disciples great news in Luke 22:28–30—in the future they would enjoy table fellowship with him in his kingdom—Jesus hits them with sobering words: "Simon, Simon, Satan has asked to sift you as wheat" (v. 31 NIV). Although he addresses Simon as leader, Jesus' words apply to all twelve of the disciples. We know this because the word "you" in verse 31 is plural—"you all."

Satan asked God for permission to afflict the disciples. It is difficult to know precisely what the picture of sifting means here, but this much is clear—Satan intends to harm the disciples, "to destroy their faith."[1] Jesus shifts from "you" plural to "you" singular in verse 32, focusing on Peter. All of the disciples will be afflicted, but Peter is Satan's special target.

Jesus' Prayer

Jesus seeks to encourage Peter: "But I have prayed for you that your faith may not fail" (v. 32). Satan will attack Peter, and Peter will feel the attack. How serious will the attack be? Jesus' next words contain a hint: "And when you have turned again, strengthen your brothers" (v. 32). Jesus implies that the attack will be very serious. Peter will be dealt such a blow that he will fall. But he will again stand on his feet; the fall will not be permanent. Jesus stands behind Peter, supporting him in prayer so that his lapse will not be without remedy. And Peter, after recovering, is to minister to the other disciples.

Peter's Boast

Jesus' words of encouragement are lost on Peter. He will not hear of his failing when Satan attacks. Jesus had just mentioned Peter's "brothers," meaning the other disciples. Peter regards them not as brothers but as rivals, boasting, "Lord, I am ready

1. Joel B. Green, *The Gospel of Luke*, New International Commentary on the New Testament (Grand Rapids: Eerdmans, 1997), 772, n. 110.

to go with you both to prison and to death." Peter implies that he will be faithful to Jesus, even if the others are not. Satan may afflict all of the disciples, but Peter has no doubt that the evil one's efforts will be futile against the power of Peter's resolve. He thinks that he needs neither Jesus' intercession nor his exhortation to minister to the others after he recovers. He will not need to recover because he—even he alone if need be—will be faithful to his Lord no matter what.

Jesus' Prediction

Jesus has strong medicine for Peter's disease of boasting: "I tell you, Peter, the rooster will not crow this day, until you deny three times that you know me" (v. 34). Jesus speaks as a prophet and makes a prediction that Peter will deny him three times on that day, before the next sunrise.

The Subsequent Story

That is exactly what happens. After Jesus is seized and taken to the high priest's house, Peter follows at a distance and sits down with some others around a fire (vv. 54–55). A servant girl recognizes Peter as one of Jesus' companions. Instead of owning up to that fact, Peter denies it: "Woman, I do not know him" (v. 57). Strike one. Not long afterward, another person asserts that Peter was with Jesus. Peter protests, "Man, I am not" (v. 58). Strike two. About an hour later still another, probably by recognizing his Galilean accent, points out that Peter was Jesus' disciple: "Certainly this man also was with him, for he too is a Galilean" (v. 59). Peter, however, denies Christ again: "Man, I do not know what you are talking about" (v. 60). Strike three.

At that moment the rooster crows (v. 60). Jesus turns to look at Peter, who recalls Jesus' prophecy. Inadvertently, Peter fulfilled exactly what his Lord had predicted. The truth of the matter slams into Peter: "And he went out and wept bitterly" (v. 62). The boaster had been humbled. He had fallen—hard—three times.

Teaching

So Jesus' words came true: "But I have prayed for you that your faith may not fail" (v. 32). Didn't Peter's faith fail? The answer is yes and no. It failed in that he disowned Jesus three times that very night, but it did not utterly fail. This is so because Jesus reinstates the repentant Peter—that is what the private meeting in John 21:15–17 is all about. Jesus brings Peter to a difficult repentance, making him affirm three times, to counter his three denials, that he loves Jesus very much. I am not claiming that it was easy to understand Jesus' prediction before it came to pass. Oftentimes biblical prophecy is like that—only its fulfillment reveals the correct way to understand its details. But looking back we possess 20/20 hindsight. Peter fell, but Jesus' prayer lifted him up.

The rest of Jesus' words ring true too: "And when you have turned again, strengthen your brothers" (v. 32). The early chapters of Acts show that after Pentecost Peter was a mighty champion for the faith. It is he who preached the first Christian sermon, took the lead in healing in Jesus' name, and brought the gospel to many. He stood faithful for Christ before the Jewish leaders, suffered imprisonment by Herod Agrippa I (Acts 12), wrote the two New Testament letters that bear his name, and, if early church history is accurate, was faithful even unto death in Rome at Nero's hands in AD 64. Indeed he "turned again" and strengthened his brothers in Christ.

Peter persevered in his faith, even after wavering terribly. Why did he succeed? Not because of the greatness of his dedication to Christ. He persevered because his Lord preserved him by praying for him. Today Jesus' dealings with Peter continue to strengthen his brothers and sisters—even us—because Jesus continues to pray for us. One of the ways that God keeps us saved is by Jesus our great High Priest's present ministry of intercession. Jesus' prayer for Peter's faith is a sample of his prayers for all believers. We will open up these passages later, but their quotation is apt now:

And I am no longer in the world, but they are in the world, and I am coming to you. Holy Father, keep them in your name, which you have given me. . . . While I was with them, I kept them in your name, which you have given me. I have guarded them, and not one of them has been lost except the son of destruction, that the Scripture might be fulfilled. . . . I do not ask that you take them out of the world, but that you keep them from the evil one. . . . Father, I desire that they also, whom you have given me, may be with me where I am, to see my glory that you have given me. . . . (John 17:11–12, 15, 24)

Who is to condemn? Christ Jesus is the one who died—more than that, who was raised—who is at the right hand of God, who indeed is interceding for us. (Rom. 8:34)

The former priests were many in number, because they were prevented by death from continuing in office, but he holds his priesthood permanently, because he continues forever. Consequently, he is able to save to the uttermost those who draw near to God through him, since he always lives to make intercession for them. (Heb. 7:23–25)

Objections

There are two main objections to this teaching about Peter's perseverance. First, Joel Green points out that "Peter will behave in ways that contradict the criteria for authentic discipleship. . . . Peter will seek to save his life by denying Jesus."[2] Green is correct to underscore the seriousness of Peter's denials. Yet, Green puts the emphasis in the wrong place when he says, "Even this can be forgiven, however, assuming that there is subsequent repentance." Of course, this too is true, but it misses Luke's point that Peter's faith did not fail precisely because of Jesus' preserving prayer for him. Luke's emphasis is not on the strength of Peter's repentance but on Jesus' strong prayers for him.

2. Ibid., 774.

Second, although Howard Marshall does put the emphasis in the right place—"Yet as a result of prayer by Jesus Peter's faith does not fail"—he concludes, "We cannot deny the efficacy of the divine protection thus extended to a disciple, but at the same time we cannot use the story to prove that disciples are inevitably and automatically preserved from the possibility of falling away; Judas was also a disciple."[3] If by "disciples" Marshall means all who profess the Christian faith, of course he is correct because not all who profess truly believe. But if by "disciples" he means "true believers," then respectfully I disagree. I say this because once we see a pattern in Jesus' prayer for Peter here and in what other Scriptures say about Jesus' ongoing intercession (John 17:11–12, 15, 24; Rom. 8:34; Heb. 7:23–25, cited above), a strong case for God's preservation of his saints emerges. It is true that Judas too was a disciple, but I will present evidence that he was a false believer and never a true disciple.[4]

John 6:35, 37–40, 44

Jesus said to them, "I am the bread of life; whoever comes to me shall not hunger, and whoever believes in me shall never thirst. . . . All that the Father gives me will come to me, and whoever comes to me I will never cast out. For I have come down from heaven, not to do my own will but the will of him who sent me. And this is the will of him who sent me, that I should lose nothing of all that he has given me, but raise it up on the last day. For this is the will of my Father, that everyone who looks on the Son and believes in him should have eternal life, and I will raise him up on the last day. . . . No one can come to me unless the Father who sent me draws him. And I will raise him up on the last day."

3. I. Howard Marshall, *Kept by the Power of God: A Study of Perseverance and Falling Away* (1969; reprint, Minneapolis: Bethany Fellowship, 1974), 89.
4. See pages 44–46 of this chapter.

After feeding the five thousand, Jesus, with echoes of God giving manna to the Israelites in the wilderness, delivers his famous "bread of life" sermon. Although the vocabulary in this passage differs from that Paul uses, John 6:37–54 gives much the same message as the apostle did in Romans 8:29–30: "For those whom he foreknew he also predestined. . . . And those whom he predestined he also called, and those whom he called he also justified, and those whom he justified he also glorified."

John doesn't use Paul's words 1) "predestined," 2) "called," or 3) "glorified," but his message is similar to Paul's. Instead, John speaks 1) of people being "given" to Jesus, 2) of their being "drawn" to him and therefore "coming" to him, and 3) of Jesus raising them on the last day.

"Coming" Means "Believing"

The parallelism between "coming" to Jesus and "believing" in him is evident in Jesus' words in John 6:35: "I am the bread of life; whoever *comes to me* shall not hunger, and whoever *believes in me* shall never thirst" (italics added). "Coming" to Jesus, therefore, is one way that John expresses believing in him. Therefore, when Jesus says, "All that the Father gives me *will come* to me" (John 6:37, italics added), he speaks of the certainty of people believing in him.

People Being Given to Jesus

John speaks frequently of people being given to Jesus. It is the Father who gives them to Jesus (10:29). Although Jesus has authority over all people, he gives eternal life only to those whom the Father gave him (17:2). He reveals the Father to them (17:6). He asks the Father to bring those the Father gave him to be with him in heaven to see his glory (17:24). The Father's giving people to the Son is one of John's ways of teaching predestination. Jesus prayed to the Father, "I am not praying for the world but for those whom you have given me, for they are yours. All mine are yours, and yours are mine" (17:9–10).

Jesus' words "All that the Father gives me will come to me" (John 6:37) mean that all of those whom the Father chose for salvation will believe in Jesus. Here John connects God's election of people for salvation with their trusting Christ as Savior. Though some teach that election is based on faith, John teaches the opposite—faith is the result of election. In fact, Jesus here teaches that all of the elect will surely believe in him. God's choice of people for himself leads unfailingly to their trusting Jesus for salvation.

Jesus Keeps Us Saved

We are ready to understand John 6:37: "All that the Father gives me will come to me, and whoever comes to me I will never cast out." Jesus teaches that all of the elect will believe in him, and he will never reject them. Indeed, Jesus will preserve God's people for final salvation. And Jesus repeats this in verse 39: "And this is the will of him who sent me, that I should lose nothing of all that he has given me, but raise it up on the last day." Jesus will lose none of the elect; he will raise them for final salvation. Jesus next ties faith and resurrection: "For this is the will of my Father, that everyone who looks on the Son and believes in him should have eternal life, and I will raise him up on the last day" (v. 40). Jesus will grant all believers eternal life now and resurrection to life at the end.

Drawing

Jesus also teaches what Paul labels "calling"—that God effectively summons people to Jesus through the gospel. Not all who hear the gospel call respond favorably. But those do who are inwardly and effectively called by the Holy Spirit. John labels this "drawing": "No one can come to me unless the Father who sent me draws him" (v. 44). People do not come to know

Jesus on their own; the Father draws them to him. Jesus' next words speak of resurrection to life: "And I will raise him up on the last day" (v. 44). Only those drawn by the Father believe in Jesus. And Jesus will raise all believers for final salvation. They are safe in his care.

Teaching

John paints a beautiful picture of harmony when he describes the work that the Father and Son undertake to save God's people. Here is a summary:

- The Father gives people to the Son (election: John 6:37).
- The Father draws those people to the Son (calling: John 6:44).
- Those people come to Jesus for salvation (faith: John 6:37, 40, 44).
- Jesus keeps them saved (preservation: John 6:37, 39).
- Jesus will raise them to life on the last day (resurrection: John 6:39, 40, 44).

It is critical to see two things: the way the Father and Son work together in salvation and the continuity of God's people. Note how the Father and Son work harmoniously. The Father chooses people and draws them to faith in the Son. They believe in him and are saved. The Son preserves them and will raise them for eternal life in the future. The Father and Son sing the song of salvation in perfect two-part harmony.

Because of the harmonious labor between the first two persons of the Godhead there is a continuity of identity to God's people. It is the same people whom the Father gives to the Son and draws to him, the same people who come to the Son, whom the Son saves and keeps, and the same people whom he will raise on the last day. The identity of those whom God saves is the same from the beginning of salvation to the end. Due to the harmonious work of the Father and Son, then, all believers are safe and will not be cast out, will not be lost (vv. 37, 39). In plain words, Jesus here teaches our preservation—he will keep us for salvation on the last day.

We are overwhelmed with such matchless grace. As we grow in Christ, he reveals to us more of our weaknesses, and this in turn makes us more grateful for his grace that saves and keeps us. Thomas Schreiner and Ardel Caneday say it well: "We know that we are prone to wander, but we have the promise that Jesus will never lose us, that the work he began he will also complete on the day of our resurrection."[5]

Objections

Craig S. Keener seeks to qualify John's witness to preservation by making it dependent on believers continuing to believe the gospel: "Those who truly came to him [Jesus] would never be 'cast out' (6:37), a fate delineated more graphically in 15:6 as relevant to those who failed to persevere. In the whole of John's theology, true 'coming' to Jesus implies more than initial faith, for it demands perseverance."[6] Keener appeals to John's wider teaching to blunt the force of his witness to preservation in John 6.

Marshall acknowledges, "Nowhere else in the New Testament is the fact of divine preservation of the disciples of Jesus so clearly presented as here, and no theology of perseverance and apostasy must fail to give these verses their full value." But he immediately implies that Jesus' power does not prevent people from falling away but only preserves those who continue in belief.[7]

These scholars disappoint because they do not do justice to the Trinitarian harmony and consequent continuity of God's people. John does not make being raised for eternal life on the last day dependent on perseverance in John 6. Rather, his

5. Thomas R. Schreiner and Ardel B. Caneday, *The Race Set Before Us: A Biblical Theology of Perseverance and Assurance* (Downers Grove, IL: InterVarsity, 2001), 250.

6. Craig S. Keener, *The Gospel of John: A Commentary* (Peabody, MA: Hendrickson, 2003), 684.

7. Marshall, *Kept by the Power of God*, 181.

strong witness to divine preservation guarantees perseverance to God's own.

John 10:25-30

> Jesus answered them, "I told you, and you do not believe. The works that I do in my Father's name bear witness about me, but you do not believe because you are not part of my flock. My sheep hear my voice, and I know them, and they follow me. I give them eternal life, and they will never perish, and no one will snatch them out of my hand. My Father, who has given them to me, is greater than all, and no one is able to snatch them out of the Father's hand. I and the Father are one."

In contrast to the unfaithful shepherds of Old Testament Israel (see Ezek. 34:10), Jesus is the Good Shepherd who loves the sheep and gives himself up for them.

Jesus Confronts Unbelief

Jesus rebukes the Jewish leaders' unbelief because he knows their hearts. Although they try, they cannot justly plead insufficient evidence for their failure to believe (v. 25). Jesus has performed many signs, many works that the Father gave him to do, in their midst. These signs and Jesus' unique words, also from the Father, have borne abundant witness to him. It is not due to a lack of evidence but due to the Jewish leaders' hard hearts that they reject Jesus. That rejection, Jesus asserts, is evidence of their rejection by God: "You do not believe because you are not part of my flock" (v. 26). By contrast, Jesus' sheep, his people, listen to him—they believe in him. Furthermore, he knows them personally, and they follow him, that is, they obey his commands.

Eternal Life Is a Gift from Jesus

One of John's major pictures portrays Jesus as the giver of eternal life. According to the prologue, even before his incarnation, the eternal Word, in whom alone was eternal life, gave life to all things by creating (1:3–4). So, it is no surprise that the incarnate Word gives physical and spiritual life to needy sinners. After giving life and health to the legs of a paralyzed man, Jesus declares, "For as the Father raises the dead and gives them life, so also the Son gives life to whom he will" (5:21). Indeed, John presents Jesus as "the bread of life" (6:35), "the resurrection and the life" (11:25), and "the way, and the truth, and the life" (14:6).

It is fitting, then, when, as clearly as anyplace in Scripture, Jesus, the giver of eternal life, proclaims in John 10:28 that eternal life is his gift to his own: "I give them eternal life" (v. 28). He does not use Paul's terminology and say that salvation is all of grace and has nothing to do with human achievement, but Jesus' meaning overlaps the apostle's. In contrast to the goats, who reject Jesus and are rejected by God, Jesus' sheep receive the gift of eternal life from their Good Shepherd.

"They Will Never Perish"

Jesus' next words are monumental: "They will never perish" (v. 28). It is difficult for English translations to convey the strength of the original Greek. Listen to Daniel B. Wallace, the author of the most respected advanced Greek grammar:

> Emphatic negation is indicated by *ou me* plus the *aorist subjunctive*. . . . This is the strongest way to negate something in Greek . . . *ou me* rules out even the idea as being a possibility. . . . Emphatic negation is found primarily in the reported sayings of Jesus. . . . As well, a *soteriological* theme is frequently found in such statements, especially in John: what is negatived is the possibility of the loss of salvation.[8]

Wallace lists some examples, the second of which is John 10:28: "I give them eternal life, and *they will not at all perish*."[9] Jesus,

8. Daniel B. Wallace, *Greek Grammar Beyond the Basics: An Exegetical Syntax of the New Testament* (Grand Rapids: Zondervan, 1996), 468, italics original.
9. Ibid. (italics original).

as emphatically as possible, states that those to whom he gives eternal life will never be lost, will never be cast into hell. That is, they will certainly obtain final salvation. This is one of the strongest statements of God's preservation of his people in the whole Bible, and it comes from the lips of Jesus, the Savior of the world.

Jesus' powerful statement is made even more powerful by his words that follow: "No one will snatch them out of my hand" (v. 28). Jesus, the Good Shepherd, holds his sheep and will allow no enemy to take them away from his strong grip. The word "snatch" speaks of a violent attempt to separate the sheep from their Shepherd. Jesus' mentioning of strong attempts includes all lesser ones. The people of God are safe in the care of their strong Savior.

Moreover, Jesus continues, "My Father, who has given them to me, is greater than all, and no one is able to snatch them out of the Father's hand" (v. 29). John teaches two complementary truths: the deity of Christ and that when he becomes a man, he subordinates himself to the Father. Here both are taught. Jesus, acting as only God can, gives eternal life as a gift. No angel or apostle can do that, but only God himself. But at the same time that John teaches Jesus' equality with God, he reminds us that in the incarnation the Son submits himself to the Father. That is the meaning of Jesus' words, "My Father . . . is greater than all." Not only does the Son of God have a solid grip on his flock; the Father does also. The sheep are safe in the strong arms of God the Father and God the Son.

"I and the Father Are One"

These words of Jesus are frequently misunderstood as teaching that the Father and the Son share God's essence. Although that is a biblical truth (taught in Heb. 1:3, for example), it is not taught here. Rather, the preceding context is the key to understanding Jesus' words. Jesus has said that he gives the sheep eternal life and they will never suffer the punishment of hell. That is because he and the Father hold them tight and no one can take the sheep out of their firm grip. Jesus means that he and the Father are one in their keeping the sheep safe. They are one in preserving the people of God for final salvation. John 10:30 does affirm the deity of Christ: it shows he is God by ascribing to him a work that God alone performs—preservation.

Teaching

This passage is justly famous as a proof text for preservation (eternal security). In three ways Jesus assures his sheep that they are safe in his care. First, he categorically states that they will never perish. Second, he declares the sheep safe in his strong arms, saying no one can seize them away from him. Third, he says that the Father also holds the sheep in his mighty arms and that no one can snatch them from him as well.

Objections

Keener thinks that such conclusions are too sweeping:

> The point in this text is not the impossibility of apostasy. . . . Sheep abandoning the fold is not the same as a wolf "snatching" them. . . . Many early Christian texts warn of apostasy; one could experience God's grace and yet fall away. Johannine theology, however, emphasizes that Jesus knows people's responses before they make them; from God's omniscient standpoint, only those who will ultimately persevere belong to Christ in any event. . . . These would never perish.[10]

Keener errs for at least three reasons. First, before Jesus denies that anyone will snatch sheep away from him or his Father, he emphatically states, "I give them eternal life, and they will never perish" (John 10:28). Keener errs in assuming that this statement is comprehensively explained and therefore limited by the

10. Keener, *The Gospel of John*, 825.

"snatching" statements that follow. To the contrary, this statement is broader than the "snatching" statements. It precludes apostasy as well as anything else that would destroy Jesus' people. Carson has it right: "The ultimate security of Jesus' sheep rests with the good shepherd."[11]

Second, Keener misunderstands Jesus' teaching: "No one will snatch them out of my hand . . . and no one is able to snatch them out of the Father's hand" (vv. 28–29). Jesus does not here limit God's preservation to one circumstance and leave the door open for the sheep to perish in other ways. Instead, he uses an extreme example—an enemy attacking the sheep—to include lesser dangers to the sheep's welfare. If no one can snatch them away, then no one can take them away in less forceful ways—by tempting or tricking them, for example. And believers themselves are included in Jesus' words: "*No one* will snatch them out of my hand . . . *no one* is able to snatch them out of the Father's hand" (vv. 28–29, italics added). Carson is right again: "The focus is . . . on Jesus' power: *no one can snatch them out of my hand*, not the marauding wolf (v. 12), not the thieves and robbers (vv. 1, 8), not anyone."[12]

Third, although it is true that John says, "Jesus knew from the beginning who those were who did not believe" (6:64), John never says that God bases his decisions upon such foreknowledge. Specifically, John nowhere teaches that God bases his people's spiritual security upon his foreknowledge of their perseverance in faith to the end. Keener simply reads his own view of election conditioned upon foreseen faith and final perseverance into the fourth gospel.

Leon Morris better grasps John's teaching in 10:28–30: "It is one of the precious things about the Christian faith that our continuance in eternal life depends not on our feeble hold on Christ, but on His firm grip on us."[13] Indeed, the wonder of this

11. D. A. Carson, *The Gospel according to John* (Grand Rapids: Eerdmans, 1991), 393.

12. Ibid., italics original.

13. Leon Morris, *The Gospel According to John*, The New International Commentary on the New Testament (Grand Rapids: Eerdmans, 1971), 521.

passage is that the sheep are in the safest place imaginable—in the almighty arms of the Son and the Father.

John 17:9–12, 15, 24

> I am praying for them. I am not praying for the world but for those whom you have given me, for they are yours. All mine are yours, and yours are mine, and I am glorified in them. And I am no longer in the world, but they are in the world, and I am coming to you. Holy Father, keep them in your name, which you have given me, that they may be one, even as we are one. While I was with them, I kept them in your name, which you have given me. I have guarded them, and not one of them has been lost except the son of destruction, that the Scripture might be fulfilled. . . . I do not ask that you take them out of the world, but that you keep them from the evil one. . . . Father, I desire that they also, whom you have given me, may be with me where I am, to see my glory that you have given me because you loved me before the foundation of the world.

In Jesus' famous prayer to the Father, Jesus prays for himself (John 17:1–5), his eleven disciples (vv. 6–19), and future believers (vv. 20–26). In the latter two sections, among other requests, four reverberate: that believers might be one (vv. 11, 21, 22, 23), holy (vv. 17, 19), witnesses (vv. 18, 21, 23), and preserved (vv. 11–12, 15, 24). The last is our present concern. At least four times in John 17, Jesus speaks of preservation.

Jesus Asks the Father to Protect the Disciples

Jesus does not pray for the world, but for those chosen by God, those whom the Father gave him (v. 9). These people belong to the Father and Son, and amazingly, Jesus says that he is glorified in them (vv. 9–10). When he says, "I am no longer in the world . . . I am coming to you" (v. 11), he envisions his work on earth completed (see v. 4). In fact, though he prays this prayer before his crucifixion, resurrection, and ascension, throughout he prays as if he has already returned to the Father's heavenly presence (v. 24)!

So, although in his mind's eye Jesus has returned to the Father, his disciples are still in the world (v. 11). Accordingly, he prays, "Holy Father, keep them in your name, which you have given me" (v. 11). Though Jesus here uses an imperative to address the Father—"Keep them"—of course he is not commanding him. Imperatives are used in prayers to express requests.[14] We might paraphrase this, "Holy Father, please keep them."

Despite his holding sway over all human beings, Jesus gives eternal life only to those the Father gave him. Jesus defines eternal life as knowing the Father and the Son (v. 3). He also says that he revealed the Father to those given to him out of the world (v. 6). This revelation involves both information and a personal knowledge of the Father (vv. 6–8). So, when Jesus asks the Father to "keep them" (v. 11), he asks the Father to ensure that they will continue to know the Father and the Son.

In verses 6, 11, 12, and 26 of this prayer, Jesus refers to "the name." He revealed the Father's name to his disciples (v. 6). Later Jesus repeats this idea and adds, "And I will continue to make it known" (v. 26). Jesus' next words show that the Father's "name" refers to the character of the Father: "that the love with which you have loved me may be in them, and I in them" (v. 26). Revealing the Father's name, therefore, means making the Father and his attributes known.

What does Jesus mean when he prays, "Holy Father, keep them *in your name, which you have given me*" (v. 11)? Here again the name stands for the character of God himself, this time as supremely revealed in Jesus.[15] Jesus prays that the Father himself will preserve believers. Jesus' words highlight the Father's person with all of his qualities, including his power, grace, and faithfulness. Believers are in very good hands.

14. Wallace, *Greek Grammar Beyond the Basics*, 487–88.
15. So Carson, *The Gospel according to John*, 562.

Notice the purpose of Jesus' prayer for the Father to keep believers. It is "that they may be one, even as we are one" (v. 11). The themes of preservation and unity overlap. Praying for believers whom he will leave behind, Jesus, soon to return to the Father, asks him to preserve them in salvation, that they might reflect the unity of the Godhead. The harmony between fellow Christians is a testimony to the fact that the Father and Son (and Holy Spirit) are one. How highly God values the spiritual oneness of his people!

Jesus Protected Them While on Earth

Even as Jesus asks the Father to protect believers in his absence, so also Jesus did keep them during his earthly ministry: "While I was with them, I kept them in your name, which you have given me" (v. 12). By his divine power, Jesus gave eternal life to his eleven disciples and kept them saved while he was with them. Seen in this light, the preceding verse is Jesus' request for the Father to continue the work Jesus began on earth—preserving the eleven for final salvation. Thus John 17 is similar to John 10. There we learned that the sheep are safe in the strong arms of the Son and the Father. Here the Son says that he kept his own while on earth and asks the Father to continue to safeguard them from heaven.

Via repetition, Jesus emphasizes his preservation of his people: "I kept them. . . . I have guarded them, and not one of them has been lost" (v. 12). Jesus adds guarding to keeping in order to underscore his work on behalf of his eleven disciples. He has protected them spiritually, so that none of them fell away.

Did Judas Lose Salvation?

Some claim that the end of verse 12 indicates that Judas lost his salvation, for Jesus says, "I kept them. . . . I guarded them, and not one of them has been lost except the son of destruction."[16]

16. So Grant R. Osborne, "Soteriology in the Gospel of John," in *The Grace of God, the Will of Man*, ed. Clark H. Pinnock (Grand Rapids: Zondervan, 1989), 249, 254.

But this claim is mistaken. Though Judas was one of Jesus' twelve disciples, he was never a believer. I say this for four reasons. First, despite the fact that Jesus chose Judas to be a disciple, from the beginning he knew that Judas would not believe but was a devil who would betray him (John 6:64, 70–71).

Second, Judas declares it wasteful when Mary, Lazarus's sister, anoints Jesus' feet with expensive ointment (John 12:3–5, 7). John's explanatory comment is telling: "He said this, not because he cared about the poor, but because he was a thief, and having charge of the moneybag he used to help himself to what was put into it" (v. 6). Judas *used to* help himself" to money given to Jesus. John uses a tense that indicates repeated or habitual action. Paul, warning against deception, says that the unrighteous will not inherit God's kingdom:

> Neither the sexually immoral, nor idolaters, nor adulterers, nor men who practice homosexuality, *nor thieves*, nor the greedy, nor drunkards, nor revilers, nor swindlers will inherit the kingdom of God. And such were some of you. But you were washed, you were sanctified, you were justified in the name of the Lord Jesus Christ and by the Spirit of our God. (1 Cor. 6:9–11, italics added)

A Christian could commit an act of stealing, even as a Christian could commit idolatry or adultery. But persons living a lifestyle of stealing, idolatry, or adultery belie their profession to be Christians. Judas was a thief who had never been washed, sanctified, or justified. His betrayal of Jesus was not an unfortunate act out of keeping with his character. Rather, it was an expression of his evil, unbelieving heart.

Third, when Jesus washes the disciples' feet, he says, "'The one who has bathed does not need to wash, except for his feet, but is completely clean. And you are clean, but not every one of you.' For he knew who was to betray him; that was why he said, 'Not all of you are clean'" (John 13:10–11). The eleven disciples, who were "bathed" (forgiven by God), needed only to have their "feet washed" (to receive forgiveness for daily sins). But Judas never knew the once-for-all forgiveness of sins that the other disciples knew.

Fourth, both the perspectives of divine sovereignty and human responsibility show Judas to be an unsaved person. God is in control of all things, even the betrayal of his Son. Jesus knew who would betray him from the beginning (John 6:64). Jesus predicted Judas' betrayal to prove that he is God (John 13:19). Jesus prayed, "I kept them. . . . I have guarded them, and not one of them has been lost except the son of destruction, *that the Scripture might be fulfilled*" (John 17:12, italics added). The betrayal of Jesus did not surprise God but was in fulfillment of his sovereign plan, as other Scriptures attest (Luke 22:22; Acts 2:23; 4:27–28).

At the same time, Scripture presents Judas as responsible and guilty for his actions. He stole repeatedly from the moneybag (John 12:6). He alone among the Twelve gives Satan an opening for him to exploit (John 13:2, 27). After Jesus identifies the betrayer—"It is he to whom I will give this morsel of bread when I have dipped it" (v. 26)—Judas freely receives the bread from Jesus.

Schreiner and Caneday sum up the matter well:

> Jesus' very point in bringing up Judas is that he was an exception from the beginning. He was never . . . among those given by the Father to the Son. He was never washed and cleansed in the saving bath. It was prophesied from the outset that he would fulfill the role of betrayer. Thus, Jesus did not lose a single one of those given to him by God, and we are strengthened immeasurably when we realize that this prayer of Jesus will certainly be answered. God will keep us to the end and will unquestionably answer the prayers of his Son.[17]

Jesus Asks the Father to Protect the Disciples from the Devil

After contrasting the joy he gives his disciples with the hatred they receive from the world, Jesus teaches that their origin, the

17. Schreiner and Caneday, *The Race Set Before Us*, 253–54.

same as his, is from heaven (John 17:14). Then, he continues, "I do not ask that you take them out of the world, but that you keep them from the evil one" (v. 15). Once more Jesus asks the Father to preserve his own, this time specifying from what—"the evil one."

The Gospel of John tells us a lot about this evil one. Jesus knows that "the devil . . . was a murderer from the beginning . . . he is a liar and the father of lies" (8:44). Three times Jesus calls him "the ruler of this world" (12:31; 14:30; 16:11), the first and third of which announce his demise. It is this "devil" called "Satan" who prompted Judas Iscariot to betray Jesus and entered into him to empower him for the evil deed (13:2, 27).

Jesus does not ask the Father to remove the other eleven disciples from this hostile world but to protect them from the evil one. Jesus knows that the devil is active and will tempt his followers. If left to their own devices the eleven would fall, just as Judas did. But because of Jesus' prayer that the Father preserve them from the devil, they are not on their own. They are kept by the Son's prayers and the Father's power, granted in answer to those prayers. Because of the ministries of the Father and Son, even frightened Christians can take heart in John's words, "He who is in you is greater than he who is in the world" (1 John 4:4).

Jesus Asks the Father to Bring the Disciples to Heavenly Glory

Throughout this prayer, Jesus adopts the posture of one who has already returned to the Father and heavenly glory. That is nowhere more evident than in verse 24: "Father, I desire that they also, whom you have given me, may be with me where I am, to see my glory that you have given me." Although Jesus is on earth, ready to go to the cross, he knows his victory of resurrection and ascension is assured. He asks the Father to take the believers to be with him. Jesus wants his own to behold his heavenly glory. The Father certainly will answer his Son's prayer. Believers will be with Jesus to see his glory. In this way, Jesus ends his famous prayer with a fourth affirmation of the preservation of the saints.

Teaching

The harmony between the Father and the Son in salvation that we saw in John 10:28–30 is evident also in John 17. As Jesus bares his heart to his heavenly Father before his death and resurrection, he emphasizes the fact that he protected his disciples spiritually (except for Judas who was never saved) while he was with them (v. 12). Now, as he prepares to return to the Father, Jesus asks his Father to continue to keep his chosen ones in his absence. Specifically, he asks the Father not to remove them from a hostile world, but to protect them from Satan. Finally, he ends his prayer by asking the Father to bring all of the chosen ones to heavenly glory to be with him.

Objections

Those who oppose eternal security point to Judas the apostle, who became an apostate (v. 12), as evidence that believers may fall away from salvation.[18] This argument has been answered on pages 44–46 and will not be repeated here.

Puzzlingly, Marshall regards Jesus' prayers for the protection of his own in John 17 as evidence that they could fall away and be lost: "Jesus found it necessary to pray that the Father would keep the disciples (John 17:11, 15, 24), even as He had kept them (John 17:12). All this indicates that the disciples stand under the threat of being lost, for otherwise they would not need to be guarded. Their safety depends upon God."[19]

It is true that Jesus found it necessary to ask the Father to preserve the eleven, even as Jesus himself had done during his earthly ministry. But far from their being in danger of being lost, Jesus' prayer for them was his way of keeping them unto the end. If he had not prayed, they would have been in danger of falling away. Indeed their safety depends upon God, and God the Son expressly prays for them three times in John 17 to pre-

18. Osborne, "Soteriology in the Gospel of John," 249, 254; Marshall, *Kept by the Power of God*, 181–82.

19. Marshall, *Kept by the Power of God*, 184.

serve them from being lost and from the evil one, and to bring them to heavenly glory. Jesus, our great High Priest, *continues* to pray for us believers now that he is in heaven—and thus we cannot fall away.

Connecting the Dots

Jesus, the great prophet, in at least four passages taught his disciples that God preserves his saints for final salvation: Luke 22:31–34; John 6:35, 37–40, 44; 10:25–30; and 17:9–12, 15, 24.

Although Peter denied Jesus three times, his faith was not extinguished, in fulfillment of Jesus' words, "But I have prayed for you that your faith may not fail" (Luke 22:32). Peter persevered in his faith, even after terrible wavering, because his Lord preserved him by praying for him. One of the ways that Jesus, our great High Priest, keeps us saved is by his present heavenly ministry—even as he made intercession for Peter, he presently makes intercession for us (Rom. 8:34; Heb. 7:23–25).

According to John 6:37–40, the Father and Son work in harmony for our salvation. The Father chooses people and draws them to faith in the Son. They believe in the Son and are saved. The Son keeps them and will raise them for eternal life in the future. Because of the harmonious labor between the Father and Son, God's people enjoy a continuous identity. The people the Father gives to the Son and draws to him are the same people who come to the Son, the same people the Son saves and keeps, and the same people he will raise on the last day. This means that the Father and Son work together to preserve the saints so that not one believer will be lost (vv. 37, 39).

Jesus assures his sheep that they are safe in his care in three ways. First, he categorically states that they will never perish (John 10:28). Second, he asserts that the sheep are safe in his mighty grip and that no one can snatch them away from him (v. 28). Third, he says that the Father also holds the sheep in his almighty arms and that no one can take them away from him

either (v. 29). In fact, Jesus and the Father are united in preserving the sheep (v. 30).

Preservation is one of the primary themes of Jesus' high-
priestly prayer (John 17). He emphasizes his spiritual protection
of his disciples (except for unsaved Judas) during his earthly
ministry (v. 12). Now, as he prepares to return to heaven, Jesus
entrusts to the Father their ongoing spiritual well-being (v. 11).
He particularly asks the Father to protect them from the evil one
(v. 15). And he ends his prayer by asking the Father to bring all
of his own to heavenly glory to be with him (v. 24).

The Lord Jesus, the Savior of the world, thus has a lot to
say about the preservation of the saints. He does not want us
to live in fear of losing our salvation. Rather, over and over he
assures us that due to the love, power, and faithfulness of the
Father and Son, we are safe. Because of Jesus' prayers, gift of
eternal life, promises, and the protection that he and the Father
together afford believers, not one of them will perish, but all will
be raised to life on the last day. All of us will be glorified with
Jesus to behold his glory. Hallelujah!

Preservation in Paul, Part 1

AS IS TRUE for so many biblical themes, Paul has much to say about God's preservation of his saints, so much that my summary of his teaching fills two chapters. In the first of these, we will look at three passages from Romans. (In the next one, we will consider six passages from four other Pauline epistles.)

- Romans 5:9–10
- Romans 8:1–4
- Romans 8:28–39

Romans 5:9-10

> Since, therefore, we have now been justified by his blood, much more shall we be saved by him from the wrath of God. For if while we were enemies we were reconciled to God by the death of his Son, much more, now that we are reconciled, shall we be saved by his life.

Before giving the famous Adam/Christ parallel in Romans 5:12–21, Paul conveys four benefits of justification. Justification views God's salvation in legal terms. God the Father, acting as judge, declares righteous every sinner who trusts Christ for salvation. This declaration is based on Christ's death that turned away God's wrath (3:25–26) and accomplished "one act

51

of righteousness" (5:18) that is applied to the spiritual bank account of all believers.

Peace, Joy, and Hope

The advantages of free justification mentioned here begin with reconciliation, peace with God (Rom. 5:1). No longer do our sins alienate us from a holy God because he has made peace by offering his Son on the cross. As a result, we have access to God and his ongoing grace (v. 2). Other blessings of justification include joy and hope: "We rejoice in hope of the glory of God" (v. 2). The sure prospect of our one day seeing and sharing Christ's glory brings us great hope and joy now.

We not only rejoice at the thought of being with Christ some-day; we also rejoice right now, even when we suffer: "More than that, we rejoice in our sufferings, knowing that suffering produces endurance, and endurance produces character, and character produces hope" (vv. 3–4). It is easy to follow some of Paul's thought here. If Christians look to the Lord when they suffer, they learn steadfastness. And if they continue to learn steadfastness, eventually their character changes, and they become steady people. But how does character produce hope? Here Paul's ideas are hard to follow. Reading between the lines, we conclude that he means that as we see God changing our character now, it increases our faith in what we cannot see—God's future blessings. When believers respond to sufferings rightly, it strengthens their hope in the future glory of God. And, Paul continues, this hope does not disappoint us because God has given us the Holy Spirit to testify within our hearts of his love for us (v. 5).

God's Amazing Love

Paul continues to speak of God's amazing love (vv. 6–8). Paul contrasts God's action with those of normal human affairs. It is unusual for a human being to lay down his life for another— such actions are heroic (v. 7). Moreover, such self-sacrifice, as rare as it is, is always done for another whom we highly value. A soldier falls on a grenade to save his buddies; no one falls on a grenade to save an enemy! But God's love transcends human love: "For while we were still weak, at the right time Christ died for the ungodly. . . . God shows his love for us in that while we were still sinners, Christ died for us" (vv. 6, 8). We did not merit God's love. He did not give Christ for us because we were deserving. On the contrary, we were "weak," "ungodly," "sinners" (vv. 6, 8).

A Pattern

Paul's extolling God's matchless love forms the center of the pattern he paints in Romans 5:1–11. We already saw four benefits of justification in verses 1–5: peace with God, joy, hope, and God's love, in that order. Paul repeats in reverse order these benefits of justification: God's love (vv. 6–8), hope (vv. 9–10), joy (v. 11), and peace with God (v. 11). This pattern (an inverted parallelism or chiasm) follows the form A B C D D C B A, where the letters stand for ideas.

> A. Peace with God, v. 1
>> B. Joy, v. 2
>>> C. Hope, vv. 2–5
>>>> D. God's love, v. 5
>>>> D. God's love, vv. 6–8
>>> C. Hope, vv. 9–10
>> B. Joy, v. 11
> A. Peace with God, v. 11

We Shall Be Saved

Since, therefore, we have now been justified by his blood, much more shall we be saved by him from the wrath of God. For if while we were enemies we were reconciled to God by the death of his Son, much more, now that we are reconciled, shall we be saved by his life. (Rom. 5:9–10)

Paul, after praising God's remarkable love that establishes our hope of eternal glory, makes a strong case for preservation. A great manifestation of God's love is keeping his people saved to the end. And this keeping guarantees that "hope does not put us to shame" (v. 5). Twice Paul employs a Jewish argument from the more difficult to the less difficult. He uses the words "much more" to signal his use of this argument. In verse 9 he argues in terms of justification and in verse 10 in terms of reconciliation.

Paul uses shorthand in verse 9 and longhand in verse 10. The full argument involves an "if" clause followed by a "then" clause, and we find both types of clauses in verse 10. But verse 9 only has a then clause. Paul expects his readers to provide an "if" clause from the preceding verses: If, when we were condemned before a holy God, he justified us through the death of his Son. . . . "Since, therefore, we have now been justified by his blood, much more shall we be saved by him from the wrath of God." Paul uses "wrath" to refer to hell, as he frequently does in his writings.[1]

Paul argues from the harder to the easier: If God did the harder thing—justified guilty sinners—he will surely do the easier thing—keep saved to the end those he has justified. This is a powerful argument for God's preservation of his saints. God did the incredible and declared the unrighteous righteous through Christ. Now he will do the expected—he will stand by his previous verdict and not condemn his justified people.

For the sake of emphasis, Paul repeats a similar argument for preservation. But now he refers to salvation as reconciliation instead of justification. "For if while we were enemies we were reconciled to God by the death of his Son, much more, now that we are reconciled, shall we be saved by his life" (Rom. 5:9–10). This time Paul writes in longhand, giving both if and then clauses: If when we were God's enemies he made us his friends

1. He also uses "wrath" to refer to hell in Rom. 1:18; 2:5, 8; 3:5; 9:22; 12:19; Eph. 2:3; 5:6; Col 3:6; 1 Thess. 1:10; 2:16; 5:9. See Douglas J. Moo, "Paul on Hell," in Christopher Morgan and Robert Peterson, eds., *Hell under Fire* (Grand Rapids: Zondervan, 2004), 91–109.

by his Son's death, now that we are his friends he certainly will keep us saved by his Son's resurrection. Here Paul does not state what we shall be saved from, but he has already told us in verse 9—God's wrath.

Teaching

Paul expounds four great benefits of justification in Romans 5:1–11: peace, joy, hope, and love. He focuses on God's love by putting it at the center of a pattern. He first speaks of God's love and the Holy Spirit who ministers that love within our hearts. He then moves to his main idea—God's compassion through Christ. God in love does what is humanly inconceivable—he gives his Son to save sinners.

Paul returns to the idea of hope and this time highlights "the certainty of Christian hope."[2] He communicates believers' safety in Christ by employing the Jewish argument from the more difficult to the less difficult. If God did the more difficult thing—justifying the guilty and reconciling his enemies by Christ's death and resurrection[3]—he assuredly will do the less difficult thing—he will keep them saved. Twice Paul says unequivocally that we shall be saved (vv. 9, 10). Our great Father loves us and wants us to rest in his promises that guarantee our final salvation in Christ. What can we do but worship and give our lives to him who loves us like that?

Judith Gundry Volf summarizes well:

In 5:9, 10, Paul draws out the significance of God's gracious love as the guarantee that Christian hope will not disappoint. . . . With the help of two arguments *ad maiori ad minus* [from the greater

2. Douglas Moo, *The Epistle to the Romans*, New International Commentary on the New Testament (Grand Rapids: Eerdmans, 1996), 309.

3. Paul's references to Christ's blood in v. 9 and his life in v. 10 do not divide the accomplishment of salvation between his death and resurrection. Rather, reminiscent of 4:25, "Christ's death and resurrection are inseparable in effecting salvation." Thomas Schreiner, *Romans*, Baker Exegetical Commentary on the New Testament (Grand Rapids: Baker, 1998), 264. As a result, either (as a metonymy) could stand for Christ's whole saving accomplishment.

to the lesser], he shows that God's accomplishment of the scarcely imaginable feat of demonstrating love toward rebellious sinners in the cross of Christ guarantees the future salvation of those who are God's own people in fulfillment of their hope.[4]

Romans 8:1–4

> There is therefore now no condemnation for those who are in Christ Jesus. For the law of the Spirit of life has set you free in Christ Jesus from the law of sin and death. For God has done what the law, weakened by the flesh, could not do. By sending his own Son in the likeness of sinful flesh and for sin, he condemned sin in the flesh, in order that the righteous requirement of the law might be fulfilled in us, who walk not according to the flesh but according to the Spirit.

In two passages in this greatest chapter in what many consider the Bible's greatest book, Paul gives the greatest affirmation of God's preservation of his people to be found in Scripture.

Background

"There is therefore now no condemnation for those who are in Christ Jesus" (Rom. 8:1). The word "therefore" points back, in decreasing order of influence, to Romans 5:12–21; 7:6; and 7:25. In Romans 5:12–21, Paul contrasts the two Adams and their effects upon their respective races: Adam's primal sin brought condemnation and death upon the human race; Christ's "one act of righteousness" brought justification and life to all believers (vv. 18–19). The fact that the word "condemnation" occurs only in Romans 5:16, 18, and 8:1 suggests that Romans 8:1–13 draws conclusions from Romans 5:12–21.

Romans 6:1–7:25 speaks of the triumph of God's grace over sin (chapter 6) and over the law (chapter 7). When Romans 7:6

---

4. Judith M. Gundry Volf, *Paul and Perseverance: Staying In and Falling Away* (Louisville: John Knox, 1990), 53.

tells of "the new way of the Spirit," it introduces a major theme that chapter 8 will develop. Romans 7:25 hints at what is to come in the next chapter when it praises "Jesus Christ our Lord" as the deliverer of believers from spiritual defeat.

No Condemnation

Paul begins with these words: "There is therefore now no condemnation for those who are in Christ Jesus" (Rom. 8:1). The apostle speaks in legal terms and affirms that Christ completely delivers his people from "condemnation," the penalty of sin for lawbreakers. Believers will not experience God's eternal wrath. Indeed, Paul's point is that they will *never* experience it because he says with emphasis, "There is *no* condemnation" (italics added).[5] Their deliverance is forever.

Paul combines the language of the courtroom with that of relationship when he says this deliverance applies to those "who are in Christ Jesus." All who died and rose with Christ (Rom. 6:1–11) are in spiritual union with him and will never experience the pains of hell. There is no divine condemnation for them, "since the condemnation which they deserve has already been fully borne for them by Him,"[6] as verse 3 explains.

Set Free

"For the law of the Spirit of life has set you free in Christ Jesus from the law of sin and death" (Rom. 8:2). Paul gives the basis for verse 1: the Holy Spirit has liberated believers from the curse of the Mosaic Law. The Spirit is called "the Spirit of life" because he brings eternal life to the spiritually dead. By so doing he sets us free from the law that leads to sin and death. A great transfer occurs. The life-giving Spirit releases us from the realm of sin and death and delivers us into the

---

5. The emphatic negative (*ouden*) is used and is placed in the emphatic first position.

6. C. E. B. Cranfield, *A Critical and Exegetical Commentary on the Epistle to the Romans*, 2 vols., International Critical Commentary (Edinburgh: T&T Clark, 1975), 1:373.

realm of life. As a result, sin's penalty and power are broken. We will never be condemned (v. 1) and need not live in sin anymore (vv. 4b–17).

God Condemned Sin in Christ's Flesh

"For God has done what the law, weakened by the flesh, could not do. By sending his own Son in the likeness of sinful flesh and for sin, he condemned sin in the flesh" (Rom. 8:3). The law of Moses is "weakened by the flesh"; that is, the law cannot save because fallen human beings fail to keep it. But what the law could not do, God did in Christ, whom he sent "in the likeness of sinful flesh."

Paul carefully chose his words. If he had said, "Christ came in sinful flesh," then Christ would be a sinner himself and unable to save others. If, on the other hand, Paul had denied that Christ identified with sinners, he again would be unable to save us, because he would not be close enough to us. But Paul hits the golden mean—the Son came "in the likeness of sinful flesh," that is, truly sharing with the sinful human condition without committing sin himself.

The Father sent his Son "in the likeness of sinful flesh and *for sin*" (italics added). Because the words "for sin" are used regularly in the Septuagint (the Greek Old Testament) to mean "sin offering," most commentators understand them that way here.[7] Paul refers to Christ's death as a sacrifice that takes away sin.

The main idea of the verse is: "God . . . condemned sin in the flesh." Paul refers to the flesh of Christ in which he made a sin offering. Paul continues to use legal language, speaking next of "the righteous requirement of the law" (v. 4). But how did God, "by sending his own Son in the likeness of sinful flesh and for sin," condemn sin in the Son's humanity? I cannot improve on Douglas Moo's explanation:

7. See James D. G. Dunn, *Romans 1–9*, Word Biblical Commentary (Waco, TX: Word, 1988), 403.

The condemnation of sin consists in God's executing his judgment on sin in the atoning death of his Son. As our substitute, Christ "was made sin for us" (2 Cor. 5:21) and suffered the wrath of God, the judgment of God upon that sin (cf. . . . Rom. 3:25; Gal. 3:13). In his doing so, of course, we may say that sin's power was broken in the sense that Paul pictures sin as a power that holds people in its clutches and brings condemnation to them. . . . The condemnation that our sins deserve has been poured out on Christ, our sin-bearer; that is why "there is now no condemnation for those who are in Christ Jesus" (v. 1).[8]

The Law's Righteous Requirement Fulfilled

". . . in order that the righteous requirement of the law might be fulfilled in us, who walk not according to the flesh but according to the Spirit" (Rom. 8:4). Although many hold that Paul's speaking of the fulfilling of the law's requirement in us here refers to our growth in holiness, I disagree. Rather, he says, "he condemned sin in the flesh, in order that the righteous requirement of the law might be fulfilled in us" to tell about Christ's fulfillment of the law. Once more I cite Moo:

If, then, the inability of the law is to be overcome without an arbitrary cancellation of the law, it can happen only through a perfect obedience of the law's demands. . . . This, of course, is exactly what Jesus Christ has done. As our substitute, he satisfied the righteous requirement of the law, living a life of perfect submission to God. In laying upon him the condemnation due all of us (v. 3b; cf. v. 1), God also made it possible for the righteous obedience that Christ had earned to be transferred to us.[9]

God's purposes in sending his Son include not only to free sinners from condemnation (vv. 1–4a), but also to change their lives (v. 4b and the following verses). Christ died not only to justify but also to progressively sanctify his people. Those whom God has

8. Moo, *The Epistle to the Romans*, 481.
9. Ibid., 483.

declared righteous are identifiable, for they "walk not according to the flesh but according to the Spirit" (v. 4).

Teaching

Paul begins one of Scripture's most powerful chapters with an affirmation that the God who saves his people will also preserve them to the end. The apostle declares, "There is therefore now no condemnation for those who are in Christ Jesus" (Rom. 8:1). How are we to account for this bold declaration? Judith Gundry Volf, commenting on Romans 8:34, answers pithily:

> "Christ Jesus is the one who died" (v. 34b). The *katakrima* [condemnation] due us (5:16, 18) fell upon the crucified Christ: "Sending his Son in the likeness of sinful flesh and for sin, God condemned (*katekrinein*) sin in the flesh" (8:3). Thus Paul can assure believers already, "there is therefore now no *katakrima* [condemnation] for those who are in Christ Jesus" (8:1).[10]

Romans 8:28–39

> And we know that for those who love God all things work together for good, for those who are called according to his purpose. For those whom he foreknew he also predestined to be conformed to the image of his Son, in order that he might be the firstborn among many brothers. And those whom he predestined he also called, and those whom he called he also justified, and those whom he justified he also glorified. What then shall we say to these things? If God is for us, who can be against us? He who did not spare his own Son but gave him up for us all, how will he not also with him graciously give us all things? Who shall bring any charge against God's elect? It is God who justifies. Who is to condemn? Christ Jesus is the one who died—more than that, who was raised—who is at the right hand of God, who indeed is interceding for us. Who shall separate us from the love of Christ? Shall tribulation, or distress, or

10. Volf, *Paul and Perseverance*, 68.

persecution, or famine, or nakedness, or danger, or sword? As it is written, "For your sake we are being killed all the day long; we are regarded as sheep to be slaughtered." No, in all these things we are more than conquerors through him who loved us. For I am sure that neither death nor life, nor angels nor rulers, nor things present nor things to come, nor powers, nor height nor depth, nor anything else in all creation, will be able to separate us from the love of God in Christ Jesus our Lord.

These words of the apostle Paul constitute the strongest preservation passage in all of Scripture for two reasons. First, their function in the context of Romans is to teach that God keeps his saints. Second, this is the longest sustained text on eternal security in Scripture; Paul teaches preservation in line after line.

The apostle begins with very familiar words: "And we know that for those who love God all things work together for good, for those who are called according to his purpose" (Rom. 8:28). "All things" points to the preceding verses that speak of "present sufferings" and the "groaning" of creation, believers, and the Holy Spirit (vv. 18, 22, 23, 26). Believers, here defined as those who love God, are to rest assured that God works all things, even their struggles and pain, for their ultimate good. Paul further describes believers as "those who are called according to his purpose." This refers to God's effectively summoning his people to Christ in salvation, a theme to which Paul returns in verse 30. Why does Paul include it here? Lest readers misunderstand his reference to Christians as "those who love God." Our love for him is a reflex action to his prior love for us; he takes the initiative in salvation—he called us according to *his* purpose.

Paul explains why believers are assured that God works even present trials for their ultimate benefit—because he has planned their greatest good, their final salvation (vv. 29–30). The apostle here begins the first of four arguments—each linked to God's character—as to why we need not fear falling away from grace. God will keep us in his sovereignty (vv. 29–30), power (vv. 31–32), justice (vv. 33–34), and love (vv. 35–39).

We Are Kept Because of God's Sovereignty (vv. 29–30)

The word "for" that begins these two verses means "because" and gives the reason why Christians know that God works all things for their good. It is because he has planned their greatest good—their eternal salvation—from beginning to end. Paul uses five verbs in the simple past (aorist) tense to describe God's plan. Each verb has God as its subject and God's people as its direct object. God foreknew, predestined, called, justified, and glorified his people. Each verb deserves our attention.

God "foreknew" his people. "Foreknow" and its related noun "foreknowledge" have various meanings in Scripture. They sometimes refer to God's ordaining or choosing Christ (Acts 2:23; 1 Peter 1:20) and sometimes to human beings knowing facts beforehand (Acts 26:5; 2 Peter 3:17). But in the places where God is the one who foreknows and his people are the ones foreknown, it refers to his loving them beforehand (Rom. 8:29; 11:2; 1 Peter 1:2).

There are two reasons why "foreknew" in Romans 8:29 does not speak of God knowing facts beforehand, especially who would believe in Christ. First, the object of God's foreknowing here is not facts but people: "*those* whom he foreknew." Second, here it is not all, as would be the case if Paul spoke of God knowing people's responses to the gospel beforehand, but only *some* who are foreknown. That is evident because those foreknown are also predestined, called, justified, and glorified, and not all human beings will be glorified. Rather God's foreknowledge of his people here is his setting his love upon them beforehand—even before creation (Eph. 1:4; 2 Tim. 1:9; Rev. 13:8; 17:8)—in such a way that it leads to their predestination.

Those foreknown "he also predestined" (v. 29). Predestination is God, in love and sovereignty, choosing people for salvation before the creation of the world.[11] Paul's second epistle to

---

11. See my *Election and Free Will*, Explorations in Biblical Theology (Phillipsburg, NJ: P&R Publishing, 2007) for the teaching of every major section of Scripture, including Paul's epistles, on predestination.

Timothy is most succinct on this: "God . . . saved us and called us to a holy calling, not because of our works but because of his own purpose and grace, which he gave us in Christ Jesus before the ages began" (1:8–9). Paul emphasizes predestination in Romans 8:29–30 because he only expands it: we were "predestined to be conformed to the image of his Son, in order that he might be the firstborn among many brothers" (v. 29). All of those who become God's children by believing in his Son (John 1:12; Gal. 3:24) will one day be conformed to the character of their unique older Brother in holiness and glory. What a thrilling prospect for all of us who struggle with temptation day after day!

When Paul writes, "And those whom he predestined he also called," he means that those whom God has chosen for salvation he also effectively summons to Christ in the gospel. God "calls" them by drawing them so that they believe in his Son.

"And those whom he called he also justified." The ones God summons to Christ he also declares righteous because of Christ's righteousness made over to their spiritual bank accounts by grace through faith.

Now Paul's words touch on God's preservation of his saints. The apostle says, "and those whom he justified he also glorified" (v. 30). This is amazing. Glorification is a future aspect of salvation, in which God's redeemed people behold Christ's glory and are transformed by that beholding to actually share his glory (Col. 3:4; 2 Thess. 2:14; 1 Peter 5:1). But when Paul here refers to this future aspect of salvation, he uses the same simple past tense that he used to refer to four past aspects of salvation: foreknowledge, predestination, calling, and justification. "Those whom he justified he also *glorified*." Why does Paul put our future glorification in the past tense? Thomas Schreiner answers correctly: "What is envisioned is the eschatological completion of God's work on behalf of believers that began before history, and the aorist [simple past tense] signifies the certainty that what God has begun he will finish."[12]

12. Schreiner, *Romans*, 454.

The sovereign God keeps every one of his foreloved, predestined, called, and justified people for final glorification. This is brought out by Paul's use of pronouns in the passage: "For *those whom* he foreknew he also predestined. . . . And *those whom* he predestined he also called, and *those whom* he called he also justified, and *those whom* he justified he also glorified" (vv. 29–30). Not one of those who believe in Christ will fail to be saved. Our Father will keep every believer in his Son for glorification on the last day.

We Are Kept Because of God's Power (vv. 31–32)

After arguing for preservation based on God's sovereignty, Paul next argues for it based on God's power. Contemplating his words in chapter 8, Paul extols, "What then shall we say to these things?" (Rom. 8:31). The greatness of God's grace overwhelms the apostle. He adds another rhetorical question: "If God is for us, who can be against us?" (v. 31). This one too, though in the form of a question, is not a true interrogative. Rather, it is Paul's way of emphasizing that no one and nothing—not Satan, demons, human enemies, even our own sin—can successfully stand against God's people if he is on their side. After all, he is almighty God! The issue is not his ability to defeat foes. Instead, it is his commitment to us.

How can we be persuaded beyond the shadow of a doubt that God is "for us" (v. 31)? Paul answers with another question: "He who did not spare his own Son but gave him up for us all, how will he not also with him graciously give us all things?" (v. 32). The supreme demonstration that God is committed to us is his giving Christ to die for us. If we ever wonder whether God is on our side, all we have to do is visit the cross of his Son. That cross is God's "yes" to all such questions once and for all! And no enemies will ever take us away from him who is the Maker of heaven and earth. Our Father will not reject us; instead, "with" Jesus he will "graciously give us *all things*" (v. 32). That is, we as children of God Almighty will inherit "all things," God himself along with the new heavens and new earth (Rom. 8:17; 1 Cor. 3:21–23).

We Are Kept Because of God's Justice (vv. 33–34)

Paul argues for the safety of Christians' salvation based on God's attributes of sovereignty, power, and now justice. He again asks a rhetorical question: "Who shall bring any charge against God's elect?" (Rom. 8:33). He is not soliciting an answer but means, "No one will successfully bring a legal accusation against God's people and make it stick." He speaks forthrightly: "It is God who justifies" (v. 33). Our case has gone to the supreme Judge of the universe, and he has acquitted us. God the Father, who knows our sins better than we, has first pronounced a verdict of "guilty" when viewing us as sinners. But then, viewing us in Christ, he has pronounced a verdict of "righteous." No one will ever overturn the verdict of God, the highest Judge. Once more, Paul teaches, we are safe because of God's qualities in action— this time his justice.

Paul repeats the same basic argument in slightly different terms. Once more he leads with a rhetorical question: "Who is to condemn" (v. 34)? In Scripture's judgment passages, the Judge who condemns is sometimes the Father and sometimes the Son. When Paul mentions Christ Jesus after asking who will condemn, therefore, readers would suppose that Paul is presenting Christ as the Judge. Nothing could be further from the truth, however. Instead, the apostle writes, "Christ Jesus is the one who died— more than that, who was raised—who is at the right hand of God, who indeed is interceding for us" (v. 34). Christ, the Judge of all the earth, will not condemn his people on the last day. That is because he is not their Judge to condemn; he is their Savior to deliver. He died, was raised, sat at God's right hand, and intercedes for them! Christians will meet the Judge as their Savior!

He presently intercedes in heaven for them to maintain their salvation. Although his intercession according to Hebrews 7:23–25 involves the presentation of his finished sacrifice in the Father's presence, in Romans 8:34 his intercession is his praying on our behalf. I say this because the same word "intercede" is used in Romans 8:26–27 of the Holy Spirit's intercession, which is plainly his praying for us:

> Likewise the Spirit helps us in our weakness. For we do not know what to pray for as we ought, but the Spirit himself intercedes for us with groanings too deep for words. And he who searches hearts knows what is the mind of the Spirit, because the Spirit intercedes for the saints according to the will of God.

The Judge who will condemn sinners to eternal punishment will not condemn his people whom he saves and keeps saved by his prayers. God's justice assures us of final salvation—because of both the Father's verdict and the Son's intercession.

We Are Kept Because of God's Love (vv. 35–39)

Paul saves his most extensive and powerful argument for last—his argument for preservation based on God's love in Christ. Yet again he asks rhetorical questions: "Who shall separate us from the love of Christ? Shall tribulation, or distress, or persecution, or famine, or nakedness, or danger, or sword?" (Rom. 8:35). He lists seven things (the number of completeness) to consider what could possibly separate believers from Christ's love. The first six refer to serious troubles culminating in death ("sword"). Paul quotes Psalm 44:22 to assure his readers that their troubles, even when severe, are not unusual; the Old Testament people of God suffered greatly too: "As it is written, 'For your sake we are being killed all the day long; we are regarded as sheep to be slaughtered'" (v. 36).

Paul has allowed the tension to build; for three lines he has considered whether anything could separate Christians from their Savior's love. Now he replies in the negative: "No, in all these things we are more than conquerors through him who loved us" (v. 37). Believers will not be taken away from their Redeemer; instead, they overcome through his love. Paul uses a word that adds the equivalent of the English *super* to the verb *conquer*. We overwhelmingly overcome through the love of Jesus.

Paul concludes his teaching on preservation by abandoning rhetorical questions for comprehensive assertions: "For I am sure that neither death nor life, nor angels nor rulers, nor things present nor things to come, nor powers, nor height nor depth, nor anything else in all creation, will be able to separate us from the love of God in Christ Jesus our Lord" (vv. 38–39). With the exception of the term "powers," the apostle uses pairs of items to underscore his point—nothing, nothing at all, will ever separate God's saints from Jesus' love.

"Neither death nor life" shall do so. Our experience is comprehensively summarized by our "life" and "death." In this context "angels" and "rulers" refer to evil angels, demons, who want to ruin us. The original readers of Romans regarded them as a greater threat than many Christians do today. Paul's point? They will not be able to take God's people away from Christ. Once again Paul speaks comprehensively—this time with temporal reference—when he says, "nor things present nor things to come." From the vantage point of the present all is present and future. Nothing now or to come will cut us off from Christ's grace.

"Powers" also refers to demons, who are pronounced powerless to disassociate believers from Christ. "Height" and "depth" view reality in spatial terms—nothing above or below, not heaven or hell, will sever us from God's Son. Once more Paul speaks comprehensively—just in case readers did not yet get his message—asserting, "nor anything else in all creation, will be able to separate us from the love of God in Christ Jesus our Lord" (v. 39). All of reality is composed of its Creator and his creatures. God has repeatedly affirmed his intention to keep his people saved. Now he declares that no creature whatsoever will accomplish our demise. We are safe in the Savior's love, from which God will allow absolutely nothing ever to separate us.

Connecting the Dots

Paul in Romans gives the strongest assurance found in God's Word that God, who saves us by his grace, will also keep us by his grace.

In Romans 5:9–10 he teaches our safety in Christ by using the Jewish argument from the more difficult to the less difficult. If God did the more difficult thing—he justified condemned sinners and reconciled his enemies by Christ's death and resurrection—he certainly will do the less difficult—he will keep them saved to the end.

In Romans 8:1–4 Paul boldly proclaims that there is "no condemnation" for God's people (v. 1). He then explains the legal reasons why this is so: Christ freed us from the law's curse, God in Christ's sacrifice condemned sin, and Christ's life and death perfectly satisfied the law's righteous requirement.

In Romans 8:29–39, the most sustained teaching on preservation in Scripture, Paul appeals to four of God's qualities—his sovereignty, power, justice, and love—to buttress his doctrine of preservation. God has committed himself to us by covenant, and nothing will prevent our final salvation. His sovereignty guarantees the fulfillment of his plan, and therefore all believers will be glorified. His power is almighty; no one will defeat us because the Father has shown his commitment to us by giving his Son to die in our place. He, the supreme Judge, has declared us righteous, and no one will overturn his verdict. In addition, nothing will ever separate God's people from his love.

Preservation in Paul, Part 2

PAUL'S MOST POWERFUL teaching on preservation appears in Romans, as we have seen. But his teaching on this theme is by no means limited to Romans. It also appears in at least six other passages, scattered over four of his letters.

- 1 Corinthians 1:4, 8–9
- 1 Corinthians 11:27–33
- Ephesians 1:13–14; 4:30
- Philippians 1:6
- 1 Thessalonians 5:23–24

1 Corinthians 1:4, 8–9

I give thanks to my God always for you because of the grace of God that was given you in Christ Jesus, that in every way you were enriched in him in all speech and all knowledge—even as the testimony about Christ was confirmed among you—so that you are not lacking in any spiritual gift, as you wait for the revealing of our Lord Jesus Christ, who will sustain you to the end, guiltless in the day of our Lord Jesus Christ. God is faithful, by whom you were called into the fellowship of his Son, Jesus Christ our Lord. (1 Cor. 1:4–9)

After his epistolary greeting (in vv. 1–3), Paul tells how he always offers thanks to God because of his grace granted to the Corinthian Christians through the Mediator. Specifically, Paul is grateful for the way God made them rich in spiritual gifts of utterance and knowledge, thereby confirming in their midst God's witness to Christ. Due to God's grace they had all the spiritual gifts as they looked forward to Christ's return.

God Will Sustain Them Guiltless

After referring to Christ by name for the seventh time in the first seven verses of the epistle, Paul writes, "who will sustain you to the end, guiltless in the day of our Lord Jesus Christ" (v. 8). Here the apostle affirms that God will keep his saints for final salvation. Paul does this by using the tense of prediction—Christ "*will* sustain you." When used of persons, the word translated "sustain" means "to establish or strengthen."[1] Christ will establish his people. How long will he do so? Paul explains: he "will sustain you to the end" (*heos telos*, v. 8). The apostle leaves no doubt as to the meaning of "the end," for he elaborates, "in the day of our Lord Jesus Christ." Christ will preserve his people until he comes again.

Paul thinks in legal terms when he writes, he "will sustain you . . . *guiltless*" (v. 8). The word "guiltless" means "blameless, irreproachable."[2] Some have mistakenly placed the emphasis on the Corinthians' moral behavior.[3] Although Paul shows concern for that later in this letter, it is not his accent here. Rather, the meaning is "that no charge can be brought by way of accusation" against them.[4]

God the Father has declared the Corinthian believers righteous based on Christ's saving work. Justification pertains especially to

1. William F. Arndt and F. Wilbur Gingrich, *A Greek-English Lexicon of the New Testament and Other Early Christian Literature*, 2nd ed. (Chicago: University of Chicago Press, 1979), 138.
2. Ibid., 64.
3. So Gordon D. Fee, *The First Epistle to the Corinthians*, The New International Commentary on the New Testament (Grand Rapids: Eerdmans, 1987), 43–44.
4. Anthony C. Thiselton, *The First Epistle to the Corinthians*, The New International Greek Testament Commentary (Grand Rapids: Eerdmans, 2000), 101–2.

God's verdict of righteousness on the last day (Matt. 12:33–37; Rom. 5:19; Gal. 5:5). The miracle of the gospel is that God's future verdict is accurately announced in the present. Every believer has already been justified and awaits with confidence God's declaration of that verdict before men and angels at the Last Judgment.

Am I saying that God's keeping the Corinthians "guiltless" only pertains to the Last Judgment? No. It applies to the time leading up to the Last Judgment as well as to the Last Judgment itself. Anthony Thiselton says clearly, "This applies to the time which leads up to the day of the Lord as well as to being presented free from any charge on the day itself."[5]

Paul's Confidence Is in God's Faithfulness

How can Paul be so sure that the Father will keep the Corinthian believers without blame for Judgment Day? Surely, his confidence is not based on their behavior! First Corinthians reveals a congregation with more problems than any church in the New Testament. There were factions (chapters 1, 3), sexual immorality (chapters 5, 6), believers taking other believers to court before unbelievers (chapter 6), severe marriage problems (chapter 7), idolatry (chapter 10), abuses at the Lord's Table (chapter 11), confusion concerning spiritual gifts and disorderly worship (chapters 12–14), and false teaching concerning the resurrection (chapter 15). Though many pastors would give up on a church in such bad shape today, Paul does not.

Paul does not give up because his confidence of final salvation is not based on the Corinthians' faithfulness to God but on God's faithfulness to them: "God is faithful, by whom you were called into the fellowship of his Son, Jesus Christ our Lord" (v. 9). He is a faithful God who effectively summoned the unsaved Corinthians into fellowship with Christ in the gospel. In the New Testament "fellowship" does not first of all convey the social sense that we customarily give to it—"We had fellowship in the church basement." Instead, it primarily means sharing in the life

5. Ibid., 102.

71

of the Father and Son (1 John 1: 3). Here Paul accents fellowship with the Son of God. Paul has in mind our adoption, based on Christ's unique sonship, as sons and daughters into the family of God.[6] As a result of our adoption by God's grace, we all share in Christ. And since all believers share in him communally, there is a secondary sense of fellowship that involves our social interaction with other Christians.

Teaching

Paul teaches preservation when he affirms that the Lord Jesus Christ will keep the struggling Corinthian Christians guilt-less until Christ's return. Because of this divine keeping they will be blameless until and on that day. This is God's preservation of his saints unto final justification. The same faithfulness of God that effectually called them into fellowship with Christ will preserve them unto the end.

1 Corinthians 11:27-33

> Whoever, therefore, eats the bread or drinks the cup of the Lord in an unworthy manner will be guilty concerning the body and blood of the Lord. Let a person examine himself, then, and so eat of the bread and drink of the cup. For anyone who eats and drinks without discerning the body eats and drinks judgment on himself. That is why many of you are weak and ill, and some have died. But if we judged ourselves truly, we would not be judged. But when we are judged by the Lord, we are disciplined so that we may not be condemned along with the world. So then, my brothers, when you come together to eat, wait for one another—if anyone is hungry, let him eat at home—so that when you come together it will not be for judgment.

This is Paul's famous passage on the Lord's Supper. First, he warns the Corinthians against defiling Christ's body and blood through

6. See my *Adopted by God* (Phillipsburg, NJ: P&R Publishing, 2001).

their partaking of the elements "in an unworthy manner" (v. 27). He then urges them to self-examination before partaking of the Supper (v. 28). In the next five verses he mentions the idea of judgment seven times. Distinguishing the meanings of "judgment" takes us a long way toward understanding his message.

Paul puts the word "judgment" (*krima*) as bookends around verses 29–34. Partaking of the Supper without spiritually distinguishing "the Lord's body in the bread which he eats" leads the believer to "judgment" (v. 29).[7] If a communicant does not attribute proper significance to the Supper, he partakes not of covenant blessing but of corresponding curse. Because the Corinthians have been abusing the love feast (the *agape* meal) associated with the Lord's Supper, he urges them to wait for one another when they come to the Lord's Table and to eat in their homes if they are hungry. His purpose for these instructions? "So that when you come together it will not be for judgment" (*krima*, v. 34).

Different Types of Judgment

In between these bookend verses, Paul speaks about different types of judgment. First, he describes the judgment of which he spoke in verse 29: "That is why many of you are weak and ill, and some have died" (v. 30). This judgment is temporal and involves weakness, sickness, or even physical death (Paul uses the word "sleep" as a euphemism for a Christian's death [KJV, NIV]). Next, he calls the Corinthians to judge themselves so as to avoid God's temporal judgments: "But if we judged ourselves truly, we would not be judged" (v. 31). The first use of "judged" in this verse means to examine oneself before partaking of the Supper, to sit in judgment on one's sins and confess them to God. If Paul's readers did this, they would be spared God's temporal judgments.

"But when we are judged by the Lord, we are disciplined so that we may not be condemned along with the world" (v. 32).

---

7. C. K. Barrett, *A Commentary on the First Epistle to the Corinthians*, Harper's New Testament Commentaries (Peabody, MA: Hendrickson, 1968), 274.

The word "judged" refers to God's temporal judgments. To be "disciplined" refers to God's fatherly correction of his children. The word "condemned" refers to the damnation of the ungodly. This is a message of comfort in the midst of hard words. Paul does not want his readers to despair. Implied is the possibility of some of them misinterpreting the woes that had befallen many in the church. Even when believers are temporally punished by the Lord, this is God's fatherly discipline of his children. It is to be distinguished from his condemning the world. God brings illness or even takes the lives of his disobedient people for this reason—so that they will not be damned along with the unsaved.

Teaching

In an unusual way, then, Paul teaches preservation. He juxtaposes God's (sometimes severe) paternal discipline of his children with the condemnation that the wicked will suffer. Judith Gundry Volf deserves quotation:

> The language of judgment employed in this passage denotes two kinds of judgment which differ in time of execution, nature and object. Paul uses the verb *krinein* here not for eternal damnation but for present pedagogical judgment on the church in contradistinction to the final condemnation to come upon the world.[8]

The following chart summarizes Volf's points.

The Judge	Those judged	Timing	Nature	Object
God	church	present	"discipline"	temporal punishment
God	"world"	future	"condemnation"	eternal punishment

8. Judith M. Gundry Volf, *Paul and Perseverance: Staying In and Falling Away* (Louisville: John Knox, 1990), 102.

Contrary to Howard Marshall, this text does not speak of apostasy. Marshall writes:

> If the discipline was successful and the person repented, he recovered from his sickness; if it was unsuccessful, the person died, and his physical death was a sign of his spiritual death. . . . If this is the correct explanation, then we would have here definite examples of people who "fell asleep" and thus forfeited their salvation.[9]

Quite the contrary: "Paul does not make repentance from a sin for which a Christian incurs temporal judgment pivotal for escape from final condemnation. Rather, Christians' relation to God as God's children is here presented as definitive for their final destiny."[10]

Ephesians 1:13–14; 4:30

> In him you also, when you heard the word of truth, the gospel of your salvation, and believed in him, were sealed with the promised Holy Spirit, who is the guarantee of our inheritance until we acquire possession of it, to the praise of his glory. (Eph. 1:13–14)

> And do not grieve the Holy Spirit of God, by whom you were sealed for the day of redemption. (Eph. 4:30)

The passages we have studied so far, in the Gospels and Paul's epistles, have presented the Father and Son as doing the work of preservation. In these two passages in Ephesians, the Holy Spirit plays a role in keeping believers saved. He is God's seal and guarantee of our final salvation.

In Ephesians 1:3–14, Paul puts the spotlight on the roles of the three persons of the Trinity in salvation. The Father is

---

9. I. Howard Marshall, *Kept by the Power of God: A Study of Perseverance and Falling Away* (1969; reprint, Minneapolis: Bethany Fellowship, 1974), 115–16.
10. Volf, *Paul and Perseverance*, 112.

praiseworthy for choosing us for salvation (vv. 4–5, 11). The Son deserves worship because he redeems us "through his blood," his violent death (v. 7).

The Spirit's Role

The Spirit too has a part to play. Paul writes, "In him you also, when you heard the word of truth, the gospel of your salvation, and believed in him, were sealed with the promised Holy Spirit" (v. 13). When the readers believed in Christ, they were sealed by God. Paul uses a divine passive—"you were sealed"—to point to the Father as sealer. Second Corinthians 1:21–22 teaches that it is God the Father who seals believers with the Spirit. This passage does this by distinguishing "God" (v. 21) from "Christ" (v. 21) and "his Spirit" (v. 22).

The seal is the Holy Spirit, who was promised in the Old Testament. Paul's language in verse 13 is hard to follow: "In him you . . . were sealed with the promised Holy Spirit" (v. 13). Having believed, we were sealed "in him," in Christ, with the Spirit. Thus the Trinity is involved in our sealing. The Father seals us with the Holy Spirit in spiritual union with Christ. Our union with Christ is sealed with the Spirit. That means our union with the Son of God, whereby all of his saving benefits become ours, is sealed or made secure.

Both Testaments witness persons sealing things to signify ownership or authentication (Gen. 41:42; 1 Cor. 9:2) and security (Dan. 6:17; Matt. 27:66). The two uses are combined in Revelation 7:2–8; 9:4 where the 144,000 believers are sealed by God. The seal marks them as God's own and protects them from the angel of death.

The Spirit as Seal

The Holy Spirit as God's seal on believers has these same two functions, denoting ownership and security. He marks us off as belonging to God. Sealing to signify ownership is seen in 2 Corinthians 1:21–22: "Now it is God who makes both us and you stand firm in Christ. He anointed us, set his seal of ownership on us, and put his Spirit in our hearts as a deposit, guaranteeing what is to come" (NIV).

Ephesians emphasizes that our being sealed with the Spirit denotes security. This is implied in 1:13–14, where immediately after speaking of our being sealed "with the promised Holy Spirit," Paul writes, "who is the guarantee of our inheritance until we acquire possession of it, to the praise of his glory" (vv. 13–14; cf. 2 Cor. 1:22). The word "guarantee" is a commercial term meaning "down payment" or "deposit." God gives us the Spirit now as a down payment on our future inheritance. In other words, our inheritance is secure because we already have the Spirit who guarantees even better things to come.

The Spirit's role as seal that brings security is clearer in Ephesians 4:30, where Paul writes, "And do not grieve the Holy Spirit of God, by whom you were sealed for the day of redemption." In the context, Christians' sins that especially sadden the Spirit include sinful anger and evil speaking (vv. 26, 29, 31). Only here does Scripture give the full name of the third person of the Trinity—the Holy Spirit of God—perhaps to accentuate how terrible it is to grieve him.

Once more we find that the divine passive ("you were sealed") points to God the Father. In this text Paul plainly states the goal of sealing when he speaks of the Spirit, "by whom you were sealed for the day of redemption." This means that the Father sealed us for the purpose of finally redeeming us. Our salvation is thus secure, being guaranteed by the Spirit who is God's seal on our lives "for the day of redemption."

Teaching

Ephesians 1:13–14 teaches preservation from a Trinitarian perspective. The Father seals with the Holy Spirit believers' union with Christ. He thus secures the permanence of our union by giving us the Spirit as seal. The idea is reinforced by the addition of

77

the image of the Spirit as guarantee. We now receive the Spirit as God's pledge of our full and final deliverance. In Ephesians 4:30, Paul adds the goal of God's sealing us when he says that by "the Holy Spirit of God" we "were sealed *for the day of redemption*." Sealing thus underlines God's preservation of his people for final salvation. Judith Gundry Volf aptly summarizes, "Those who have been sealed with the Spirit thus come under divine protection until the end, when God will fully redeem God's own possession."[11]

Philippians 1:6

> And I am sure of this, that he who began a good work in you will bring it to completion at the day of Jesus Christ.

After Paul greets the church at Philippi with its leaders, he says that whenever he thinks of them, he thanks God with a smile on his face because of their "partnership in the gospel" from the time they met until the present (vv. 1–5).

God Will Continue

Paul immediately states his conviction that God will continue his work in their midst. "And I am sure of this, that he who began a good work in you will bring it to completion at the day of Jesus Christ" (v. 6). Paul expresses confidence when he writes, "And I am sure of this." The words that follow tell the content of Paul's confidence. He is confident that God will not abandon his saints in Philippi.

Paul does this by using two temporal indicators—a beginning point and an end point. First, he tells of God's beginning "a good work" in the Philippians. This refers to the gospel coming to them as recorded in Acts 16:11–40. Then Paul speaks of an end point—"the day of Jesus Christ." That, of course, refers to Christ's second coming.

11. Ibid., 32.

A Good Work Indeed!

What does Paul say God will do in between this beginning and end? God will continue "the good work" he began in the Philippians until Christ's return. What is this "good work"? Paul refers to one of his favorite themes—that of the new creation. The apostle, following Isaiah's lead, uses the language of Genesis 1–2 to speak of the new era of salvation inaugurated by the death and resurrection of Christ, "the last Adam," "the second man" (1 Cor. 15:45, 47). This era will only be fully realized in the new heavens and the new earth, but it has already begun in Jesus' resurrection (1 Cor. 15:20; Col. 1:18).

Genesis 2:2 tells of God's original good work: "And on the seventh day God finished his work that he had done, and he rested on the seventh day from all his work that he had done." Paul speaks of another "good work" that God will finish: "that *work* of grace in the readers' lives that began with their reception of the gospel,"[12] as Peter T. O'Brien notes. Isaiah uses creation language to speak of God's calling Israel to be his people, to belong to him:

> Thus says God, the LORD,
>> who created the heavens and stretched them out,
>> who spread out the earth and what comes from it,
> who gives breath to the people on it
>> and spirit to those who walk in it:
> "I am the LORD; I have called you in righteousness;
>> I will take you by the hand and keep you."
>>> (Isa. 42:5–6)

> But now thus says the LORD,
>> he who created you, O Jacob,
>> he who formed you, O Israel:
> "Fear not, for I have redeemed you;
>> I have called you by name, you are mine." (Isa. 43:1)

12. Peter T. O'Brien, *The Epistle to the Philippians*, The New International Greek Testament Commentary (Grand Rapids: Eerdmans, 1991), 64, italics original.

Teaching

Paul's mention of "a good work" that God began in the Philippians speaks of his mighty work of salvation in their midst. Seen against its background in Genesis and Isaiah, Philippians 1:6 states powerfully that the Almighty Creator of the heavens and the earth, who redeems his people Israel in the Old Testament, can surely be trusted to complete the work of salvation he had begun in the church at Philippi. Indeed, "the final time note"—until the day of Jesus Christ—"draws attention to the faithfulness of God in completing that good work on the day of Christ, a reference to the second coming or *parousia* of the Lord."[13]

Later Paul will tell the Philippians, "it is God who works in you, both to will and to work for his good pleasure" (Phil. 2:13). It is no surprise, then, when he begins his letter assuring them that "he who began a good work in you will bring it to completion at the day of Jesus Christ" (1:6). Paul begins his letter to the Philippians with assurance that God, who began a work of new creation in them when they believed the gospel, will carry that work through to completion until Jesus comes again.

1 Thessalonians 5:23–24

> Now may the God of peace himself sanctify you completely, and may your whole spirit and soul and body be kept blameless at the coming of our Lord Jesus Christ. He who calls you is faithful; he will surely do it.

At the end of 1 Thessalonians, Paul includes a wish-prayer. As the name suggests, this is at the same time an expression of good will (a wish) and a prayer to God that the wish be granted. Paul prays that God would bring about the sanctification of his hearers that he had earlier in this letter prayed for (in 3:11–13)

13. Ibid., 65.

and urged (in 4:3–6). He asks God to consecrate the Thessalonians completely, or through and through. He knows that though believers have a part in their growth in holiness, only God can complete it. That is why he says, "Now may the God of peace *himself* . . ."

This final sanctification is so important to the apostle that he repeats the thought. He prays that the Thessalonians would be kept blamelessly until the Lord Jesus comes again. He expands on the concept of their being "completely" sanctified when he prays that their "whole spirit and soul and body be kept blameless at the coming of our Lord Jesus Christ." "Your whole spirit and soul and body" is an expansion of "completely." Paul thus emphasizes through repetition. Once more this is a wish-prayer.

In these two sentences, Paul asks God to bring about the entire and perfect sanctification of the Thessalonians at Christ's return. Verse 24 is important for our study of the doctrine of preservation. It shows that the apostle not only prays for the complete consecration of his readers; he also expects God to do it, citing God's faithfulness as his confidence: "He who calls you is faithful; he will surely do it." As surely as God is faithful, so surely will he finally and completely sanctify the Thessalonian church.

Teaching

Leon Morris's comments on 1 Thessalonians 5:24 capture Paul's message:

> Paul's prayer is no despairing wail, but a cry of faith. He is supremely confident that what he has asked will be done, and this verse reveals that the ground of his trust is in the nature of God. . . . Now we see that he is sure that God will indeed supply their need in this matter, because He is "faithful." . . . It is not in the unstable qualities of men that trust must be placed, but in the eternal faithfulness of God. . . .
>
> But God, besides being a Caller, is a Doer. . . . The God to whom Paul prays is not a God who is inactive or ineffective. Paul

thinks of Him as One who will certainly bring to completion that which he has begun. "Hath he said, and will he not do it?" (Num. 23:19). Because He is the faithful One, and because He is the One who has called them, they may know that He will do perfectly all that is involved in their call. It is profoundly satisfying to the believer that in the last resort what matters is not his feeble hold on God, but God's strong grip on him.[14]

Connecting the Dots

The epistle to the Romans is the key to Paul's teaching on preservation. The attention that he gives to eternal security in Romans is fundamental to understanding it. He lays a large and firm foundation for the doctrine in Romans 5:9–10; 8:1–4; and 8:28–39. The references to preservation we have looked at in this chapter are not as substantial, but that does not make them unimportant. These references are more incidental, given in conjunction with abuses at the Lord's Supper in Corinth (1 Cor. 11:27–33), explaining the Holy Spirit's role in salvation (Eph. 1:13–14; 4:30), or as a part of the introduction (1 Cor. 1:4, 8–9; Phil. 1:6) or conclusion (1 Thess. 5:23–24) of Paul's epistles.

We should not allow the incidental mention of preservation in these various epistolary contexts to lead us to disregard them. To the contrary, they reveal that the apostle could refer to God's keeping his people in a variety of contexts and for various purposes. The incidental references show all the more how preservation is ingrained in Paul's thinking. When he places the doctrine at the beginning of two of his letters and at the end of another, he shows the importance that he attaches to it. He wants the Corinthians and Philippians to hear of God's keeping them before he goes on to other matters. And he wants the Thessalonians to have the doctrine still

14. Leon Morris, *The First and Second Epistles to the Thessalonians*, New International Commentary on the New Testament (Grand Rapids: Eerdmans, 1959), 182–83.

ringing in their ears when the congregational reading of his first epistle to them is over.

All in all, preservation has a significant role to play in Paul's teaching ministry. And it appears in letters of other New Testament writers as well, as our next chapter shows.

Preservation in the General Epistles

JOHN (in the fourth gospel) and Paul (in his letters) are the major biblical theologians of preservation; but they are not the only ones. The writer to the Hebrews, Peter, and John again (in 1 John) add their voices to the biblical chorus.

- Hebrews 6:17–20
- Hebrews 7:23–25
- 1 Peter 1:3–5
- 1 John 2:18–19
- 1 John 5:18

Hebrews 6:17–20

> So when God desired to show more convincingly to the heirs of the promise the unchangeable character of his purpose, he guaranteed it with an oath, so that by two unchangeable things, in which it is impossible for God to lie, we who have fled for refuge might have strong encouragement to hold fast to the hope set before us. We have this as a sure and steadfast anchor of the soul, a hope that enters into the inner place behind the curtain, where Jesus has gone as a forerunner on our behalf, having become a high priest forever after the order of Melchizedek.

The warning passage in Hebrews 6:4–12 is justly famous. But too few realize that it is followed by a strong preservation passage. The writer to the Hebrews reminds his readers that after Abraham offered up Isaac, God swore by himself and promised Abraham physical and spiritual progeny (in Gen. 22:17; cf. Heb. 2:16; 11:12). And Abraham persevered in faith and gained what was promised (Heb. 6:13–15). Buist Fanning puts the emphasis where it belongs: "What is surprising about the verses that follow [Heb. 6:12b], however, is that they focus far more on God's absolute fidelity than on Abraham's persevering faith."[1]

God Swears an Oath!

Human beings take oaths to confirm their words (Heb. 6:16). Amazingly, God stooped and took an oath when he made promises to Abraham (v. 17). God swore "by two unchangeable things." What are they? They are God's promise to Abraham and the oath he added to it. Why did God add an oath to his promise? Was not his promise sufficient for Abraham's faith? Astonishingly, God added oath to promise to fortify the faith of Abraham and his spiritual descendants, including us. God wanted to assure us by these two things that "it is impossible for God to lie." Now, of course, it is impossible for God who is truth to lie! But God, following the example of human beings who swear to confirm their words, promised and also swore to establish Abraham's faith.

Why would Almighty God do such a thing? God did so "to show more convincingly to the heirs of the promise the unchangeable character of his purpose . . . so that . . . we who have fled for refuge might have strong encouragement to hold fast to the hope set before us" (vv. 17–18). God swore by himself to convince us of his purpose so we might be encouraged to persevere! God condescends and meets the requirements of his own law—he himself provides two witnesses to assure all those who take refuge

---

1. Buist M. Fanning, "A Classical Reformed View," in Herbert W. Bateman IV, ed. *Four Views on the Warning Passages in Hebrews* (Grand Rapids: Kregel, 2007), 193.

in his Son for salvation. God did this to give great confidence to Abraham's spiritual descendants by underscoring his decision to save forever those who believe in Jesus.

William Lane explains how God's promise to Abraham assures believers in Jesus:

> In 6:13–20 the writer depicts Abraham as a paradigm of trust and steadfast endurance. But he wanted to do more. He wished to describe God's promise and oath to Abraham as a type of the way in which God has acted with the Christian community. The promise to bless Abraham is a prefiguration of the salvation God has given to the new people in Jesus. Abraham's experience with God was first and foremost a demonstration that God is faithful, that his words are reliable, and that he stands behind his promise. The promised salvation secured through the high priestly ministry of Jesus is certain because it is guaranteed by God.[2]

Believers in Christ, then, have strong reasons for assurance of final salvation: God's immutable will and God's oath. How good of God to stoop and take an oath in order to guarantee our salvation!

We Have an Anchor of the Soul in the Most Holy Place!

The writer further describes our hope as "a sure and steadfast anchor of the soul" (Heb. 6:19). He does this to strengthen our assurance. Our heavenly hope in Christ secures our souls as an anchor does a ship. This spiritual anchor is described as "sure and steadfast," intensifying the idea of security. Furthermore, the writer mixes metaphors effectively when he says that this anchor is "a hope that enters into the inner place behind the curtain." It rests firmly in the holy of holies, the very presence of God. This too builds his readers' confidence. Their hope of salvation is secured by an anchor already in the presence of God. This makes their assurance of final salvation certain.

2. William L. Lane, *Hebrews 1–8*, Word Biblical Commentary (Waco, TX: Word, 1991), 155.

The most holy place is further described as "where Jesus has gone as a forerunner on our behalf, having become a high priest forever after the order of Melchizedek" (Heb. 6:19). Jesus, in his role as High Priest, has already gone into the most holy place for us. He has done this as a forerunner, ensuring that we will follow in his train. This too guarantees salvation because:

> Jesus has entered into the eternal world not only on His own behalf but on His people's too. . . . But the errand of this Fore-runner . . . proclaims an accomplished work of redemption and signalizes the first fruits of a mighty aftercrop. . . . He is there as His people's forerunner, the surety of their admission to the dwelling-place of God.[3]

In addition, Christ is "a high priest forever after the order of Melchizedek" (v. 20). Because he remains our High Priest *forever*, his sacrifice always avails for us, and we are saved *forever*.

Teaching

This passage affirms preservation repeatedly. God guarantees believers' final salvation by:

1. promising it (v. 13),
2. confirming the promise with an oath (v. 14),
3. labeling his resolve "unchangeable" (v. 17),
4. reminding us of his veracity (v. 18),
5. calling our hope of salvation an "anchor of the soul" (v. 19),
6. three times describing this anchor as utterly reliable (v. 19),
7. teaching that Christ our forerunner has already entered heaven for us (vv. 19–20), and
8. affirming the eternity of Christ's priesthood (v. 20).

3. F. F. Bruce, *The Epistle to the Hebrews*, New International Commentary on the New Testament (Grand Rapids: Eerdmans, 1964), 131–32.

Why does Hebrews so strongly affirm preservation? To afford believers "strong encouragement" (v. 18). Their heavenly hope is "a sure and steadfast anchor of the soul" (v. 19), stabilizing them even in the midst of persecutions. I conclude, then, that the purpose of the strong accent on preservation is to strengthen the assurance and perseverance of the readers and, in God's providence, ours as well.

Hebrews 7:23–25

The former priests were many in number, because they were prevented by death from continuing in office, but he holds his priesthood permanently, because he continues forever. Consequently, he is able to save to the uttermost those who draw near to God through him, since he always lives to make intercession for them.[4]

Hebrews 7:11–22 shows the superiority of Christ's priesthood to that of Levi. The Levitical priesthood was temporary; none of its priests could perform the ultimate priestly service. An eschatological high priest in the order of Melchizedek had to come and make the final sacrifice for sin. His coming necessitated a change in the priestly regulations, a superseding of the old order. This messianic High Priest was not a descendant of Levi; he hailed from the tribe of Judah (Heb. 7:11–14).

Jesus Is a Superior High Priest

This great High Priest has better credentials than the Levitical priests. They became priests based on their ancestry, but he became one "by the power of an indestructible life" (Heb. 7:16). They became high priests of the Old Covenant based on lineage from Aaron and without an oath from God.

4. In this section I have used my article, "'Though All Hell Should Endeavor to Shake': God's Preservation of His Saints," *Presbyterion*, 17.1 (1991), 52–54.

Christ became a High Priest of the new covenant in the order of Melchizedek by God's oath. Due to his superior qualifications, he is a superior High Priest and guarantees a better covenant (vv. 15–22).

"The former priests were many in number, because they were prevented by death from continuing in office" (v. 23). Their very numbers testify to the inferiority of their priesthood. Mere men, they lived and died and were succeeded in office by their sons, grandsons, and so on. Death prohibited any one of them from performing the great work of the final high priest.

Jesus Saves Forever

"But he holds his priesthood permanently, because he continues forever" (Heb. 7:24). The Son of God's priesthood is superior to that of the old covenant. His priestly work is not suspended by death. No successor replaces him. Instead, he and his priesthood continue forever. His perpetuity, guaranteed by his resurrection, makes his priesthood permanent.[5] As a result, his priestly service is effective, as the following verses explain.

"Consequently, he is able to save to the uttermost those who draw near to God through him, since he always lives to make intercession for them" (v. 25). Because the Son, unlike the Aaronic priests, lives after death and remains forever, he has a permanent priesthood (vv. 23–24). His priesthood, therefore, has eternal efficacy; he is able to rescue his people permanently. The words translated "to the uttermost" could be rendered "forever."[6] But it is probably better to render them "completely," meaning "fully, wholly," as the ESV, "to the uttermost."[7] This

5. *Aparabaton* means "permanent, unchangeable," William F. Arndt and F. Wilbur Gingrich, *A Greek-English Lexicon of the New Testament and Other Early Christian Literature*, 2nd ed. (Chicago: University of Chicago Press, 1979), 80.

6. As does James Moffatt, *A Critical and Exegetical Commentary on the Epistle to the Hebrews*, International Critical Commentary (Edinburgh: T&T Clark, 1924), 100.

7. Both meanings are possible, according to Arndt and Gingrich, *A Greek-English Lexicon*, 608.

includes salvation with reference to time ("forever") but also with reference to extent—he saves "fully," in every conceivable way.

It is because, as the risen One, he always lives[8] that he is able to save fully. The power of his indestructible life enables him to save completely. Because he always lives to intercede for his people, they are secure in his care. The great Mediator of the new covenant performs a priestly work on the cross (v. 27) and in heaven that perfectly meets the needs (v. 26) of his own.

Teaching

Although Arminians have studied salvation in Hebrews, they have neglected this passage when treating perseverance and apostasy.[9] But it is worthy of attention. Due to his identity, God's Son surpasses the Levitical priests. His priestly service, therefore, also surpasses theirs. "Repeatedly" they offer "the same sacrifices, which can never take away sins. . . . By a single offering he has perfected for all time those who are being sanctified" (Heb. 10:11, 14).

Hebrews 7:23–25 teaches the Son's preservation of his people. Because his life is indestructible, he saves completely. Because he is alive from the dead, his sacrifice is perfect, his priesthood permanent, his intercession never-ending, "and therefore the salvation which He secures to them is absolute."[10] Indeed, as Philip Hughes summarizes: "How can we who draw near to God through Christ fail to be eternally secure in view of the fact not only that *he always lives* but also that as our ever living priest he never ceases *to make intercession* for us in the heavenly sanctuary?"[11]

8. *Zon* is a circumstantial participle of cause; so NIV, NASB, and ESV.
9. It is missing from I. Howard Marshall, *Kept by the Power of God: A Study of Perseverance and Falling Away* (1969; reprint, Minneapolis: Bethany Fellowship, 1974), 137–157, 247–250 and Grant R. Osborne, "Soteriology in the Epistle to the Hebrews," in *Grace Unlimited*, ed. Clark H. Pinnock (Minneapolis: Bethany, 1975), 144–66.
10. Bruce, *The Epistle to the Hebrews*, 155.
11. Philip E. Hughes, *A Commentary on the Epistle to the Hebrews* (Grand Rapids: Eerdmans, 1977), 269, italics original.

1 Peter 1:3–5

> Blessed be the God and Father of our Lord Jesus Christ! According-ing to his great mercy, he has caused us to be born again to a living hope through the resurrection of Jesus Christ from the dead, to an inheritance that is imperishable, undefiled, and unfading, kept in heaven for you, who by God's power are being guarded through faith for a salvation ready to be revealed in the last time.

When Peter praises God the Father who "has caused us to be born again," he emphasizes God's initiative in granting us new life. Why did the Father do this for us? The apostle points to his "great mercy" as the reason. Peter's words comfort his largely Gentile audience that is suffering painful trials (1:6; 4:12). He points to a result of regeneration—"a living hope." The cause of Christians' having this sure hope lies in the fact that Jesus arose from the grave (v. 3).

An Eternal and Kept Inheritance

Peter gives another result of God's gift of new life: Christians have "an inheritance that is imperishable, undefiled, and unfad-ing, kept in heaven" for them. Peter describes this inheritance with four adjectives. "Each of these words in its own way drives home the point that the inheritance of which Peter speaks is an eternal one."[12] It is "imperishable" and will not be destroyed, as will all material inheritances. It is "undefiled," that is, pure, and will not be stained by sin. It is "unfading," unlike flowers that wither and die, and will never lose its beauty.

Furthermore, it is "kept in heaven" for God's people. Here Peter explains that our heavenly inheritance awaits us because God himself reserved it in time past. This is Peter's way of say-ing that our inheritance is sure. It cannot be lost, as Thomas Schreiner underscores:

12. J. Ramsey Michaels, *1 Peter*, Word Biblical Commentary, 49 (Waco, TX: Word, 1988), 21.

The verse concludes with the promise that the inheritance is "kept in heaven for you." The passive of the word "kept" (*teteremenen*) is a divine passive, referring to God as the one who reserves the inheritance for believers. Peter emphasized in the strongest possible terms the security and certainty of the reward awaiting believers.[13]

A Kept People

It is important to see that God keeps two things in this passage: the saints' inheritance and the saints themselves. Peter describes those for whom heaven is reserved as protected for future "salvation," a synonym of "inheritance" (vv. 4–5). Specifically, they "by God's power are being guarded." In addition, this protection by God's power is "through faith." Peter's mention of faith anticipates his emphasis on the ordeals that will be mentioned in verses 6–9 and the rest of the letter. It is in light of these trials that God protects his people.

How are we to construe the relation between divine keeping power and human faith implied in verse 5? Here opinions vary. Some claim that God keeps us as long as we exercise faith: "God's chosen stand in need of protection; they are guaranteed this through . . . God's power, which as a result of their faith makes victory certain."[14] Others disagree because such a view makes believers' "faith the cause of their preservation by God, i.e. they are saved because they cling steadfastly to God; this really makes the reference to God's power unnecessary and provides no assurance to the believer since what he doubts is his own power to cling to God in trial."[15]

In this context, the second view is correct, as Wayne Grudem explains: "God's power does not work apart from the personal faith of those being guarded, but *through* their faith. . . . God's

13. Thomas R. Schreiner, *1, 2 Peter, Jude*, The New American Commentary (Nashville: Broadman & Holman, 2003), 63.

14. J. N. D. Kelly, *A Commentary on the Epistles of Peter and Jude* (Grand Rapids: Baker, 1969), 52.

15. Ernest Best, *1 Peter*, The New Century Bible (Grand Rapids: Eerdmans, 1971), 77.

power in fact energizes and continually sustains individual, personal faith."[16] Grudem is right. God's keeping power, the power that raised Jesus from the dead (v. 3), is not dependent on our faith. To the contrary, his power strengthens our faith, which is one means he uses to protect us. What is the practical import of this? As we walk with God by faith, we are confident that God works in us to guard us.

Believers are protected by God's power through the instrumentality of faith "for a salvation ready to be revealed in the last time." Peter here views salvation as our final deliverance. Salvation is "ready," but its full realization still awaits. It will not be "revealed" until Christ's return.

Teaching

Peter affirms God's preservation of the persecuted saints to whom he writes via two themes: 1) God's reservation of their heavenly inheritance and 2) his keeping them to the end by his power. Concerning the first, believers' inheritance "will never be denied them, for Peter tells them that it has been kept 'for you.'"[17] Concerning the second, God in his power "will protect them, not like a guard watching prisoners who will in the end be condemned when the judge gives his verdict, but like a soldier guiding and protecting people as they move through hostile territory toward the freedom of friendly lines."[18]

1 John 2:18–19

Children, it is the last hour, and as you have heard that antichrist is coming, so now many antichrists have come. Therefore we know that it is the last hour. They went out from us, but they were not of us; for if they had been of us, they would have con-

16. Wayne Grudem, *1 Peter*, Tyndale New Testament Commentaries (Leicester, UK: Inter-Varsity Press, 1988), 58–59.
17. Ibid., 57.
18. Peter H. Davids, *The First Epistle of Peter*, The New International Commentary on the New Testament (Grand Rapids: Eerdmans, 1990), 54.

tinued with us. But they went out, that it might become plain that they all are not of us.

John distinguishes between an antichrist figure (who is still to come) and "many antichrists" who have already come.[19] The antichrists are the false teachers who have injured believers in the churches to which John writes (cf. 1 John 4:1–3). The apostle interprets the presence of these false teachers as evidence that the end times have already come. This adds urgency to his words in verse 19. The antichrists were members of his readers' churches. Later, however, they came out of those churches and thereby revealed their true identity, as Colin Kruse relates:

> Those whom the author describes as antichrists were in fact once members of his own Christian community, but they had seceded from it: "they went out from us." Their secession, as far as the author is concerned, only showed that they had never really been true members of his Christian community, and this is reiterated in his next statements.[20]

Their leaving, John teaches, signifies that the antichrists were not really God's children. Their "voluntary secession from the fellowship"[21] was apostasy. Though they were in the midst of the believers and appeared to belong to Christ and the church, they did not belong. And their leaving revealed their true stripe, as John Stott explains: "Only on the final day of separation will the wheat and the tares be completely revealed. Meanwhile, some are shown up in their true colours by their defection."[22] Such were the antichrists whom John condemns.

19. In this section I have used material from my article "Apostasy," *Presbyterion*, 19.1 (1993), 29–31.

20. Colin G. Kruse, *The Letters of John*, The Pillar New Testament Commentary (Grand Rapids: Eerdmans, 2000), 102.

21. Stephen S. Smalley, *1, 2, 3 John*, Word Biblical Commentary (Waco, TX: Word, 1984), 102.

22. John R. W. Stott, *The Letters of John*, rev. ed., Tyndale New Testament Commentaries (Grand Rapids: Eerdmans, 1964, 1988), 111.

In fact, if they had been true believers, they would have remained. John's use of the second class condition here is important. Daniel Wallace, a recognized linguist, says that such a Greek conditional sentence "indicates *the assumption of an untruth (for the sake of argument)*" and includes 1 John 2:19 in this category.[23] D. E. Hiebert brings out the force of the second class condition: "For if they were from us (but they weren't), they would have remained with us (but they didn't)."[24] John's message is plain: The false teachers did not belong, and that is why they left. But true believers persevere in Christian fellowship.

Teaching

John teaches that the opposition to God characteristic of the last times is present in the first century. Already many antichrists are attacking God's truth. John instructs his readers to protect them from potential despair. They should not be dismayed when the false teachers desert them, because this desertion serves to distinguish true believers from false. The apostates left because they did not really belong to God's people. If they had, they would have remained. John here correlates the doctrines of perseverance and apostasy. True believers do not apostatize; on the contrary, they persevere.

Because God preserves his own for final salvation, true Christians persevere to the end in faith. And by implication, apostates are false Christians, as D. A. Carson points out:

> The same stance is reflected in 1 John 2:19: Those who have seceded from the church are described in telling terms: "They went out from us, but they did not really belong to us. For if they had belonged to us, they would have remained with us; but their going showed that none of them belonged to us." In other

23. Daniel B. Wallace, *Greek Grammar Beyond the Basics: An Exegetical Syntax of the New Testament* (Grand Rapids: Zondervan, 1996), 694, 696, italics original.
24. D. E. Hiebert, "An Exposition of 1 John 2:18–28," *Bibliotheca Sacra* (1989): 81, as reported in Daniel L. Akin, *1, 2, 3 John*, The New American Commentary (Nashville: Broadman and Holman, 2001), 116.

words, genuine faith, by definition, perseveres; where there is no perseverance, by definition the faith cannot be genuine.[25]

1 John 5:18

We know that everyone who has been born of God does not keep on sinning, but he who was born of God protects him, and the evil one does not touch him.

The believers to whom John writes have been rejected by false teachers, who subsequently left the church (1 John 2:19, 26–27; 4:1–6). In the purpose statement for his epistle, John says that he writes to assure these rejected Christians that they know Christ and have eternal life (5:13). In 1 John 5:18—"everyone who has been born of God does not keep on sinning"—John teaches that each person whom the Father has regenerated does not practice sin the way he did before regeneration. "He who was born of God" refers not to believers, but to the unique Son of God.[26] The implied reason for this perseverance in holiness is that the unique Son "protects" each regenerate person. It is Christ's protection that causes us to live godly lives.

The Son of God Protects Us from the Devil

Christ also protects us from the devil. Because Christ keeps us, "the evil one does not touch" us. "Touch" (*haptetai*) here means "'touching' or 'laying hold' to the point of doing harm."[27] The devil is more powerful than we and certainly desires to harm us: "Your adversary the devil prowls around like a roaring lion, seeking someone to devour" (1 Peter 5:8). Why doesn't he? One answer is because Christ protects us from falling into sin that destroys us. Stott says it memorably:

25. D. A. Carson, "Reflections on Assurance," in *Still Sovereign*, ed. Thomas R. Schreiner and Bruce A. Ware (Grand Rapids: Baker, 1995, 2000), 264.

26. For a summary of evidence for this predominant view, see Smalley, *1, 2, 3 John*, 303.

27. Ibid. Cf. Arndt and Gingrich, *A Greek-English Lexicon*, 103.

The devil, *the evil one*, is maliciously active. Strong and subtle, he is more than a match for him [the believer alone]. But the Son of God came to destroy the devil's work (3:8), and if he *keeps . . . safe (terei)* the Christian, the devil will not be able to *harm* him. . . . The devil does not touch the Christian because the Son keeps him, and so, because the Son keeps him, the Christian does not persist in sin.[28]

Unlike the world which "lies in the power of the evil one," believers "are from God" (1 John 5:19); they have been begotten by the Father and belong to him.

Teaching

"In 1 John 5:18, John draws on this image [from John 10:7–18, 28–29] of Christ protecting and preserving the life and soul of the one who trusts in him because this one has been born of God (cf. 1 John 5:1; Jude 1)."[29] The Son of God protects us from sin and Satan.

Connecting the Dots

It is not only Jesus and Paul who testify to God's keeping his people saved. The general epistles do the same. So that readers will not misunderstand his famous warning passage, the writer to the Hebrews tells how God's promise and oath undergird our hope of salvation "as a sure and steadfast anchor of the soul" that Jesus our forerunner and High Priest has taken into heaven itself for us (Heb. 6:19–20). Jesus, the superlative High Priest, uniquely offered up himself as a sacrifice, and "by a single offering he has perfected for all time those who are being sanctified" (Heb. 10:14). Furthermore, he arose, guaranteeing the permanence of his priesthood. Because he is alive from

---

28. Stott, *The Letters of John*, rev. ed., 195, italics original.
29. Robert W. Yarbrough, *1–3 John*, Baker Exegetical Commentary on the New Testament (Grand Rapids: Baker Academic, 2008), 316.

the dead, he saves us forever and makes intercession for us in heaven (Heb. 7:24–25).

Peter concurs. God has reserved our eternal heavenly inheritance (1 Peter 1:4). Not only so, but our destiny is sure because God's power keeps us through the agency of faith "for a salvation ready to be revealed in the last time" (v. 5).

John assures his troubled readers and us when he teaches that—unlike the false teachers—true believers do not fall away but persevere (1 John 2:19). It is not that we are so strong or that our enemy is so weak; to the contrary, in ourselves we are weak, and the devil is far stronger than we. But the Son of God is on our side, and he protects us from sin and Satan, so that we do not fall away from the faith (1 John 5:18).

The writer to the Hebrews, Peter, and John witness along with Jesus and Paul that God preserves his people to the end. The words of a familiar hymn, based on Hebrews 6:19–20, capture the thoughts we have been exploring in chapters 3 through 6:

> Will your anchor hold in the storms of life,
> When the clouds unfold their wings of strife?
> When the strong tides lift and the cables strain,
> Will your anchor drift, or firm remain?
>
> It is safely moored, 'twill the storm withstand,
> For 'tis well secured by the Savior's hand;
> And the cables, passed from His heart to mine,
> Can defy that blast, thro' strength divine.
>
> It will surely hold in the Straits of Fear—
> When the breakers have told that the reef is near;
> Though the tempest rave and the wild winds blow,
> Not an angry wave shall our bark o'erflow.
>
> It will firmly hold in the Floods of Death—
> When the waters cold chill our latest breath,
> On the rising tide it can never fail,
> While our hopes abide within the Veil.

When our eyes behold through the gath'ring night
The city of gold, our harbor bright,
We shall anchor fast by the heav'nly shore,
With the storms all past forevermore.

Refrain

We have an anchor that keeps the soul
Steadfast and sure while the billows roll,
Fastened to the Rock which cannot move,
Grounded firm and deep in the Savior's love.[30]

But what about the many warning passages in Scripture, especially those that warn of apostasy? How are we to understand them? If preservation is biblical and it is impossible for believers to lose salvation, why did God include warnings in his Word? The next five chapters are devoted to answering these questions.

30. Words: Priscilla J. Owens, 1882. Music: William J. Kirkpatrick.

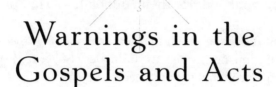

Warnings in the
Gospels and Acts

WE HAVE EXAMINED eighteen passages that teach preservation. Scripture also contains warning passages. These concern a host of topics, but some of the warnings pertain to salvation. Do any of these passages teach that saved persons can lose their salvation? The next five chapters address this question. We will look at warnings in the Gospels and Acts (chapter 7), Romans, 1 Corinthians, Galatians, and Colossians (chapter 8), 1 and 2 Timothy (chapter 9), Hebrews (chapter 10), and the other General Epistles (besides Hebrews) and Revelation (chapter 11).

Warnings in the Gospels and Acts include:

A. The Gospels
- Matthew 7:21–23: Miracles do not save.
- Matthew 10:33: "Whoever denies me before men, I also will deny before my Father."
- Matthew 24:24: ". . . So as to lead astray, if possible, even the elect."
- Luke 8:5–15: No fruit means no life!
- John 15:1–8: Fruitless branches.
B. The Acts of the Apostles
- Acts 5:5, 10: Ananias and Sapphira.
- Acts 8:13, 20–24: Trying to buy the Holy Spirit!

The Gospels

Matthew 7:21–23: Miracles Do Not Save

Even miraculous deeds do not guarantee genuine faith. Immediately preceding this passage, Jesus warns, "Beware of false prophets, who come to you in sheep's clothing but inwardly are ravenous wolves" (Matt. 7:15). Although they look good, they are anything but good. He then enunciates a vital principle:

> You will recognize them by their fruits. Are grapes gathered from thornbushes, or figs from thistles? So, every healthy tree bears good fruit, but the diseased tree bears bad fruit. A healthy tree cannot bear bad fruit, nor can a diseased tree bear good fruit. Every tree that does not bear good fruit is cut down and thrown into the fire. (vv. 16–19)

You Will Recognize Them by Their Fruits. False prophets often can be detected by their sinful lives. Even as trees produce fruit corresponding to their kind, so do false prophets: in spite of their words, they produce bad fruit. It is a settled principle: healthy trees only can and do produce good fruit, and unhealthy ones only can and do produce bad fruit (vv. 17–18). And just as trees that bear bad fruit are good for nothing but burning, so false prophets will be cast into hell (v. 19).

Jesus then shifts attention from false prophets to false disciples:

> Not everyone who says to me, "Lord, Lord," will enter the king-dom of heaven, but the one who does the will of my Father who is in heaven. On that day many will say to me, "Lord, Lord, did we not prophesy in your name, and cast out demons in your name, and do many mighty works in your name?" And then will I declare to them, "I never knew you; depart from me, you workers of lawlessness." (vv. 21–23)

The early Christian confession was, "Jesus is Lord," as evidenced in Romans 10:9: "If you confess with your mouth that Jesus is

Lord and believe in your heart that God raised him from the dead, you will be saved." One must trust Jesus as risen Lord and Savior to be saved. But mere profession of Jesus' lordship is insufficient: "Not everyone who says to me, 'Lord, Lord,' will enter the kingdom of heaven" (Matt. 7:21). Entrance into God's kingdom is limited to those who sincerely confess Christ. This sincerity is borne out by a life that submits to God's will: Jesus says that only he or she will enter the kingdom who "does the will of my Father who is in heaven" (v. 21).

Inadequate Confession of Jesus' Lordship. Jesus gives three examples of inadequate confession of his lordship: "On that day many will say to me, 'Lord, Lord, did we not prophesy in your name, and cast out demons in your name, and do many mighty works in your name?'" (v. 22). On judgment day many false disciples will confess Jesus as Lord and appeal to their doing supernatural deeds by his authority. Shockingly, Jesus will retort, "I never knew you; depart from me, you workers of lawlessness" (v. 23).

Profession of Jesus with supernatural deeds is insufficient to gain entrance into the kingdom. Rather, one must genuinely believe and repent to gain entrance. But these false disciples did not do this, for Jesus calls them "workers of lawlessness" (v. 23). His principle applies here too: "You will recognize them by their fruits" (vv. 16, 20). We know they were unsaved because of Jesus' words of rejection: "I never knew you." Of course, he does not deny that he knows all things. Instead, he denies that he ever knew them with the knowledge of salvation. The disciples of Matthew 7:21–23 do not show that persons can lose salvation because Jesus never knew them—they were never saved.

Matthew 10:33: "Whoever Denies Me before Men, I Also Will Deny before My Father"

Jesus sent out his twelve disciples to preach, heal, and cast out demons (Matt. 10:5–15). They will meet serious opposition but can rely on the Holy Spirit for words when they are hauled into courts due to their following Jesus (vv. 16–25). The disciples are not to fear men but God who will judge the dead (v. 28). The previous verses "focused on the message of the kingdom, which the disciples must proclaim even in the face of opposition and suffering. . . . Now it is the person of Jesus that takes center stage."[1]

"Whoever Denies Me . . . I Also Will Deny." Then Jesus boldly proclaims, "So everyone who acknowledges me before men, I also will acknowledge before my Father who is in heaven, but whoever denies me before men, I also will deny before my Father who is in heaven" (vv. 32–33). Merely claiming to be Jesus' disciple is not enough. One must publicly confess him, even if hauled before rulers in earthly courts (vv. 18–20). The result of confessing him before men? "The acknowledgment his followers will receive will avail in the highest of all courts"[2]—that of Jesus' Father himself. But as Jesus' parallelism presses home, rejecting him also brings permanent consequences—rejection before the Father. Those who finally deny Christ will be cast into hell.

Does Jesus here threaten his followers with the loss of salvation if they fail to confess him? No. Rather, Jesus said "everyone" and "whoever" in Matthew 10:32–33 to separate true disciples from false ones. D. A. Carson encapsulates Jesus' message:

> Though addressed to the Twelve (vv. 1–5), like much of vv. 17–42, this saying looks beyond the apostles to the disciples at large. The point is made by "Whoever" (v. 32). A necessary criterion for being a disciple of Jesus is to acknowledge him publicly. . . . This will vary in boldness, fluency, wisdom, sensitivity, and frequency from believer to believer . . . but consistently to disown Christ . . . is to be disowned by Christ.[3]

1. Donald A. Hagner, *Matthew 1–13*, Word Biblical Commentary (Dallas: Word, 1993), 288.
2. Leon Morris, *The Gospel According to Matthew*, The Pillar New Testament Commentary (Grand Rapids: Eerdmans, 1992), 265.
3. D. A. Carson, "Matthew," in *The Expositor's Bible Commentary*, ed. Frank E. Gaebelein, vol. 8 (Grand Rapids: Zondervan, 1984), 256.

Matthew 24:24: ". . . So As to Lead Astray, If Possible, Even the Elect"

> And if those days had not been cut short, no human being would be saved. But for the sake of the elect those days will be cut short. Then if anyone says to you, "Look, here is the Christ!" or "There he is!" do not believe it. For false christs and false prophets will arise and perform great signs and wonders, so as to lead astray, if possible, even the elect. (Matt. 24:22–24)

In his famous eschatological discourse, Jesus uses "prophetic foreshortening" to intermingle predictions that will come to pass shortly with those that will come to pass at the end.[4] In the same message he predicts the destruction of Jerusalem and his own return. Speaking of the latter, he foretells terrible times to come of persecution, false prophets, and apostasy and urges perseverance (Matt. 24:9–13). He announces, "If those days had not been cut short, no human being would be saved" (v. 22). Does that mean that no one is to be saved? No, because "for the sake of the elect those days will be cut short" (v. 23). Jesus tells of God's mercifully shortening the time of his wrath on earth for the sake of his people.

He predicts that false messiahs and false prophets will appear, make claims, and seek to authenticate them by performing "great signs and wonders" (v. 24). He cautions his hearers ahead of time not to believe these claims because the supernatural occurrences will be so persuasive "as to lead astray, *if possible*, even the elect" (v. 24, italics added).

"If Possible." I. Howard Marshall regards the words "if possible" in this verse as raising the "remote" possibility that the elect could fall away from salvation: "The possibility that the elect may be led astray cannot be ruled out."[5] On the contrary,

---

4. For this concept see Anthony A. Hoekema, *The Bible and the Future* (Grand Rapids: Eerdmans, 1979), 148–49.

5. I. Howard Marshall, *Kept by the Power of God: A Study of Perseverance and Falling Away* (1969; reprint, Minneapolis: Bethany Fellowship, 1974), 72–73.

D. A. Carson points out that the phrase "if possible" does not call into question God's preservation of the elect any more "than it calls into question the inevitability of Jesus' cup."[6] Carson recalls Jesus in Gethsemane: "And going a little farther he fell on his face and prayed, saying, 'My Father, *if it be possible*, let this cup pass from me; nevertheless, not as I will, but as you will'" (Matt. 26:39, italics added). Even as it was not possible for the cup of God's judgment to pass from Jesus, so it is not possible for the elect to be led astray by the signs and wonders of the false prophets.

Not Possible! In fact, Jesus' words underscore the power of the false signs and wonders to persuade. And in so doing, ironically they teach God's preservation of his own, as Leon Morris underlines: "They will impress *even the elect*. Since the elect are God's own, and are kept by the power of God, it will not be possible for them to be led astray by these charlatans. But Jesus brings out the impressive character of the things they will do by saying that if it were possible to lead the elect astray, they would do it."[7] Morris is correct. Jesus is speaking hypothetically to emphasize the persuasive power of the false prophets. Paradoxically, then, Jesus' words actually emphasize the fact that the elect cannot be finally and totally deceived because they are kept safe by God.

Luke 8:5–15: No Fruit Means No Life!

> A sower went out to sow his seed. And as he sowed, some fell along the path and was trampled underfoot, and the birds of the air devoured it. And some fell on the rock, and as it grew up, it withered away, because it had no moisture. And some fell among thorns, and the thorns grew up with it and choked it. And some fell into good soil and grew and yielded a hundredfold. . . .
>
> The seed is the word of God. The ones along the path are those who have heard; then the devil comes and takes away

6. Carson, "Matthew," in *The Expositor's Bible Commentary*, 503.
7. Morris, *The Gospel According to Matthew*, 607, italics original.

the word from their hearts, so that they may not believe and be saved. And the ones on the rock are those who, when they hear the word, receive it with joy. But these have no root; they believe for a while, and in time of testing fall away. And as for what fell among the thorns, they are those who hear, but as they go on their way they are choked by the cares and riches and pleasures of life, and their fruit does not mature. As for that in the good soil, they are those who, hearing the word, hold it fast in an honest and good heart, and bear fruit with patience. (Luke 8:5–15)

The Parable of the Sower. Luke's account of Jesus' parable of the sower gives insight into inadequate faith. Jesus tells of a sower who scattered his seed in various locations. Some fell on a path, was trampled underfoot, and was eaten by birds; some landed on rocks, where it sprang up but withered due to a lack of moisture; some landed among thorns, which choked it; some fell on good soil, grew, and yielded a harvest (Luke 8:5–8).

At his disciples' request, Jesus explains. The seed is God's word, and the soil that fell on the path stands for hearers from whom the devil snatches the word so they cannot believe and be saved (v. 12). The rocky soil stands for those who joyfully welcome the word. "But these have no root; they believe for a while, and in time of testing fall away" (v. 13). Some take this to speak of believers who fell away from salvation because Jesus says they received the word with joy, believed for a time, and then fell away. "One cannot escape the fact that Jesus focuses so heavily on the possibility of short-term faith. . . . Jesus' parable leaves open the possibility that some will fall away."[8]

A Mistake. This is a mistaken conclusion, however, because it misses the point that only the fourth soil bears fruit. The first three represent various responses to the word that fall short of saving faith. Receiving the word with joy is not enough.

---

8. Joel B. Green, *The Gospel of Luke,* The New International Commentary on the New Testament (Grand Rapids: Eerdmans, 1997), 329.

Admittedly, the words "they believe for a while" could describe saving faith. But they do not in this context because they are preceded by the words, "But these have no root." True disciples are rooted and bear fruit. The falling away likewise is incommensurate with saving faith. True believers not only profess—they persevere in faith to the end.

D. A. Carson agrees:

> The person who receives "the word" . . . in a thoughtless way may show immediate signs of life and promise to be the best of the crop: he receives the truth "with joy" (v. 20 [in Matt. 13]). But without real root, there is no fruit; and external pressures, trouble, and persecution (cf. [Matt.] 24:9, 21, 29), like sun beating on a rootless plant, soon reveal the shallowness of the soil. "At once" (*euthys*) he receives the word with joy, and as "quickly" (*euthys*) "falls away." . . . Such temporary disciples are always numerous in times of revival and were so in Jesus' ministry.[9]

No Fruit Indicates No Life! The seed that fell among thorns stands for persons who hear the word but are unfruitful because the "thorns" of worldly cares, the desire for wealth, and fleeting pleasures choke the word (v. 14). Note that once more fruitlessness indicates no salvation. It is only the last and good soil that stands for those who hear the word, truly believe it, and "bear fruit with patience" (v. 15). Matthew's version distinguishes different degrees of fruitfulness among believers: "He indeed bears fruit and yields, in one case a hundredfold, in another sixty, and in another thirty" (13:23). It is true to life that there are various degrees of fruitfulness among Christians. This reinforces the principle: Eternal life yields fruit; but no fruit indicates no eternal life.

The seed that fell among thorns, then, does not picture believers in Christ who forfeited salvation. Rather, their unfruitfulness—despite their initial joy and apparent faith—reveals that their faith fell short of genuine salvation.

9. Carson, "Matthew," in *The Expositor's Bible Commentary*, 314.

John 15:1–8: Fruitless Branches

I am the true vine, and my Father is the vinedresser. Every branch in me that does not bear fruit he takes away, and every branch that does bear fruit he prunes, that it may bear more fruit. Already you are clean because of the word that I have spoken to you. Abide in me, and I in you. As the branch cannot bear fruit by itself, unless it abides in the vine, neither can you, unless you abide in me. I am the vine; you are the branches. Whoever abides in me and I in him, he it is that bears much fruit, for apart from me you can do nothing. If anyone does not abide in me he is thrown away like a branch and withers; and the branches are gathered, thrown into the fire, and burned. If you abide in me, and my words abide in you, ask whatever you wish, and it will be done for you. By this my Father is glorified, that you bear much fruit and so prove to be my disciples. (John 15:1–8)

When Jesus teaches about the vine and the branches, he applies to himself the Old Testament picture of Israel as the Lord's vineyard (for example, see Isa. 5:1–7). As the true vine, he replaces the rebellious nation that failed to fulfill its mission. Jesus' Father, the wise Gardener, severs fruitless branches and prunes those that bear fruit (15:2). Is Jesus speaking of two kinds of Christians here, fruitful and fruitless ones? No, in John's thought, people either love the light or hate it (John 3:19–21). They either believe in God's Son or reject him (John 3:36). They either have eternal life or are spiritually dead (John 5:24). They either are children of God or children of the devil (John 8:42–44). They either obey Christ's commandments or disobey them (John 14:23–24). For John there are only two possibilities: Either people are Christians or they are not. As a result there is no middle position between fruitfulness and fruitlessness.

Fruitless Branches. The fruitless branch in John 15 is an unsaved person who has in one sense been "in the vine"—he has firsthand experience of the teachings and power of Jesus.

109

In fact, the unfruitful branch that Jesus immediately is thinking of is Judas. Judas has acted outwardly as a disciple should, appearing to be a fruitful branch, even deceiving the other disciples (13:28–29). But actually he is a fruitless branch whose wicked deeds will soon expose him. All along he has been a thief (12:4–6) and now has left to betray the Son of God (13:27, 30). One reason, then, that Jesus tells of the vine and the branches is to prepare his disciples for Judas's betrayal. The Gardener will cut off the fruitless branches so they can be cast into the flames (John 15:2, 6). This is an image of the eternal punishment that Judas and those like him will experience.

Jesus does not threaten his disciples with hellfire; he tells them that he regards them as fruitful branches. He employs a speech figure in verses 2–3 (in the original Greek) called *paronomasia*, which uses words with similar sounds but different meanings. Though the Gardener takes away *(airei)* unfruitful branches, he prunes *(kathairei)* fruitful ones. When Jesus, therefore, informs the eleven that they are already clean *(katharoi)* because of the word he had spoken to them, he assures them that they are fruitful branches.

The Disciples Are Not Headed for Condemnation. In addition, Jesus warns of condemnation in 15:1–8 in the third person: "every branch of mine that does not bear fruit" (v. 2) and "If anyone does not abide in me he is thrown away like a branch" (v. 6). But in the surrounding verses, Jesus employs the second person to address his disciples: "Already you are clean" (v. 3); "apart from me you can do nothing" (v. 5); "If you abide in me" (v. 7). In this way, Jesus makes a distinction between his disciples and the unfruitful branches that are headed for condemnation.

Jesus sums up the chief reason that he teaches his disciples about the vine and the branches. "By this my Father is glorified, that you bear much fruit and so prove to be my disciples" (v. 8). Because eternal life reveals itself in fruitfulness, the disciples are to prove their genuineness by bearing fruit.

What does Jesus mean when he speaks over and over of "abiding" in the vine? He means continuing in his love (v. 9). Abiding is remaining in a personal relationship with Christ. Although Judas appears to have such a relationship with the Son of God, he really does not. The other disciples, however, are genuine fruit-bearing branches. They remain in the vine by continuing to love him who loved them first—Jesus. By this means they will bear much fruit.

What Is the Fruit? Some point to winning souls, others to the fruit of the Spirit. Although these are not excluded, the text does not mention them. Rather, the fruit Jesus speaks about is obedience to his commands (v. 10) and love for other Christians (vv. 12–14). Furthermore, Jesus models both of these for his disciples: he keeps his Father's commands (v. 10), and he gives the greatest example of love by laying down his life for them (vv. 12–13).

The disciples cannot even take credit for bearing fruit. In the final analysis, they did not choose Jesus, but he chose them and appointed them to go and bear lasting fruit (v. 16). Because he chose them out of the world, they no longer belong to the world, but they now belong to him (v. 19).

The Acts of the Apostles

Acts 5:5, 10: Ananias and Sapphira

But a man named Ananias, with his wife Sapphira, sold a piece of property, and with his wife's knowledge he kept back for himself some of the proceeds and brought only a part of it and laid it at the apostles' feet. But Peter said, "Ananias, why has Satan filled your heart to lie to the Holy Spirit and to keep back for yourself part of the proceeds of the land? While it remained unsold, did it not remain your own? And after it was sold, was it not at your disposal? Why is it that you have contrived this deed in your heart? You have not lied to men but to God." When Ananias heard these words, he fell down and breathed his last.

And great fear came upon all who heard of it. The young men rose and wrapped him up and carried him out and buried him. After an interval of about three hours his wife came in, not knowing what had happened. And Peter said to her, "Tell me whether you sold the land for so much." And she said, "Yes, for so much." But Peter said to her, "How is it that you have agreed together to test the Spirit of the Lord? Behold, the feet of those who have buried your husband are at the door, and they will carry you out." Immediately she fell down at his feet and breathed her last. When the young men came in they found her dead, and they carried her out and buried her beside her husband. And great fear came upon the whole church and upon all who heard of these things. (Acts 5:1–11)

Luke testifies to the great unity of the early Christians in Jerusalem, which issued in the voluntary sharing of material goods (Acts 4:32). God's grace and power were evident in the apostles' witness to Jesus' resurrection and in there being no one in material need among them (v. 33–34). Why was no one in need? Luke explains: "For as many as were owners of lands or houses sold them and brought the proceeds of what was sold and laid it at the apostles' feet, and it was distributed to each as any had need" (vv. 34–35). He cites the example of Joseph, whom we know as Barnabas, who "sold a field that belonged to him and brought the money and laid it at the apostles' feet" (vv. 36–37).

The dynamic, grace-filled early Christian church, however, was not without problems, because Luke immediately cites another example, this time of things gone awry. Ananias and Sapphira, a couple who belonged to the Jerusalem church, also sold a piece of property and laid money at the apostles' feet. But there was a stark difference between their deed and that of Barnabas. For they conspired to lie about how much they received for selling the field, to keep part for themselves, and to tell the apostles that they had given the full amount.

Lying to the Holy Spirit! Peter does not rebuke them for keeping part of the proceeds but for lying: "Ananias, why has

Satan filled your heart to lie to the Holy Spirit and to keep back for yourself part of the proceeds of the land? While it remained unsold, did it not remain your own? And after it was sold, was it not at your disposal? Why is it that you have contrived this deed in your heart? You have not lied to men but to God" (vv. 3–4). Upon hearing these words, Ananias fell down dead (v. 5).

About three hours after Ananias's burial, Peter asked Sapphira about the proceeds from their land sale. She too lied (vv. 7–8). Peter had hard words for her too: "How is it that you have agreed together to test the Spirit of the Lord? Behold, the feet of those who have buried your husband are at the door, and they will carry you out" (v. 9). She too immediately died (v. 10).

What was the couple's sin? Witherington answers well: "In Luke's view this couple is guilty of secrecy, collusion, and attempting to lie to the Holy Spirit."[10] There is no doubt that Luke regards their sin as a serious business—sinning against the covenant community and more importantly against God himself. Adding to the severity of their sin is its parallelism to an infamous Old Testament transgression—Achan's sin in the book of Joshua. Dennis Johnson summarizes this comparison's most important point: "This couple, like their Old Testament counterpart, dared to deceive in the presence of the Holy One of Israel."[11]

Conclusion. Are Ananias and Sapphira believers? If so, should they be viewed as Christians who fell away from salvation? Or should we see them as Christians who reaped God's temporal judgment of death, similar to God's treatment of the sinning Corinthians so that they would "not be condemned along with the world" (1 Cor. 11:32)? Or should we regard the unfortunate couple as having made false professions of faith in the first place with their lying revealing their unsaved condition before God?

10. Ben Witherington III, *The Acts of the Apostles: A Socio-Rhetorical Commentary* (Grand Rapids: Eerdmans, 1998), 215.

11. Dennis Johnson, *The Message of Acts in the History of Redemption* (Phillipsburg, NJ: P&R, 1997), 171–81.

It is difficult to reach a settled conclusion on the matter, and perhaps that is the best conclusion to reach. I agree with the wisdom of F. F. Bruce:

> It is idle to ask if Ananias and Sapphira were genuine believers or not. Certainly they did not behave as if they were. But we cannot be sure that they were not, unless we are prepared to say that no one who is guilty of an act of deliberate deceit can be a true Christian. The fear which fell upon the whole community suggests that many a member of it had reason to tremble and say to himself, "There, but for the grace of God, go I."[12]

Acts 8:13, 20-24: Trying to Buy the Holy Spirit!

The story of Simon of Samaria in Acts 8 illustrates Luke's message of the seed that fell on rocky soil (Luke 8:13). Philip preached Christ in Samaria, cast out demons, and performed healings, and many professed faith. Amazingly, among them was a man named Simon, a practitioner of magic who made great claims and amazed many people, causing them to proclaim, "This man is the power of God that is called Great" (Acts 8:10). They revered Simon "because for a long time he had amazed them with his magic" (v. 11). Luke records, "Even Simon himself believed, and after being baptized he continued with Philip. And seeing signs and great miracles performed, he was amazed" (v. 13).

Simon Believed and Was Baptized? The preceding verse explained, "But when they believed Philip as he preached good news about the kingdom of God and the name of Jesus Christ, they were baptized, both men and women" (v. 12). We would, therefore, normally interpret Luke's statement that Simon too believed and was baptized as describing a genuine conversion. His fascination with the signs and miracles after his profession of faith might raise eyebrows, but given his past, this fascina-

---

12. F. F. Bruce, *The Book of Acts*, rev. ed., The New International Commentary on the New Testament (Grand Rapids: Eerdmans, 1988), 115.

tion is understandable. But the following verses—which tell of Simon's subsequent actions and Peter's evaluation of them—call this normal interpretation into question.

Peter and John came from Jerusalem to see what God was doing in Samaria. Unique to Acts (and in fact to Scripture), the Holy Spirit was given to believers at the hands of the apostles (Acts 8:14–17). Simon was awestruck when he saw this and tried to buy this power from the apostles: "He offered them money, saying, 'Give me this power also, so that anyone on whom I lay my hands may receive the Holy Spirit'" (vv. 18–19).[13]

Peter, stunned by Simon's evil words, blasts him:

> May your silver perish with you, because you thought you could obtain the gift of God with money! You have neither part nor lot in this matter, for your heart is not right before God. Repent, therefore, of this wickedness of yours, and pray to the Lord that, if possible, the intent of your heart may be forgiven you. For I see that you are in the gall of bitterness and in the bond of iniquity. (vv. 20–23)

Peter is offended at Simon's obsession with power and his attempt to purchase the Holy Spirit. He warns Simon that his heart "is not right before God" and urges repentance (vv. 21–22). Dennis Johnson evaluates accurately: Simon has "no share in the word of salvation that the apostles and Philip were proclaiming (Acts 8:20–21)," and "despite his claim to divine power, Simon was chained to unrighteousness as its slave."[14]

Writing in the Arminian tradition, Ben Witherington III agrees:

> There are at least several hints in the text that ... Simon was never converted at all. These hints include: (1) the way Simon is introduced in the narrative in pejorative terms (vv. 9–11); (2) the fact that

---

13. From Simon's request the word *simony* has entered our vocabulary, meaning "the buying or selling of a church office," *Merriam-Webster's Collegiate Dictionary*, 11th ed. (Springfield, MA: Merriam-Webster, 2003), 1162.

14. Johnson, *The Message of Acts in the History of Redemption*, 171–72.

while it is said that Simon believed, we are not told *what* he believed, unlike the case with the Samaritans (see vv. 12–13). Apparently Luke means that Simon affirmed the reality of the miracles and the power that accomplished them and sought to have such power himself. . . . (4) . . . As vv. 20ff. make clear, Simon's heart is not right before God, and he is in danger of going to destruction or hell. . . . (5) v. 23 is as telling a description of an unregenerate person as one could want—trapped in the chains of wickedness. . . . In short, Luke portrays Simon as not converted, only strongly impressed with the apparent miracle-working power of Philip and Peter.[15]

Simon's Profession Was Not Genuine. Therefore, though we normally would interpret at face value Luke's statement that Simon believed—that is, as indicating genuine saving faith—the words that follow lead us to conclude otherwise. Simon's action of trying to buy the ability to bestow the Spirit and Peter's words of condemnation lead us to conclude that Simon's profession was not genuine.

Commentators vary in their estimation of the sincerity of Simon's response to Peter: "Pray for me to the Lord, that nothing of what you have said may come upon me" (v. 24). Some regard it as "uncertain" whether or not it shows true repentance;[16] others regard it as showing "no sign of repentance, or even contrition."[17] Regardless of the sincerity of Simon's response, Luke's overall picture of him leads me to regard him as an example of the seed that fell on the rock, lacked roots, and produced no fruit. Simon is not a true believer who fell away from salvation, for his was an inadequate faith.

Connecting the Dots

We have looked at seven warning passages in the Gospels and Acts and have drawn conclusions dealing with preservation

15. Witherington, *The Acts of the Apostles*, 288–89.
16. William J. Larkin Jr., *Acts*, The IVP New Testament Commentary (Downers Grove, IL: InterVarsity, 1995), 130.
17. John R. W. Stott, *The Message of Acts*, The Bible Speaks Today (Downers Grove, IL: InterVarsity, 1990), 151.

and apostasy. It is useful to summarize those conclusions by putting them into categories.

First, sometimes it is hard to know whether or not some persons in the biblical story were saved. The fatal judgment on Ananias and Sapphira in Acts 5:5, 10 fits here. We cannot be sure if they were genuine believers or not. Furthermore, if they were saved, their judgment may have been only temporal—loss of life. There is no indication that they perished eternally. They are not examples of Christians who forfeited salvation.

Second, Jesus' true followers confess him publicly. How are we to tell true disciples from false ones? Those who publicly acknowledge Jesus, he will acknowledge before his Father. But as Matthew 10:33 indicates, those who publicly repudiate him, he will repudiate before his Father. This passage, therefore, concerns distinguishing true from false disciples, not the loss of salvation.

Third, one passage ironically emphasizes the eternal security of God's people. Jesus said that the false messiahs' and false prophets' signs and wonders were so persuasive that they would "lead astray, if possible, even the elect" (Matt. 24:24). Jesus, speaking hypothetically, means that it is not possible totally to deceive God's chosen people because he keeps them safe.

Fourth, we come to the dominant category in the warning passages in the Gospels and Acts. Four of the seven passages illustrate Jesus' dictum, "You will recognize them by their fruits" (Matt. 7:16, 20). True believers show their faith by their deeds, while false ones show their lack of faith in the same way.

This is the case with the false disciples of Matthew 7:21–23. Though they have done supernatural deeds, when they stand before Jesus on judgment day, he will deny them entrance into the kingdom. He explains that he never knew these "workers of lawlessness" with saving knowledge (v. 23).

Luke 8:5–15 fits in this category too. The seed among thorns does not portray Christians who forfeited salvation. Instead, their lack of fruit, in spite of apparent faith, shows that their profession fell short of saving faith. If it had been saving, it would have produced fruit—like the seed that fell among good soil (v. 15).

John 15:1–8 belongs here too. The fruitless branch is an unsaved person who has in a sense been "in the vine"—he has personally experienced Jesus' sermons and signs. But fruitless disciples are not true disciples. By contrast it is through bearing fruit that true disciples prove their genuineness (v. 8).

Acts 8:13, 20–24 likewise fits here. Luke must give us reason to regard his statement that Simon the magician believed as not indicating genuine faith (v. 13). And Luke does that very thing. When Simon tries to buy the ability to bestow the Holy Spirit and Peter subsequently condemns him, Luke shows that Simon did not truly believe in Jesus.

In summary, each of the four passages in this category—consistent with the rest of Scripture—demonstrates the biblical principle that genuine faith proves itself in deeds. Believers vary in degrees of fruitfulness, as Jesus' words at the end of the parable of the sower reveal: "As for what was sown on good soil, this is the one who hears the word and understands it. He indeed bears fruit and yields, in one case a hundredfold, in another sixty, and in another thirty" (Matt. 13:23). But every real believer brings forth fruit. As a result, a fruitless Christian is an oxymoron, a contradiction in terms.

Warnings in Paul, Part 1

WARNINGS TO CHURCHES and individuals appear in every part of the New Testament. In fact, there are so many warnings in Paul's epistles that we will consider them in two chapters, the second devoted to 1 and 2 Timothy. Here we will look at four warning passages in Romans, 1 Corinthians, and Colossians:

- Romans 8:13: "If You Live according to the Flesh You Will Die."
- Romans 11:20–22: Corporate Judgment.
- 1 Corinthians 9:27: Disqualification from Service.
- Colossians 1:21–23: "If Indeed You Continue in the Faith."

Romans 8:13: "If You Live according to the Flesh You Will Die"[1]

> For if you live according to the flesh you will die, but if by the Spirit you put to death the deeds of the body, you will live.

Romans 8:13 connects to the verses before it by the idea of "life." It is "the Spirit of life" who has liberated Christians "from the law of sin and death" through Christ's atonement

---

1. Because Galatians 6:7–8 is similar to Romans 8:13, and space constraints prevent a separate treatment, our conclusions for Romans 8:13 will serve for Galatians 6:7–8 too.

(vv. 2–4). The mind-set of unbelievers leads to "death," but the mind-set of believers leads to "life and peace," where "death" and "life and peace" refer to the final destinies of the lost and saved respectively (v. 6).

Unbelievers' minds oppose God and cannot please him (vv. 7–8). Believers, however, are not ruled by the sinful nature but by the Holy Spirit. In fact, anyone who lacks the Spirit does not belong to Christ (v. 9). But if the Spirit, and Christ from whom he is inseparable, dwells in people, though their bodies will die, the Spirit has given them eternal life now and will one day raise their bodies to life and immortality (vv. 10–11).

A Stark Contrast

As a result of the above, Christians are obligated not to live for sin but, by implication, for the Spirit (vv. 12–13). "For if you live according to the flesh you will die, but if by the Spirit you put to death the deeds of the body, you will live" (Rom. 8:13). It is crucial to note that "you will die" and "you will live" denote the final states of damnation and salvation respectively. Paul thus speaks in strong terms. To "live according to the flesh" is to live with a mind-set that is hostile to God, that disobeys God, and that leads to spiritual death (vv. 5–8). Paul speaks bluntly: living in such a manner leads to hell.

By contrast, to live in such a manner as to "put to death the deeds of the body" is to live the godly life that God requires of his children. Living in this way leads to eternal life. Paul breaks up the symmetry in the contrast between the two modes of living by adding to the second the words "by the Spirit" (v. 13). Observing this is essential to understanding Paul's message. The apostle certainly expects his readers to dedicate their wills to obeying his message. But he does not advocate a self-help program for Christians. Instead, as Thomas Schreiner explains, "Victory is by means of the Spirit . . . which means that believers conquer sinful passions by relying on and trusting in the Spirit to provide the strength to resist the passions that wage war within us."[2] By creating asymmetry, then, Paul emphasizes the Spirit, by whose work alone victory in the Christian life is possible and ultimately assured.

Can Christians Lose Salvation?

It is striking that after Paul's strong words of God's preservation in Romans 8:1–4 and before his even stronger words on the subject in verses 28–39, he urgently exhorts his readers to live not for sin but for God. There is no mistaking his forceful words: "For if you live according to the flesh you will die, but if . . . you put to death the deeds of the body, you will live" (Rom. 8:13). Does Paul here teach that Christians can lose salvation if they stop living for God? At first glance it may appear so, but it would be strange if he would contradict the message he gives before and after this verse. And a good look at the following verses confirms that Paul is not threatening believers with the loss of salvation.

The next verse reads, "For all who are led by the Spirit of God are sons of God" (v. 14). Christians are identifiable: God's children obey the Holy Spirit. This verse helps us understand verse 13, as Schreiner explains:

> Verse 14 clarifies by saying that those who are the children of God, that is, truly part of the people of God, are those who are led by the Spirit of God. . . . All those who have the Spirit manifest that fact by their submission to the Spirit, and conversely those who do not possess the Spirit are not led by the Spirit. . . . The passive form of the verb is significant, in that it suggests that the Spirit is the primary agent in Christian obedience, that it is his work in believers that accounts for their obedience. . . . Although this does not exclude the need for believers to follow the Spirit . . . it emphasizes that any human obedience is the result of the Spirit's work. A link is forged with verse 13, for those who are led by the Spirit put to death the deeds of the body by the agency of the Spirit.[3]

2. Thomas R. Schreiner, *Romans*, Baker Exegetical Commentary on the New Testament (Grand Rapids: Baker, 1998), 421–22.
    3. Ibid., 422.

Conclusion

In Romans 8:13, Paul presents two bold truths: "For if you live according to the flesh you will die, but if by the Spirit you put to death the deeds of the body, you will live." Although this passage could be taken to teach that believers can fall from saving grace, it should not be so taken for three reasons. First, it is very hard to reconcile such an interpretation of Romans 8:13 with the strong preservation passages surrounding it (8:1–4, 28–39). Paul does not contradict himself in the same chapter.

Second, the next verse, Romans 8:14, clarifies verse 13 by assuring readers that God's children obey the Spirit; that is, they "put to death the deeds of the body" (v. 13). Paul thus presents God's condition for attaining eternal life in one verse and gives believers confidence that they will meet that condition and reap life in the next verse.

Third, already in Romans 8:13 itself, Paul, by creating imbalance in the two sections of the verse, draws attention to the words "by the Spirit" in its second half. This underlines the fact that God enables Christians to do what he demands—kill the deeds of the body—by the power of the Holy Spirit within them. Christians *do* live for God because they have God's Spirit, whom they obey.

Romans 11:20–22: Corporate Judgment

> But if some of the branches were broken off, and you, although a wild olive shoot, were grafted in among the others and now share in the nourishing root of the olive tree, do not be arrogant toward the branches. If you are, remember it is not you who support the root, but the root that supports you. Then you will say, "Branches were broken off so that I might be grafted in." That is true. They were broken off because of their unbelief, but you stand fast through faith. So do not become proud, but fear. For if God did not spare

122

the natural branches, neither will he spare you. Note then the kindness and the severity of God: severity toward those who have fallen, but God's kindness to you, provided you continue in his kindness. Otherwise you too will be cut off. And even they, if they do not continue in their unbelief, will be grafted in, for God has the power to graft them in again. For if you were cut from what is by nature a wild olive tree, and grafted, contrary to nature, into a cultivated olive tree, how much more will these, the natural branches, be grafted back into their own olive tree. (Rom. 11:17–24)

Paul shares his burden for his fellow-Israelites in Romans 11. He begins, "I ask, then, has God rejected his people? By no means! For I myself am an Israelite, a descendant of Abraham, a member of the tribe of Benjamin" (v. 1). God has not utterly forsaken the descendants of Abraham because Paul (like many other Jews) has trusted Jesus as Messiah. And this is in keeping with the Old Testament story of God's dealings with Israel, as the account of Elijah shows. The prophet despaired, fearing he was the only true worshipper of Yahweh left. God, however, reassured him that he had reserved for himself seven thousand Israelites who had not worshipped Baal. Paul writes, "So too at the present time there is a remnant, chosen by grace" (v. 5).

Hardened Hearts

But first-century Jewish believers are only a remnant because Israel has largely rejected its Messiah, in keeping with Old Testament descriptions of hardened hearts in Israel (vv. 7–10). Paul then asks, "Did they stumble in order that they might fall?" He answers, "By no means! Rather through their trespass salvation has come to the Gentiles, so as to make Israel jealous" (v. 11). First-century Israel's rejection of Christ led to the gospel going to the Gentiles. Paul expects that God's work among the Gentiles will make Israel "jealous" for the gospel and bring many of them to Christ also (vv. 12–16).

Wild Olive Branches

The apostle next speaks hard words to his Gentile readers:

But if some of the branches were broken off, and you, although a wild olive shoot, were grafted in among the others and now share in the nourishing root of the olive tree, do not be arrogant toward the branches. If you are, remember it is not you who support the root, but the root that supports you. (vv. 17–18)

Paul cautions the Gentile members of the church in Rome to be respectful toward their Jewish Christian brothers, for God's dealings with humanity in salvation did not begin with the Gentiles but with the Jews, with God's covenant with Abraham. Now Israel's rejection of the gospel brought it to the Gentiles. But the Gentile believers must never forget that they were far from God and have now participated in the blessings originally meant for Israel.

Paul crushes Gentile pride by issuing a severe warning:

Then you will say, "Branches were broken off so that I might be grafted in." That is true. They were broken off because of their unbelief, but you stand fast through faith. So do not become proud, but fear. For if God did not spare the natural branches, neither will he spare you. Note then the kindness and the severity of God: severity toward those who have fallen, but God's kindness to you, provided you continue in his kindness. Otherwise you too will be cut off. (vv. 19–22)

These verses, of course, contain the bone of contention. Grant Osborne, to cite one example, understands Paul's words "otherwise you too will be cut off" (v. 22) as a warning that Christians can lose their salvation: "Therefore it seems a valid warning that any believing Gentile who falls away (as many Jews have) will also be *cut off* . . . so long as they are cut off they are headed for divine judgment and eternal death."[4]

4. Grant R. Osborne, *Romans*, The IVP New Testament Commentary (Downers Grove, IL: InterVarsity, 2003), 300–301, note on 11:22.

Corporate and Not Individual Judgment

Is Osborne right? Does Paul here teach that saved people can be lost? I respectfully disagree for three reasons. First, when Paul speaks of Jewish branches being cut off and grafted in again (vv. 17, 19, 23, 24), he is not speaking of individual Jews losing their salvation and then regaining it. His focus is not on the stories of individuals but on the roles of Jews and Gentiles in God's plan.

The olive tree represents Israel, which before Christ's coming was the people of God. When Christ came, many Jews believed in him and continued to be God's people. But the majority rejected him and were broken off as branches. Though they continued to be Jews ethnically, they were no longer a part of the people of God. Their rejection of the Messiah cut them off from salvation.

Paul warns the Gentiles that although the Jews' rejection has brought the Gentiles the gospel, they too must fear lest they lapse into unbelief and be cut off. Paul does not have individual Gentiles in view but refers to their place in God's plan as an ethnic group. As a group, they were unsaved ("a wild olive shoot," v. 17) and now have become a part of God's people ("were grafted in," v. 17). If they do not pass the gospel on to their children and grandchildren, they too risk being cut off as an ethnic group.

Second, Paul does not threaten Gentile Christians with the loss of salvation because he has taught God's preservation of his people—as plainly as anywhere in the Bible—in Romans 5:9–10, 8:1–4, and 8:28–39. He does not contradict this teaching in the same book.

Third, it is better to identify the branches that are broken off from the olive tree with families and generations than with individuals. I agree with Charles Hodge:

> This passage, however, has no legitimate bearing on this subject [the final perseverance of believers]. Paul is not speaking of the connection of individual believers with Christ, which

125

he had abundantly taught in chap. viii. and elsewhere, to be indissoluble, but of the relation of communities to the church and its various privileges. There is no promise or covenant on the part of God, securing to the Gentiles the enjoyment of these blessings through all generations, any more than there was any such promise to protect the Jews from the consequences of their unbelief. The continuance of these favours depends on the conduct of each successive generation. Paul therefore says to the Gentile, that he must continue in the divine favour, "otherwise thou also shalt be cut off."[5]

Hodge is correct. Paul is not threatening individuals with the loss of salvation if they fail to persevere in faith to the end. Rather, he is warning Gentiles as an ethnic group that the truth of the gospel will not continue unless each generation walks in the way of the Lord and transmits the gospel to its successor.

1 Corinthians 9:27: Disqualification from Service

Do you not know that in a race all the runners run, but only one receives the prize? So run that you may obtain it. Every athlete exercises self-control in all things. They do it to receive a perishable wreath, but we an imperishable. So I do not run aimlessly; I do not box as one beating the air. But I discipline my body and keep it under control, lest after preaching to others I myself should be disqualified. (1 Cor. 9:24–27)

Paul has been speaking of his service for Christ. He is obligated by God to preach the gospel (v. 16). He is God's steward who presents the good news free of charge (v. 18). He demonstrates flexibility in order to bring the gospel to different groups of people (vv. 19–22). In summary, "I have become all things to all people, that by all means I might save some. I do it all for the sake of the gospel" (vv. 22–23).

5. Charles Hodge, *Commentary on the Epistle to the Romans*, rev. ed. (Philadelphia: James S. Claxton, 1864), 582.

The Isthmian Games

Next the apostle shifts to an athletic metaphor, speaking of athletes who compete in the Pan-Hellenic Isthmian games. These games were held in Corinth in the spring of AD 49 and 51. As the name implies, athletes from across Greece came to compete in contests, including foot races, wrestling, boxing, etc. The games attracted huge crowds and brought in significant revenue for the Corinthian tradespeople. "The fame of the Isthmian Games is well attested in Greek literature and philosophy."[6]

Paul focuses on runners in the Isthmian games, prodding his hearers to diligence: "Do you not know that in a race all the runners run, but only one receives the prize? So run that you may obtain it" (v. 24). The runner's discipline captures his interest: "Every athlete exercises self-control in all things" (v. 25). And why do they run? "They do it to receive a perishable wreath, but we an imperishable" (v. 25). The athletes in the Greek games seek the laurel wreath, whose leaves suffer decay and ruin, but Christians seek an "imperishable" wreath, even the reward of eternal life.

Paul the Athlete

Similar to an athlete, Paul disciplines himself: "So I do not run aimlessly; I do not box as one beating the air. But I discipline my body and keep it under control" (vv. 26–27). Why does Paul take such pains? He does so "lest after preaching to others I myself should be disqualified" (v. 27). Some claim that Paul teaches that if he leads a careless life he would fall away from grace and forfeit salvation. Among them is C. K. Barrett: "Paul clearly envisages the possibility that, notwithstanding his work as a preacher, he may himself fall from grace and be rejected. . . . His conversion, his baptism, his call to apostleship, his service in the Gospel, do not guarantee his eternal salvation."[7]

6. Anthony C. Thiselton, *The First Epistle to the Corinthians*, The New International Greek Testament Commentary (Grand Rapids: Eerdmans, 2000), 710.
7. C. K. Barrett, *A Commentary on the First Epistle to the Corinthians*, Harper's New Testament Commentaries (New York: Harper, 1968), 218.

When Paul fears being "disqualified," does he refer to the possibility of losing his salvation? Inspection of 1 Corinthians 9:27 in its context leads me to answer the question in the negative. First, it is important to see, in the words of Anthony Thiselton, that "Paul does not specify that he would be *not approved* . . . as if to imply eschatological rejection or loss of salvation. . . . The test reveals failures of an unspecified nature, not utter rejection."[8] This is correct. Paul does not specify from what he fears disqualification. We must, therefore, study his use of "disqualified" elsewhere and the context in 1 Corinthians 9 to supply the specifics.

Second, 2 Corinthians 13:5 uses the concept of "disqualified" with regard to the test of salvation: "Examine yourselves, to see whether you are in the faith. Test yourselves. Or do you not realize this about yourselves, that Jesus Christ is in you?—unless indeed you fail to meet the test!" But in the next verse Paul applies the term to himself with regard to the test of apostleship: "I hope you will find out that we have not failed the test" (2 Cor. 13:6). The context shows that the Corinthians were not questioning Paul's salvation but were seeking "proof that Christ is speaking in" him (v. 3). In fact, "a survey of Paul's self references with *adokimos* ["disqualified"] and cognates has shown that Paul always has in mind the test of apostleship when he applies the terminology of testing to himself."[9] The fact that when Paul applies "disqualified" to himself in every other instance he refers to his fitness as an apostle and not to the test of salvation suggests that the same is true for 1 Corinthians 9:27. But does a consideration of the context corroborate this?

Disqualified from Service

The answer is yes. Interpreters err because they misunderstand Paul's references to athletic discipline in 1 Corinthians 9:24–27. Marshall, for example, sees the athletic terminology as speaking

---

8. Thiselton, *The First Epistle to the Corinthians*, 717.
9. Judith M. Gundry Volf, *Paul and Perseverance: Staying In and Falling Away* (Louisville: John Knox, 1990), 233, 236.

of "the general concept of the Christian's self-discipline" in light of "the temptations of the body" and Paul's possible disqualification, then, as referring to "rejection on the day of judgment."[10] But more recent study has overturned this view.

> Rather, Paul is illustrating discipline with regard to the use of Christian rights and freedom, which has been his main concern since 8:1. Like the athlete's practice of *egkrateia* ["discipline"], Paul's subjugation of the body consists in renunciation of physical desires which are satisfied through normal, accepted behavior. The athlete was deprived of wine, meat and sexual activity for a ten month training period. Similarly, Paul gave up practices to which he had a rightful claim. He renounced his right to marry (9:5) and to receive the Corinthians' financial support (9:12, 15, 18). . . . Moreover, he so radically limited his freedom in Christ that he became a slave to all (. . . 9:19) by becoming all things to all people in order by all means to save some (9:22). The use of similar verbs to denote "slavery" in apostolic service in 9:19 . . . and the "enslavement" of the *soma* ["body"] in 9:27 . . . is significant. It illustrates Paul's practice of connecting the metaphor to its context through a catchword. . . . This parallel and the abundance of references to Paul's renunciation of his rights immediately preceding the athletic metaphor make it most natural to define the attacks by Paul against his *soma* ["body"] as his self-subjection to physically trying circumstances as a result of renouncing his apostolic rights and limiting his use of Christian freedom.[11]

Seen in its context, then, 1 Corinthians 9:24–27 sums up Paul's words (in vv. 1–22) about putting aside his rights as an apostle and freedom as a Christian in order better to preach the gospel. He is an example to other believers of renunciation out of love for Christ and the lost. Like an athlete, Paul subdues his physical desires by giving up his rights and freedom. Also, like

10. I. Howard Marshall, *Kept by the Power of God: A Study of Perseverance and Falling Away* (1969; reprint, Minneapolis: Bethany Fellowship, 1974), 120–21.

11. Volf, *Paul and Perseverance*, 239–40.

an athlete, Paul has a goal toward which he presses: "But I discipline my body and keep it under control, lest after preaching to others I myself should be disqualified" (v. 27). That goal is to avoid disqualification and to be approved by God.

Volf asks a timely question:

> Is it likely that Paul could lose his salvation by exercising his very apostolic *rights* and Christian *freedom* instead of renouncing them? The apostolic right to financial support even rests on a command of Jesus . . . (9:14). And Paul mentions that other apostles make use of their rights in the gospel without this practice calling their salvation into question (9:4–6). Paul's going beyond the call of duty in his apostolic ministry does not mean that he fears for his salvation.[12]

If, then, we take into account Paul's use of "disqualified" referring to himself and the flow of thought of 1 Corinthians 9, we learn that his fear of disqualification has to do with the success or failure of his apostolic service and not the loss of his salvation.

Colossians 1:21–23: "If Indeed You Continue in the Faith"

> And you, who once were alienated and hostile in mind, doing evil deeds, he has now reconciled in his body of flesh by his death, in order to present you holy and blameless and above reproach before him, if indeed you continue in the faith, stable and steadfast, not shifting from the hope of the gospel that you heard, which has been proclaimed in all creation under heaven, and of which I, Paul, became a minister.

In the preceding verses Paul teaches that Christ deserves first place over the creation (1:15–17) and the new creation, the church (vv. 18–20). At the end of that section, Paul introduces the theme of reconciliation: "For in him all the fullness of God was pleased to dwell, and through him to reconcile to himself

12. Ibid., 241–42.

all things, whether on earth or in heaven, making peace by the blood of his cross" (vv. 19–20). Reconciliation is God, through Christ's death and resurrection, making peace between him and us and between us and him. In verse 20 the apostle teaches that Christ accomplished "cosmic restoration or renewal"[13] that will result not only in the resurrection of believers unto eternal life but also the renewal of their destination—the new earth.

Returning to "the theme of a 'transfer' from one spiritual realm to another from vv. 12–14,"[14] Paul describes the background for reconciliation: "And you . . . once were alienated and hostile in mind, doing evil deeds" (v. 21). Before the Colossians came to know Christ, they were estranged from God. Paul singles out their mind-set of rebellion again their Maker. Sinful actions flowed from their rebellious thinking.

Reconciliation

When the Colossians were God's enemies, he acted: "And you . . . he has now reconciled in his body of flesh by his death" (vv. 21–22). Christ suffered and died to make peace between the Colossians and God. What is the goal of this reconciliation? Paul answers, "in order to present you holy and blameless and above reproach before him" (v. 22). The goal is nothing less than final and complete sanctification in God's presence at the last judgment. God will do this for us, as Paul indicates: "he has now reconciled . . . in order to present you . . ." (v. 22). God will present believers, including the Colossians, to himself in moral perfection.

A Condition

Christ's reconciliation, then, is for the purpose of final sanctification. Paul correlates another important theological truth— perseverance: "And you . . . he has now reconciled . . . to present you holy and blameless and above reproach before him, *if indeed you*

13. So Douglas J. Moo, *The Letters to the Colossians and to Philemon* (Grand Rapids: Eerdmans, 2008), 136.
14. Ibid., 138.

131

continue in the faith, stable and steadfast, not shifting from the hope of the gospel that you heard" (vv. 21–23, italics added). The apostle is emphatic, adding to "faith," these words: "stable and steadfast, not shifting from the hope of the gospel" (v. 23). There is no doubt that Paul plainly teaches the necessity of perseverance in faith to the end as a condition of final salvation. Schreiner and Caneday are straightforward: "Thus, once again Paul admonished us to remain steadfast in faith in order that we may attain unto salvation in the last day."[15] This is "the central concern of the letter: to encourage the Colossian Christians to resist the blandishments of the false teachers and to continue to grow in their knowledge of Christ."[16]

Loss of Salvation?

If Paul makes continuing to believe the gospel a condition of final salvation, does that imply that a believer could fail to do this and fall away from grace? Some answer affirmatively. One such is F. B. Westcott: "This blessed consummation can only be attained provided they maintain faith unimpaired. To lose that is to lose all. Therefore the proviso [of v. 23] follows."[17] I. Howard Marshall agrees: "The need for perseverance in faith is also stressed in Colossians 1:23 . . . here the construction, 'provided that . . .' (*ei ge*), allows, but by no means demands, the possibility that the condition may not be fulfilled."[18]

Other capable scholars, including P. T. O'Brien, disagree. Colossians 1:23 does not imply that Christians can lose salvation. In fact, "The Greek construction *ei ge*, translated 'provided that,' does not express doubt." He insists, "The words in this sentence may be paraphrased: 'At any rate if you stand firm in the faith—and I am sure that you will.'"[19]

15. Thomas R. Schreiner and Ardel B. Caneday, *The Race Set Before Us: A Biblical Theology of Perseverance and Assurance* (Downers Grove, IL: InterVarsity, 2001), 193.

16. Moo, *The Letters to the Colossians and to Philemon*, 143.

17. Frederick Brooke Westcott, *Colossians: A Letter to Asia* (Minneapolis: Klock & Klock, 1981; orig. pub. 1914), 75.

18. Marshall, *Kept by the Power of God*, 243, n. 64.

19. Peter T. O'Brien, *Colossians, Philemon*, Word Biblical Commentary (Waco, TX: Word, 1982), 69. Murray J. Harris agrees with O'Brien in *Colossians and Philemon*,

Amidst these differing opinions, I value Doug Moo's fair and balanced judgment:

> The precise nuance of the conditional construction that Paul uses here is debated. Some believe that the construction (*ei ge*) suggests uncertainly—"if, though I doubt it"—while others think it connotes confidence—"if, as I am sure." Pauline evidence points in both directions, Galatians 3:4 falling into the former category and 2 Corinthians 5:3 and Ephesians 3:2; 4:21 into the latter. Since most of the parallels point to the idea of confidence, and because Paul expresses confidence in the Colossians elsewhere (see esp. 2:5), it is this direction that we should probably take here. Nevertheless, the condition is a real one, and it is very important not to rob the words of their intended rhetorical function.[20]

Moo speaks wisely. Although the evidence is debated, its preponderance and Paul's tone in Colossians favor the confidence view, but we must not blunt the force of the condition. Fairness leads me to conclude from Paul's making final sanctification dependent upon Christians' perseverance in faith that one could deduce the possibility of their losing salvation. But it is important to note that the apostle himself does not draw that conclusion here. Frankly, Colossians 1:21–23 can be integrated into either an Arminian or Calvinist systematic theology. The passage by itself does not prove or disprove either theological system. Theologians must bring other passages to bear on their understanding of Colossians 1:21–23, including not only other warning passages but preservation passages as well. This passage, then, is inconclusive.

Connecting the Dots

Once again it is helpful to put our findings into categories. A first category is for a passage that boldly distinguishes the

Exegetical Guide to the Greek New Testament (Grand Rapids: Eerdmans, 1991), 60.
20. Moo, *The Letters to the Colossians and to Philemon*, 144.

lifestyles of those who will perish from those who finally will be saved: "For if you live according to the flesh you will die, but if by the Spirit you put to death the deeds of the body, you will live" (Rom. 8:13).[21] I admit that this text could be understood as teaching that believers can forfeit salvation, but I do not reach that conclusion for three reasons. First, it would conflict with Paul's teaching of preservation in ten passages: Romans 5:9–10; 8:1–4, 28–39; 1 Corinthians 1:4, 8–9; 11:27–32; Ephesians 1:13–14; 4:30; Philippians 1:6; 1 Thessalonians 5:23–24. Second, the context of Romans 8:13 provides assurance to believing readers—in verse 14. Third, the passage itself turns readers away from their own resources to the Holy Spirit to assure them that they belong to God and will not fail (Rom. 8:13).

A second category concerns redemptive history and not individuals' salvation. It has to do with God's plan for Israel and the Gentiles and not the stories of individual Jews and Gentiles. Paul warns the Gentiles, "You stand fast through faith. So . . . fear. For if God did not spare the natural branches, neither will he spare you. Note then . . . God's kindness to you, provided you continue in his kindness. Otherwise you too will be cut off" (Rom. 11:20–22). The apostle speaks of God's dealings with the Gentiles as an ethnic group. He does not threaten individuals with the loss of salvation. Instead he warns ethnic Gentiles as a group that the gospel will not continue in their families unless each successive generation trusts that gospel and commits it to the next one.

A third category speaks of disqualification from office rather than loss of salvation. Paul explains, "But I discipline my body and keep it under control, lest after preaching to others I myself should be disqualified" (1 Cor. 9:27). Considering Paul's use of "disqualified" with reference to himself and the context of 1 Corinthians 9 shows that his fear of disqualification concerns the possibility of failure as an apostle and not the forfeiture of salvation.

21. I intend for these conclusions to also serve for Galatians 6:7–8.

A fourth category makes persevering in faith to the end a condition of final salvation. The majority usage of "if indeed" (Col. 1:23) and Paul's overall tone in Colossians favor the view that Paul is confident of his readers' salvation, but the matter cannot be decided based on this verse alone. The truth that believers must continue to trust Christ for final salvation fits both Calvinist and Arminian theological models. But since this passage by itself neither proves nor disproves either model, it is inconclusive.

9

Warnings in Paul, Part 2

THE WARNING passages in Paul's letters to Timothy are numerous and important enough to warrant a separate chapter. There are so many warnings that we cannot examine them all, but we will treat six key ones.

- 1 Timothy 1:18–20: Rejection of the Gospel.
- 1 Timothy 4:1: "Teachings of Demons."
- 1 Timothy 5:8: "Worse Than an Unbeliever."
- 1 Timothy 5:11–12: Condemnation for Abandoning Their Former Faith.
- 2 Timothy 2:11–13: "If We Deny Him, He Also Will Deny Us."
- 2 Timothy 2:17–19: Hymenaeus and Philetus.

1 Timothy 1:18–20: Rejection of the Gospel

This charge I entrust to you, Timothy, my child, in accordance with the prophecies previously made about you, that by them you may wage the good warfare, holding faith and a good conscience. By rejecting this, some have made shipwreck of their faith, among whom are Hymenaeus and Alexander, whom I have handed over to Satan that they may learn not to blaspheme.

Paul resumes the personal exhortation to his disciple Timothy that he had begun in verses 3–7, now urging him to fight the good fight of a Christian and a minister (v. 18). Specifically, Timothy is to hold fast to "faith and a good conscience" (v. 19). In 1 Timothy "faith" sometimes refers to trust in Jesus and other times to the content of Christian belief. Here, because it is used with the phrase "a good conscience," faith means trust in Christ. "Conscience" is one's moral compass, and Timothy is to keep his in good working order by obeying God from a pure heart characterized by a sincere faith, as described in verse 5.

A Telling Contrast

As he does frequently in the pastoral epistles, Paul teaches by way of contrast. Over against Timothy's "faith and a good conscience," the false teachers have repudiated a good conscience and "have made shipwreck of their faith" (v. 19). Paul first spoke of the false teachers in verse 3, where he said that his purpose for leaving Timothy at Ephesus was to confront them: "so that you may charge certain persons not to teach any different doctrine." By "different doctrine" Paul means that which diverges from the true gospel. The apostle described the false teachers' legalistic perversion of the gospel and its ethic in verses 8–11.

Now Paul names Hymenaeus and Alexander as two leaders who "have made shipwreck of their faith," (vv. 19–20).[1] Is he saying that these two have forfeited their salvation? Quoting John Wesley, Thomas Oden thinks so: "Hymenaeus and Alexander . . . ran their ships onto rocks. Their lives and others' were strewn with the wreckage of bad conscience and unsound teaching. Once their faith had rested securely in good conscience, for 'none can make shipwreck of faith who had never had it.'"[2]

1. For discussion of their identities, see William D. Mounce, *Pastoral Epistles*, Word Biblical Commentary (Nashville: Nelson 2000), 67–68.
2. Thomas C. Oden, *First and Second Timothy and Titus*, Interpretation (Louisville: John Knox, 1989), 123–24.

A Rejection of the Gospel

The false teachers deliberately rejected Paul's message: "Paul's opponents made a deliberate decision to abandon their faith and to sear their consciences."[3] Plainly, "shipwreck" refers to the destruction of the false teachers' faith. But does Paul regard Hymenaeus and Alexander as lapsed believers or as those who were never saved? Paul provides a clue in his earlier words in verses 5–7, where he says that the goal of his instruction is "love that issues from a pure heart and a good conscience and a sincere faith. Certain persons, by swerving from these, have wandered away into vain discussion." Philip Towner masterfully ties this earlier passage to 1 Timothy 1:19–20:

> The condition of the conscience is determined by one's disposition toward the gospel (by conversion), which suggests the ordering of "faith" followed by "a good conscience." Paul is obviously setting faithfulness to his gospel as the prerequisite of Timothy's success. Together, then, these two items link the ministry of opposition Timothy is to be engaged in to godly faith and behavior, just as they distance authentic Christian ministry from the activities of the opponents.
>
> In fact, this distance between authentic and inauthentic faith is now explained in terms of the opponents' act of rejection. . . . This decision of rejection does indeed have practical and visible results in the form of behavior that does not conform to godliness, but the root error seems to have been rejection of Paul's gospel.[4]

Inauthentic Doctrine and Conduct

This is correct. Just as Paul juxtaposed true and false faith in verses 3–7, so now he does the same in verses 18–20. Timothy is to "wage the good warfare, holding faith and a good conscience" (vv. 18–19). But Hymenaeus and Alexander, though they were leaders in the Ephesian churches, were never saved and showed it by

---

3. Mounce, *Pastoral Epistles*, 67.

4. Philip H. Towner, *The Letters to Timothy and Titus*, The New International Commentary on the New Testament (Grand Rapids: Eerdmans, 2006), 158–59.

rejecting Paul's message of grace to embrace a message of legalism and a corrupted conscience that led them to depart from Christian norms of godliness, which in turn led to their disaster. "Their rejection of the Pauline conception of the faith, with its insistence on the internalizing of the norm of godliness, for an external law structure without the Spirit, rendered their conscience incapable of discerning authentic from inauthentic doctrine and conduct."[5]

Though Paul at this point does not regard the false teachers as true believers, he has not given up on them entirely. Rather, he "handed [them] over to Satan that they may learn not to blaspheme" (v. 20). God may still reclaim them.

1 Timothy 4:1: "Teachings of Demons"

> Now the Spirit expressly says that in later times some will depart from the faith by devoting themselves to deceitful spirits and teachings of demons, through the insincerity of liars whose consciences are seared, who forbid marriage and require abstinence from foods that God created to be received with thanksgiving by those who believe and know the truth. For everything created by God is good, and nothing is to be rejected if it is received with thanksgiving, for it is made holy by the word of God and prayer. (1 Tim. 4:1–5)

Paul has been speaking of the qualifications of elders and deacons and of his desire to visit Timothy, and in the meantime he writes to teach him "how one ought to behave in the household of God" (1 Tim. 3:15). Next, the apostle, in quoting an early church confession, extols "the mystery of godliness," which is Christ in his incarnation to ascension:

> He was manifested in the flesh,
>   vindicated by the Spirit,
>   seen by angels,

5. Ibid., 158.

proclaimed among the nations,
      believed on in the world,
            taken up in glory. (v. 16)

"Some Will Depart from the Faith"

Then Paul, returning to the theme of the false teaching that is disturbing the Ephesian church, warns of terrible times to come: "Now the Spirit expressly says that in later times some will depart from the faith" (1 Tim. 4:1). The word used for "departing" from the faith (*aphistemi*) "acquired the technical meaning 'apostatize.'"[6] It is critical to understand that, in the words of I. Howard Marshall, "What is prophesied is in fact already happening."[7] "Some," therefore, includes the false teachers whom Paul has warned his readers about (1 Tim. 1:3–7, 19–20) and those within "the household of God . . . the church" (3:15) infected with their false teaching.

By "the faith" here is meant the Christian faith, the beliefs that make up orthodoxy. This faith, which some will leave, includes the content of the confession just quoted (1 Tim. 3:16). "The 'mystery of godliness' means the revelation of Jesus Christ in which Christian existence has its origin."[8] That mystery includes Christ's incarnation (being "manifested in the flesh"), resurrection from the grave ("vindicated by the Spirit, seen by angels"), ascension ("taken up in glory"), and the consequent spread of the gospel ("proclaimed among the nations, believed on in the world").

"Deceitful Spirits and Teachings of Demons"

Since the Spirit predicted such a defection from Christianity, the fact that false teachers have done that very thing should not surprise the believers in Ephesus. In fact, some within their church already have turned away from these basic tenets of the

6. Ibid., 289.
7. I. Howard Marshall, *The Pastoral Epistles*, International Critical Commentary (New York: T&T Clark, 1999), 531.
8. Towner, *The Letters to Timothy and Titus*, 277.

faith. But where did they turn? Paul says they will depart "by devoting themselves to deceitful spirits and teachings of demons" (1 Tim. 4:1). They will turn to false teaching, teaching inspired by "deceitful spirits" and "demons." Gordon Fee speaks plainly: "The ultimate source of the false teachings is Satan himself."[9] And the demons are not the only source of deceit, for Paul characterizes the false teachers' conduct as "the insincerity of liars whose consciences are seared" (v. 2). So there are two sources of the false teaching—demons and the false teachers energized by them.

The false teachers, driven by demons, "forbid marriage" and "require abstinence from foods that God created" (v. 3). While it is difficult to pinpoint the heresy, clearly these are both affronts to the Creator, who instituted marriage in the garden of Eden and who made all things good, including foods. Rather than abstaining from marriage or certain foods, "those who believe and know the truth" are to receive them "with thanksgiving," as befits grateful creatures of a good Creator (vv. 3–5).

Loss of Salvation?

Does Paul here teach that saved persons become unsaved by abandoning the apostolic teaching? I answer no for two reasons. First, Paul's evaluation of the spiritual status of the false teachers is evident from their first mention:

> As I urged you when I was going to Macedonia, remain at Ephesus so that you may charge certain persons not to teach any different doctrine, nor to devote themselves to myths and endless genealogies, which promote speculations rather than the stewardship from God that is by faith. The aim of our charge is love that issues from a pure heart and a good conscience and a sincere faith. Certain persons, by swerving from these, have wandered away into vain discussion, desiring to be teachers of the law, without understanding either what they

9. Gordon D. Fee, *1 and 2 Timothy, Titus*, New International Biblical Commentary (Peabody, MA: Hendrickson, 1984, 1988), 98.

are saying or the things about which they make confident
assertions. (1 Tim. 1:3–7)

In these words, at the very beginning of Paul's epistle, he highlights
the false teachers' serious doctrinal and moral deficiencies—
deficiencies incompatible with a true knowledge of Christ, as
Towner makes clear:

> In this opening restatement of Timothy's commission (vv. 3–7),
> Paul has set out the goal his coworker is to pursue, and under-
> scored that the opponents' ministry in the community runs
> contrary to this goal. Paul has not provided a detailed critical
> analysis of the false teaching . . . but by naming the goal and
> linking it to the apostolic gospel, he establishes at the outset
> that the opponents in Ephesus are in direct opposition to his
> and Timothy's mission. By stating the goal—love—Paul focuses
> the critique of the heresy on visible Christian living. What these
> opponents teach and the disputes resulting from their teach-
> ing run counter to God's order of life. The opponents, in fact,
> are incapable of understanding God's purposes or of serving
> them because they have departed from the gospel and lack
> the inward components (cleansed heart, good conscience, and
> sincere faith) that take the believer from apprehension of the
> gospel to authentic Christian love.[10]

Second, 1 Timothy 4:1–5 repeats the truth already taught in
1:3–7—namely, that by word and deed the false teachers reveal
their unsaved status. Despite their claims, their teaching and
lives expose them as people who have never been saved. When
they purport to deliver Christian teachings, they do not know
what they are talking about. And they lack the faith and internal
purity characteristic of those who believe the gospel. Indeed,
their departure "from the faith," "devoting themselves to deceitful spirits and teachings of demons," reveals that though they
insist otherwise, in reality they are "liars whose consciences are
seared" (1 Tim. 4:1–2). William Mounce offers a terse summary:

10. Towner, *The Letters to Timothy and Titus*, 121.

"The opponents are hypocritical liars who know that what they are teaching is wrong and yet continue to teach, claiming to be Christians and yet bearing Satan's brand of ownership."[11]

1 Timothy 5:8: "Worse than an Unbeliever"

> But if anyone does not provide for his relatives, and especially for members of his household, he has denied the faith and is worse than an unbeliever.

Paul instructs Timothy how to relate to church members both young and old and of both genders: "Do not rebuke an older man but encourage him as you would a father, younger men as brothers, older women as mothers, younger women as sisters, in all purity" (1 Tim. 5:1–2). He then begins a long section treating widows (vv. 3–16) before teaching about elders (vv. 17–25) and Christian slaves (6:1–2).

Two Problems Concerning Widows in Ephesus

Paul here gives his most extensive teaching about any group in 1 Timothy when he turns his attention to widows. Paul deals with two problems: the care of some widows was unnecessarily burdening the church, and the scandalous lives of some younger widows gave the church a bad reputation. The two problems were related. Some families who were able to care for their widows were not doing so, and as a result other truly needy and deserving widows were left out. Also, younger women were on the list of widows for whom the church provided when they should not have been. The results were idleness, promiscuity, and their taking places on the rolls that belonged to deserving older widows.

Paul begins with a command: "Honor widows who are truly widows," that is, those who are in need with no family to support

11. Mounce, *Pastoral Epistles*, 233.

them (1 Tim. 5:3). If a widow has children or grandchildren able to take care of her, they should do so (v. 4). Those who are truly widows, for whom the church is to provide, are those who are alone and godly (vv. 4–7).

Timothy is warned that some women, including widows, are ungodly and spiritually dead; such a woman "is dead even while she lives" (v. 6). Paul instructs Timothy to "command these things as well" to the widows in the church "so that they may be without reproach" (v. 7). There is a problem because some widows, especially younger ones, are leading sinful lives and come in for special correction in verses 11–15.

Worse Than an Unbeliever!

In the midst of this discussion Paul writes hard words: "But if anyone does not provide for his relatives, and especially for members of his household, he has denied the faith and is worse than an unbeliever" (1 Tim. 5:8). In verse 4, Paul had commended family members who care for their widows. Now he condemns those who fail to do so. Paul, in speaking of householders with means, moves from the general "relatives" to the specific "members of his household."

"To deny the faith" here means "'repudiate' or 'disown,' in the sense of apostasy from the Christian faith . . . referring to Christianity as that which one professes to believe."[12] A Christian who does not provide for his or her indigent widow "is worse than an unbeliever" (v. 8). This is a dishonoring of parents and hence a violation of the fifth commandment. The implication is that unbelieving families were taking care of their widows. For professed believers to fail to do so, therefore, was tantamount to a denial of the faith. This is apostasy, this time meaning not doctrinal abandonment of an orthodox profession but practical abandonment of family responsibilities that even pagan society fulfilled.

12. George W. Knight III, *Commentary on the Pastoral Epistles*, New International Greek Testament Commentary (Grand Rapids: Eerdmans, 1992), 221.

Fallen from Grace?

Does Paul here teach that previously saved persons by sinning have fallen from grace and are unsaved? No; rather, he means that such behavior is inconsistent with genuine Christianity and reveals that people whose lives are characterized by such behavior are unsaved. This is Paul's evaluation of two groups mentioned in this passage: the negligent householders and the promiscuous younger widows. We treat the former here and the latter in our next passage.

When he speaks of negligent householders as "denying the faith" and being "worse than an unbeliever," he means that they have turned away from the gospel they formerly professed. Their lives discredit their profession of faith. Towner's words are apt:

> Paul places the capable relatives (presumably householders) who fail in this duty into the category of unbelievers. To understand this, the dynamic and holistic meaning of "godliness" in v. 4, which makes care for family an outworking of genuine faith, must be kept in mind. Shirking this responsibility is, thus, denial of "the faith" . . . an act that reveals a breach in the integrity of the faith-generated behavior that is authentic Christianity.[13]

1 Timothy 5:11–12: Condemnation for Abandoning Their Former Faith

> But refuse to enroll younger widows, for when their passions draw them away from Christ, they desire to marry and so incur condemnation for having abandoned their former faith.

The context for this text is the same as the last. In his long section treating widows at Ephesus, Paul condemns those family members with means who fail to provide for their widows (the previous passage) and also immoral younger widows. When giving instructions for identifying "real widows" who should receive church aid, he includes requirements of age (sixty years)

13. Towner, *The Letters to Timothy and Titus*, 344–45.

and lifestyle: devotion to family, a good reputation, and having engaged in ministries of hospitality and mercy (vv. 9–10).

Their Passions Draw Them Away from Christ

Next Paul issues a warning: "But refuse to enroll younger widows, for when their passions draw them away from Christ . . ." (v. 11). Not only were some of the widows on the list much younger than sixty and thus burdening the congregation financially, but they also were guilty of sexual sin. Mounce is correct: "The basic thrust of these verses is straightforward: these younger widows are turning against Christ. . . . The real problem is that the younger widows have given themselves over to a self-centered, self-indulgent lifestyle and have followed after Satan (v. 15)."[14]

This much is clear, but the rest of the passage is not: "But refuse to enroll younger widows, for when their passions draw them away from Christ, *they desire to marry* and so incur condemnation for having abandoned their former faith" (vv. 11–12, italics added). Why would Paul condemn younger widows for wanting to remarry when he encourages the very thing two verses later: "So I would have younger widows marry" (v. 14)?

This question has fostered much discussion that space forbids me even to summarize.[15] I will only share what I consider the right answer, in the words of Towner:

> Apparently, Paul envisions young widows led by their enjoyment of promiscuous behavior to marry unbelievers. Since typically the wife would adopt the religion of the husband, remarriage to unbelievers would involve actual rejection of the widow's "first/ prior faith in (commitment to) Christ. . . ." When Paul turns to encourage young widows to remarry in v. 14, he assumes marriage to believers.[16]

14. Mounce, *Pastoral Epistles*, 67.
15. For discussion, see ibid., 289–92.
16. Towner, *The Letters to Timothy and Titus*, 352 cites Bruce W. Winter, *Roman Wives, Romans Widows: The Appearance of New Women and the Pauline Communities* (Grand Rapids: Eerdmans, 2003), 137.

Forfeiture of Salvation?

The spiritual condition of these widows is the same as that of the promiscuous ones Paul condemns a few verses earlier as "self-indulgent" and "dead even while she lives" (1 Tim. 5:6). He means such a widow is spiritually dead. The unsaved status of such widows is revealed by their immoral lifestyle, a result of which is that they "incur condemnation for having abandoned their former faith" (v. 12). The widows' immorality amounted to a practical apostasy and revealed their unsaved condition.

2 Timothy 2:11-13: "If We Deny Him, He Also Will Deny Us"

> The saying is trustworthy, for: If we have died with him, we will also live with him; if we endure, we will also reign with him; if we deny him, he also will deny us; if we are faithless, he remains faithful—for he cannot deny himself.

In the preceding verses, through various means, Paul seeks to strengthen Timothy in his ministry (2:1–10). Now Paul urges him to remember Christ as Paul preached him, divine—"risen"— and human—"the offspring of David"—(v. 8). Though Paul is in jail, God's word is not bound (v. 9), and Paul perseveres even in imprisonment in order to bring the gospel to God's people. "Therefore I endure everything for the sake of the elect, that they also may obtain the salvation that is in Christ Jesus with eternal glory" (v. 10).

"We Will Live with Him"

The apostle next gives his fifth faithful saying, inserting a confession or hymn from the early church. It is easy to imagine whole churches confessing these words in unison. "If we have died with him, we will also live with him" (v. 11). Paul, bringing to mind Romans 6:3–5, means: If we have been united to Christ

148

in his death, we will also be united to him in his resurrection. If we have been joined spiritually to Christ by trusting him as our crucified Savior, we will be raised from the dead in union with him, our risen Lord, unto eternal life.

"We Will Reign with Him"

"If we endure, we will also reign with him" (v. 12). Paul means: If we professed believers endure to the end, we will be saved finally and will reign with Christ in glory. Just as Paul exhorted Timothy to do (vv. 1–7) and as Paul himself does (vv. 8–10), so all who name the name of Christ must persevere if they would be saved. We must persevere in suffering with him if we would reign with him. Such suffering is evidence of true union with Christ in his death, which will issue into union with him in his resurrection.

"He Will Deny Us"

"If we deny him, he also will deny us" (v. 12). Behind Paul's words are those of Jesus, whose saying comes in the context of sending out his twelve disciples to preach, heal, and exorcise demons (Matt. 10:5–8). They will meet serious opposition but can rely on the Holy Spirit for words when they are hauled into courts for Jesus' sake (vv. 16–20). The disciples are not to fear men but God who will judge the dead (vv. 26, 28). Then Jesus says, "So everyone who acknowledges me before men, I also will acknowledge before my Father who is in heaven, but whoever denies me before men, I also will deny before my Father who is in heaven" (vv. 32–33). Merely claiming to be Jesus' disciple is not enough. One must publicly confess him. The result? "The acknowledgment his followers will receive will avail in the highest of all courts"[17]—that of Jesus' Father himself. But, as Jesus' parallelism presses home,

17. Leon Morris, *The Gospel According to Matthew*, The Pillar New Testament Commentary (Grand Rapids: Eerdmans, 1992), 265.

rejecting him also brings permanent consequences—rejection before the Father.

Although there are important similarities between Jesus' words and Paul's, there is an important difference too. Jesus said "everyone" and "whoever" in Matthew 10:32–33 to separate true disciples from false ones. Paul says, "If we deny him, he also will deny us" (2 Tim. 2:12). Paul's words are a part of a profession of faith made in common by church members. Those who persevere will reign with Christ (v. 12). "However, if some deny Christ, if through their lives they deny knowing him by their word and deed, then before the judgment seat Christ will also deny knowing them."[18] Scripture affords assurance to those who walk in faith; but it does not promise salvation to those who profess Christ but later reject him. Such persons, according to 1 and 2 Timothy, commit final apostasy, show they were never saved, and will be lost forever.

"He Cannot Deny Himself"

God is very gracious to his people! As soon as the hard words of the previous saying come out of the people's mouths, words of comfort follow: "If we are faithless, he remains faithful—for he cannot deny himself" (v. 13). Even if we fail, and at times fall, he still is our solid rock. He is dependable even when we are not. Being unfaithful here is less serious than denying him in the previous line. We are all unfaithful at times, but true believers do not deny him totally and finally, as apostates do. Paul exhorts God's people to perseverance in faith in this passage, but he puts that perseverance in a larger context at the end of the confession. Though the church is composed of unsteady people, its ultimate success depends on the faithfulness of God, who cannot deny himself. "Even if there are false teachers and false believers in the church, God will not fail to preserve his people; that is, whatever happens

18. Mounce, *Pastoral Epistles*, 519.

150

to the church and its leadership, God will remain faithful to his covenant."[19]

2 Timothy 2:17–19: "Hymenaeus and Philetus"

> But avoid irreverent babble, for it will lead people into more and more ungodliness, and their talk will spread like gangrene. Among them are Hymenaeus and Philetus, who have swerved from the truth, saying that the resurrection has already happened. They are upsetting the faith of some. But God's firm foundation stands, bearing this seal: "The Lord knows those who are his," and, "Let everyone who names the name of the Lord depart from iniquity." (2 Tim. 2:16–19)

Paul deals with the same false teachers in 2 Timothy as he did in his first epistle. In this passage he names two of them. He had urged Timothy to remind his flock of important truths concerning Christ, the gospel, and perseverance (2 Tim. 2:8–14). Next Paul warned his understudy to charge the people "not to quarrel about words," for this only harms those who hear (v. 14). By contrast, Timothy is to work hard to handle God's Word correctly and thereby commend himself to God (v. 15). Once more Paul returns to the theme of the harmful effects of sinful speech: "But avoid irreverent babble, for it will lead people into more and more ungodliness" (v. 16). Furthermore, such talk "will spread like gangrene," that is, it will infect others with its deadly disease (v. 17).

The apostle gets specific: "Among them are Hymenaeus and Philetus" (v. 17). "Because the name Hymenaeus is unusual, it may be assumed that he is the same person paired with Alexander and excommunicated by Paul in 1 Tim 1:20."[20] Philetus appears only here in the New Testament. Due to the prominence Paul gives them, these two men must have been leaders among the false teachers he opposes. Paul's judgment

19. Towner, *The Letters to Timothy and Titus*, 514.
20. Mounce, *Pastoral Epistles*, 527.

is plain: they "have swerved from the truth" (v. 18). These two departed from orthodoxy.

Specifically, Hymenaeus and Philetus teach "that the resurrection has already happened" (v. 18). They claim that the resurrection of the righteous had already occurred, and this bad teaching has harmed others in the church: "They are upsetting the faith of some" (v. 18). They are damaging believers in the churches. Towner summarizes: "Thus, one way or another, the opponents had come to believe that the eschatological resurrection of believers had already occurred, and they had popularized this view."[21] People's faith was disrupted if they allowed the false teachers to take away their future hope in the resurrection of the body and resulting blissful life on the new earth.

Paul reminds his readers that despite this malicious teaching, God still is in control. The apostle first points to God's sovereign grace: "But God's firm foundation stands, bearing this seal: 'The Lord knows those who are his'" (v. 19). Next, he points to our responsibility in light of God's grace: "Let everyone who names the name of the Lord depart from iniquity" (v. 19).

Fallen from Grace?

Are we to regard Hymenaeus and Philetus as true believers who have lost their salvation or as professors of Christian faith whose defection revealed their true stripe? This passage alone does not provide enough information for us to say. The way we answer the question concerning their spiritual status depends upon our conclusions reached from other passages in 1 and 2 Timothy. I will deal with these matters in the next section.

Connecting the Dots

Once again the conclusions from the warning passages can be gathered helpfully into categories. When used of human beings,

21. Towner, *The Letters to Timothy and Titus*, 529.

"faith" has two prominent meanings in the New Testament. Sometimes it means saving trust in Jesus: "For by grace you have been saved through *faith*" (Eph. 2:8, italics added). At other times, it means the content of what is believed. Jude urges Christians "to contend for *the faith* that was once for all delivered to the saints" (Jude 3, italics added).

The first category of warning passages in this chapter involves faith in the first sense—belief in Jesus. It warns of people believing inadequately and so remaining unsaved. The second category deals with faith in the second sense—the content of belief. These warnings speak of people rejecting the sound teaching of the gospel and falling short of salvation. A third category treats people whose lives contradict their profession of faith. Because there is overlap between the categories, some passages could be placed in more than one.

Warnings of People Believing Inadequately

Many Scriptures speak of people apparently believing in Christ for salvation, only to have the context reveal that their faith was inadequate in some way. In the opening words of 1 Timothy Paul alerts his readers to this. He urged Timothy to "charge certain persons not to teach any different doctrine." He says, "certain persons, by swerving from these [a pure heart and a good conscience and a sincere faith], have wandered away into vain discussion, desiring to be teachers of the law, without understanding either what they are saying or the things about which they make confident assertions" (1 Tim.1:3, 6–7). This passage is fundamental to all that follows concerning these "certain persons," that is, the false teachers, whom Paul condemns often in 1–2 Timothy. Here he highlights the false teachers' serious doctrinal and moral deficiencies—deficiencies incompatible with a true knowledge of Christ. The false teachers stand opposed to the apostolic gospel in word and deed. Contrary to their claims, they lack and have always lacked inner purification and a clear conscience that come from sincere faith in Christ.

153

We must read the rest of 1–2 Timothy in light of Paul's opening statement in 1 Timothy 1:3–7. This is the case for 1 Timothy
1:18–20, where church leaders Hymenaeus and Alexander were
never saved and revealed that fact by rejecting Paul's message
of grace for one of legalism that led to a corrupted conscience,
ungodliness, and disaster.

This is also the case for 2 Timothy 2:11–13, where Paul cites
words from a church's profession of faith: "If we endure, we
will also reign with him; if we deny him, he also will deny us"
(v. 12). Those who continue will rule with Christ. But those who
deny knowing him by their words and actions, he also will deny
knowing at the last judgment. As soon as the people recite these
hard words, God graciously supplies comforting words: "If we
are faithless, he remains faithful—for he cannot deny himself"
(v. 13). Even when we fail, God is dependable. Being unfaithful
here is less serious than denying him in the previous line. We
are all unfaithful at times, but true believers do not deny him
totally and finally, as apostates do. Those who deny him and
never repent show, by their denial, that they have never known
him as Lord and Savior.

Warnings of People Rejecting Sound Teaching

Paul also warns of people who know the truth but walk away
from it, showing they never embraced it. First Timothy 4:1–5 demonstrates that, despite the false teachers' claims, their teaching
and lives reveal that they are unsaved. They do not deliver sound
doctrine. And they fall short of the true faith and inner godliness
characteristic of authentic believers. Indeed, their leaving "the
faith" to follow "teachings of demons" shows that they are "liars
whose consciences are seared" (vv. 1–2).

Though some read 2 Timothy 2:17–19 as teaching that Christians can lose saving grace, this is a mistake.[22] It is true that this
text does not repeat Paul's evaluations of the false teachers' spiri-

---

22. My conclusions for 2 Timothy 2:17–19 pertain also to 1 Timothy 6:9–10, which I
could not include due to a lack of space.

tual status, but we should not expect it to do so. Paul previously—in 1 Timothy 1:3–7; 4:1–5—described his opponents as apostates who were never saved. He intends for his later condemnations of false teachers to be seen in this light. This includes "Hymenaeus and Philetus, who have swerved from the truth, saying that the resurrection has already happened" (2 Tim. 2:17–18).[23]

Warnings of People's Lives Contradicting Their Profession of Faith

Paul's words in Titus 1:16, describing "the defiled and unbelieving" (v. 15) epitomize this category: "They profess to know God, but they deny him by their works." His evaluation of a negligent householder as one who "has denied the faith and is worse than an unbeliever" (1 Tim. 5:8) means that such a person has turned away from the gospel he formerly professed and is living like an unsaved person. Such a life nullifies a profession of faith, proving it to be insincere.

The spiritual condition of the promiscuous younger widows spoken of in 1 Timothy 5:11–12 is the same as that Paul condemns a few verses earlier as "self-indulgent" and "dead even while she lives" (v. 6)—they are devoid of eternal life. Such widows' immoral lifestyle exposes their unsaved status so that they "incur condemnation for having abandoned their former faith" (v. 12). Though the young women once professed Christ, their profession was discredited by their lives.

23. This holds true too for the false teachers of whom Paul writes, "by professing it [what is falsely called knowledge] some have swerved from the faith" (1 Tim. 6:20–21).

Warnings in Hebrews

OUR STUDY of the Bible's formidable witness to preservation, especially in John and Romans, would be incomplete without an investigation of the most famous warnings of all—those in Hebrews.

There is a general consensus that Hebrews contains five warning passages, and there is agreement as to their general location, but differences emerge when we try to delineate the passages exactly. Here I follow the suggestion of Scot McKnight: Hebrews 2:1–4; 3:7–4:13; 5:11–6:12; 10:19–39; and 12:1–29.[1] All five passages are worthy of study, but we will concentrate on the two that have attracted the most attention: those in Hebrews 6 and 10.

- Hebrews 5:11–6:12: "It Is Impossible to Restore Again to Repentance . . ."
- Hebrews 10:19–39: "If We Go on Sinning Deliberately . . ."

Almost all agree that these two passages warn of the sin of apostasy, which is the abandonment of the Christian faith by someone who formerly professed it. But the big question is: Do these passages teach that persons who were once saved by God's grace sometimes later reject Christ and forfeit their salvation?

1. Scot McKnight, "The Warning Passages of Hebrews: A Formal Analysis and Theological Conclusions," *Trinity Journal*, n.s. 13 (1992): 22.

Before addressing that question we will summarize inadequate Reformed treatments of these great passages.

Inadequate Treatments

Some who hold to God's preservation of his saints, as I do, have not adequately handled the key warning passages in Hebrews 6 and 10. Here are three such views. First, to say that the warning passages are hypothetical is mistaken and deserves Roger Nicole's criticism that such a view "tends to artificiality."[2] It is hard to believe that the following words did not issue an actual warning:

> Anyone who has set aside the law of Moses dies without mercy on the evidence of two or three witnesses. How much worse punishment, do you think, will be deserved by the one who has spurned the Son of God, and has profaned the blood of the covenant by which he was sanctified, and has outraged the Spirit of grace? (Heb. 10:28–29)

Even as the penalties for rejecting the Mosaic Covenant were real and not hypothetical, so those for rejecting the new covenant are also real. Clearly at least some of the original readers of Hebrews were in danger, as Philip Hughes stresses: "The danger of apostasy was real, not imaginary, and the situation called for the gravest possible warning."[3]

Second, Verlyn D. Verbrugge correctly holds that many have misunderstood Hebrews' warnings as only speaking of individuals repudiating their faith in Christ. Instead, he proposes what he calls "the covenant community" view—the idea that the author is "not so much interested in each separate individual as he is in

---

2. Roger Nicole, "Some Comments on Hebrews 6:4–6 and the Doctrine of the Perseverance of God with the Saints," in *Current Issues in Biblical and Patristic Interpretation*, ed. G. F. Hawthorne (Grand Rapids: Eerdmans, 1975), 356.

3. Philip Hughes, "Hebrews 6:4–6 and the Peril of Apostasy," *Westminster Theological Journal* 35 (1973): 138; see also 143–44. Buist M. Fanning agrees, "A Classical Reformed View," in ed. Herbert W. Bateman IV, *Four Views on the Warning Passages in Hebrews* (Grand Rapids: Kregel, 2007), 186.

the congregation as a whole."[4] Verbrugge's community emphasis is welcome, and I will incorporate it in my conclusions. Nevertheless, he overreacts to the previous overemphasis on individuals. As Scot McKnight has shown, this view clashes with the concern of Hebrews for each reader, evidenced by 6:11, for example: "And we desire *each one of you* to show the same earnestness to have the full assurance of hope until the end"[5] (italics added).

A third inadequate view is that of Thomas Kem Oberholtzer, who maintains that Hebrews' warnings were written to warn Christians of possible loss of rewards in a future earthly millennium.[6] Respectfully, I must disagree and insist along with the majority of commentators that words such as the following warn of eternal damnation: "a fearful expectation of judgment, and a fury of fire that will consume the adversaries. . . . It is a fearful thing to fall into the hands of the living God. . . . But we are not of those who shrink back and are destroyed" (Heb. 10:27, 31, 39).[7]

Admitting that it is much easier to criticize erroneous views than to give a correct one, I now turn to what all acknowledge are the two most difficult of the five warning passages in Hebrews: 5:11–6:12 and 10:19–39.

Hebrews 5:11–6:12: "It Is Impossible to Restore Again to Repentance . . ."

In Hebrews 5:11–6:3 the writer rebukes his readers for their spiritual laziness. He wants to tell them more about Melchizedek,

4. Verlyn D. Verbrugge, "Towards a New Interpretation of Hebrews 6:4–6," *Calvin Theological Journal*, 15 (April 1980): 67.

5. McKnight, "The Warning Passages of Hebrews," 53–54. Verbrugge, "Towards a New Interpretation of Hebrews 6:4–6," 61–73.

6. Thomas Kem Oberholtzer set forth this view in a series of articles in *Bibliotheca Sacra*: "The Eschatalogical Salvation of Hebrews 1:5–2:5" (145 [January–March 1988]: 83–97); "The Kingdom Rest in Hebrews 3:1–4:13" (145 [April–June 1988]: 185–96); "The Thorn-Infested Ground in Hebrews 6:4–12" (145 [July–September 1988]: 319–28); "The Danger of Willful Sin in Hebrews 10:26–39" (145 [October–December 1988]: 410–19); and "The Failure to Heed His Speaking in Hebrews 12:25–29" (146 [January–March 1989]: 67–75).

7. See Fanning, "A Classical Reformed View," in Bateman, *Four Views*, 190.

whom he began to talk about in 5:6, 10, but must postpone doing so until 7:1. Why? Due to the religious sluggishness of his audience. Even though enough time has passed since their profession of faith in Christ for them to teach others God's truth, they themselves need to be reminded of the ABC's of the spiritual life (5:12). They are immature in their faith, and this is reflected in their spiritual diet: They drink milk rather than eat solid food. Is their problem solely intellectual, then? No, their problem is not even primarily intellectual. Rather, it is moral, because "solid food is for the mature, for those who have their powers of discernment trained by constant practice to distinguish good from evil" (5:14). The readers have become spiritually flabby; they lack the discernment that comes from exercising their spiritual "muscles" by saying no to sin and yes to righteousness.

The writer, then, urges them to spiritual maturity, wanting them to build on the foundation of basic Christian truths. And by God's grace they will do so (Heb. 6:3). Next, the author issues Scripture's most famous warning.

> For it is impossible, in the case of those who have once been enlightened, who have tasted the heavenly gift, and have shared in the Holy Spirit, and have tasted the goodness of the word of God and the powers of the age to come, and then have fallen away, to restore them again to repentance, since they are crucifying once again the Son of God to their own harm and holding him up to contempt. (Heb. 6:4–6)

This passage explains the impossibility of bringing back to repentance persons who have experienced the blessings mentioned and who then commit apostasy.

A Description of Christians?

The description seems to depict believers in Christ. Gareth Cockerill speaks for Arminians when he states, "In Hebrews 6:4–8 the Greek article joins five substantive participles to form a

160

description of true believers who fall away."[8] And Buist Fanning speaks for many Calvinists: "On the face of it these seem to reflect different facets of a full experience of true Christian conversion."[9] "Those who have once been enlightened" (Heb. 6:4) are people whose minds have been illuminated by the gospel and who know the way of salvation. Those "who have tasted the heavenly gift" are those who have experienced supernatural blessings. Attempts by Calvinists to interpret "tasted" (here and in the words "have tasted the goodness of the word of God and the powers of the age to come") and "shared" ("in the Holy Spirit" in the next description) as indicating less than full participation fail.[10] Though it is difficult to precisely identify "the heavenly gift," those described have personal experience with good things from God.

Those who "have shared in the Holy Spirit" are people who have participated in the Spirit of God. They have experienced the Spirit's working in the congregation. They have firsthand acquaintance with the Spirit's supernatural activity. The description "have tasted the goodness of the word of God and the powers of the age to come" refers to the readers' personal experience of the Word and miracles. They have not merely observed the Christian faith from afar, vicariously through Christian friends. Instead, they have vital Christian experience; they know the Word is God's Word from personal experience. They have witnessed supernatural works of God.

I find helpful Hughes's understanding that "these six blessings [of 6:4–5] . . . are but different aspects and manifestations of the one great blessing which the reception of the gospel brings."[11] Although the description appears to describe Christians, the following is an overstatement: "If this passage [Heb. 6:4–6] were found in Romans 8, we would all hail it as the greatest description of Christian blessings in the entire Bible."[12]

8. Gareth L. Cockerill, "A Wesleyan Arminian View," in Bateman, *Four Views*, 273.
9. Fanning, "A Classical Reformed View," in Bateman, *Four Views*, 177.
10. So Nicole, "Some Comments," 360–61.
11. Ibid., 143.
12. Grant R. Osborne, "A Classical Arminian View," in Bateman, *Four Views*, 112.

The Burden of Proof

The burden of proof rests with those who claim verses 4–5 do not describe Christians. Before investigating that, I note that Arminian interpreters also have trouble with this passage. For they hold that when the text says, "It is impossible" for those who have "fallen away, to restore them again to repentance," it speaks of believers forfeiting salvation. If this is true, it follows that the passage also teaches that these fallen believers cannot be restored. Though some Arminian interpreters accept this implication,[13] many are uncomfortable with it. The problem is not solved by softening the meaning of "impossible" (*adynaton*) in verse 4 by saying that it means impossible for man, not God, or impossible as long as the rebels continue in apostasy, as Hughes shows.[14]

It is important to see why "it is impossible . . . to restore" the apostates "again to repentance" (vv. 4, 6). It is because "they are crucifying once again the Son of God to their own harm and holding him up to contempt" (v. 6). This describes a public repudiation of the Christ whom they formerly had professed. In the words of Gareth L. Cockerill, "These causal participles, 'crucifying again' and 'exposing to public disgrace,' describe a severance from the benefits of Christ that leaves no basis for renewed repentance."[15]

I now assume the previously mentioned burden of proof. Grant Osborne insists concerning the description of the apostates in Hebrews 6:4–5: "This is truly a remarkable list of experiences, and there is hardly anything to compare with it elsewhere in terms of a brief creedal-like presentation of the privileges in being a Christian."[16] Indeed, the description is strong, and there must be clear indicators in the context for one to deny that this text describes Christians. The writer gives just such clear indicators and thereby teaches that if any of his readers commit

13. So McKnight, "The Warning Passages of Hebrews," 34–35.
14. Hughes, "Hebrews 6:4–6 and the Peril of Apostasy," 144–45.
15. Cockerill, "A Wesleyan Arminian View," in Bateman, *Four Views*, 276.
16. Osborne, "A Classical Arminian View," in Bateman, *Four Views*, 114.

apostasy, by doing so they manifest their unsaved status. The deserters knew the truth of the gospel, enjoyed God's blessings, participated in the Spirit, and saw miracles. Nonetheless, the writer employs an agricultural illustration and encouraging words to distinguish the believing majority of his readers from potential apostates.

Two Kinds of Land

Immediately following the warning of Hebrews 6:4–6, we read, "For land that has drunk the rain that often falls on it, and produces a crop useful to those for whose sake it is cultivated, receives a blessing from God. But if it bears thorns and thistles, it is worthless and near to being cursed, and its end is to be burned" (vv. 7–8). This illustration sheds light on the preceding verses. The author depicts two kinds of land, both of which receive rain. The first kind of land yields useful vegetation and reaps God's blessing; the second yields only thorns and thistles and is about to be cursed by God and burned. In this manner, the writer describes both believers and unbelievers who have been exposed to the Word and blessings of God, because both kinds of land receive rain. But only the good land produces fruit; the bad land produces only weeds. The fruit and weeds stand for the good deeds of believers and the sinful deeds (especially apostasy) of unbelievers. God's blessing and cursing stand for eternal life and death respectively, as the burning of the bad land implies.

The writer invites readers to identify those who fall away in Hebrews 6:6 with the unfruitful land. They have had much exposure to spiritual things but have not continued in their professed faith. Their defection is "thorns and thistles" that show they are unsaved. And what they can look forward to is the judgment of God. Calvinist interpretation fares better here than does Arminian. The writer does not portray the fruitless land as once having borne fruit. The apostates are not Christians who lost their salvation but people who were never saved. In contrast, the fruitful soil stands for the preponderance of readers, who have persevered and displayed true Christian love and service (v. 10).[17]

A Strong Word of Encouragement

The key to understanding Hebrews 6:4–8, in my judgment, is verse 9: "Though we speak in this way, yet in your case, beloved, we feel sure of better things—things that belong to salvation." The writer is convinced of better things concerning most of his readers than those things he has just said. He highlights this by changing from third person (in Heb. 6:4–6) to second person (in vv. 9–12). He is confident that the greater part of his readers are not unfruitful land heading for judgment; they are not apostates. He explains that the "better things" are "things that belong to salvation" (v. 9). After the warning of verses 4–6, he assures his believing readers (the majority) that they are fruitful land that will receive God's blessing.

"Though we speak in this way . . ." Although the writer speaks of departure from the faith in Hebrews 6:4–6 and of barren and worthless land in verse 8, he is persuaded of better things than these concerning the majority of his readers. He is convinced that they are good soil, genuine believers. Even his form of address is designed to encourage them, because only here in Hebrews he calls them "beloved" (v. 9).

The writer rounds off his warning by exhorting every one of his readers to persevere in faith until the end: "And we desire each one of you to show the same earnestness to have the full assurance of hope until the end, so that you may not be sluggish, but imitators of those who through faith and patience inherit the promises" (Heb. 6:11–12). He ties 5:11–6:12 together by means of the literary device known as inclusion—the placing of a similar word or idea at two ends of a unit of literature. The word "sluggish" in 6:12 is the same Greek word (*nothroi*)

17. Wayne Grudem agrees in "Perseverance of the Saints: A Case Study from the Warning Passages in Hebrews," in *Still Sovereign: Contemporary Perspectives on Election, Foreknowledge, and Grace*, ed. Thomas R. Schreiner and Bruce A. Ware (Grand Rapids: Baker, 1995, 2000), 157.

translated "dull" (of hearing) in 5:11. The writer chastises some of his audience for being "dull" of hearing at the beginning of the passage and encourages each one of them not to be "sluggish" at its end.

A Summary

The author warns a minority of his readers whom he fears may not know Christ and may show it by apostatizing. At the same time he encourages the preponderance of them, whom he is confident are saved, to continue and thereby increase in faith and gain greater assurance. The objections to my interpretation of Hebrews 6 and 10 are important, and I will deal with them together after treating the latter passage.

Hebrews 10:19–39: "If We Go on Sinning Deliberately . . ."

Hebrews 10:19–25 introduces this warning passage. The writer draws conclusions from the preceding verses, which praise the new covenant and Jesus Christ its Mediator. Because we have confidence to enter God's presence due to Jesus our High Priest's death for us, four results follow. First, having been cleansed by his sacrifice, we are to draw near to God confidently in worship (10:22). Second, the author exhorts his readers to persevere steadfastly, resting in God's faithfulness (v. 23). Third, he encourages them to provoke each other to "love and good works" (v. 24). Fourth, they are to continue meeting for worship (despite persecution) and fervently in light of Christ's return (v. 25).

The following words sound as strong a warning as any in Scripture:

> For if we go on sinning deliberately after receiving the knowledge of the truth, there no longer remains a sacrifice for sins, but a fearful expectation of judgment, and a fury of fire that

will consume the adversaries. Anyone who has set aside the law of Moses dies without mercy on the evidence of two or three witnesses. How much worse punishment, do you think, will be deserved by the one who has spurned the Son of God, and has profaned the blood of the covenant by which he was sanctified, and has outraged the Spirit of grace? For we know him who said, "Vengeance is mine; I will repay." And again, "The Lord will judge his people." It is a fearful thing to fall into the hands of the living God. (Heb. 10:26–31)

Apostasy

"Receiving the knowledge of the truth" (v. 26) signifies understanding the way of salvation and professing faith. Due to the severity of the warnings in this passage, people on both sides of the preservation issue interpret "sinning deliberately" as referring to apostasy—a deliberate renunciation of a faith once professed—rather than speaking generally of intentional sin.[18] For those who profess faith in Jesus and then repudiate him, there is no atonement since they have spurned the only means of forgiveness provided by God. Instead of forgiveness they will know only God's wrath because they have gone over to the side of God's enemies. Indeed, they can expect "a fearful expectation of judgment, and a fury of fire that will consume the adversaries" (v. 27).

Breakers of the Mosaic Covenant, convicted by the testimony of two or more witnesses, paid a terrible penalty: "Anyone who has set aside the law of Moses dies without mercy on the evidence of two or three witnesses" (v. 28). The Old Testament background concerns the sin of idolatry, and it condemns any Israelite who "in transgressing his [God's] covenant . . . has gone and served other gods and worshiped them" (Deut. 17:2–3). Apostates who exchanged the worship of Yahweh for that of other gods paid the penalty of capital punishment.

18. For one holding to preservation, see Hughes, "Hebrews 6:4–6 and the Peril of Apostasy," 138, 143–44. For one holding that believers may fall from grace, see McKnight, "The Warning Passages of Hebrews," 39–40.

"How much worse punishment, do you think, will be deserved by the one who has spurned the Son of God, and has profaned the blood of the covenant by which he was sanctified, and has outraged the Spirit of grace?" (Heb. 10:29). The writer's argument is based on a comparison between the old covenant and the new. If violators of the old covenant were punished by death, what a terrible fate awaits transgressors of the new covenant! The three expressions "who has spurned . . . has profaned . . . and has outraged . . ." are three ways of saying, "who despised the new covenant." As Gareth Cockerill explains, "Together they refer to a studied contempt and repudiation of everything the Godhead has done in salvation."[19] Those in danger of committing apostasy had professed faith in God's Son and thus laid claim to his purifying blood and had come into the church, the sphere of the Holy Spirit's special influence.

A Strong Description

As in Hebrews 6:4–5, so here the description of those who may fall away is very strong. Those warned of the penalties for desertion had come within the sphere of God's covenant blessings, personally tasted his grace, and had then risked sinning against the Trinity by thinking of walking away. "The blood of the covenant by which he was sanctified" (Heb. 10:29) would appear to refer to a true believer. Stephen Ashby is sure of it: "This is clearly referring to a saved person, because his or her sanctification has been accomplished by the blood of Christ."[20] But this is not a necessary conclusion, as Wayne Grudem shows.[21] It could refer to a covenantal sanctification in which persons are set apart (sanctified) as part of God's covenant community, the church, and may or may not be saved. Examples include people who have made an inadequate

19. Osborne, "A Classical Arminian View," in Bateman, *Four Views*, 121.
20. Stephen M. Ashby, "A Reformed Arminian View," in *Four Views on Eternal Security*, ed. J. Matthew Pinson (Grand Rapids: Zondervan, 2002), 177.
21. Grudem, "Perseverance of the Saints," 178.

profession of faith and children who walk away from the faith of their Christian parents.[22] The idea of a "sanctification" that is covenantal but not saving occurs in 1 Corinthians 7:14 and Hebrews 9:13. In view of the contrast here between the old and new covenants, I take "sanctified" in Hebrews 10:29 to mean set apart covenantally as belonging to God.[23]

As in the other Hebrews warning passages, so here the consequences of apostasy are devastating. "For we know him who said, 'Vengeance is mine; I will repay.' And again, 'The Lord will judge his people.' It is a fearful thing to fall into the hands of the living God" (10:30–31). These Old Testament quotations (from Deut. 32:35–36) speak of God's delivering Israel by punishing its enemies. The author quotes the Old Testament to remind his readers that the living God also knows how to judge his covenant people in order to distinguish true from false believers. Those who do not measure up will "fall into the hands of the living God" (Heb. 10:31), that is, experience his wrath.

In Hebrews 10:32–34, the writer reminds his readers of their past faithfulness while suffering persecution to encourage them to keep persevering in present trials. He praises them because they "endured a hard struggle with sufferings," including public humiliation and loss of property (vv. 32–34). All of this they accepted "joyfully" (v. 34). My thesis is that the warnings (of vv. 26–31) are addressed to professed believers in the congregation who have come short of faith and may be tempted to apostatize. The encouragements (vv. 32–34) are addressed to the believing (although struggling) majority.

The writer then connects assurance of salvation to perseverance. His readers began well; they need to finish well to enjoy the full confidence of faith. "Therefore do not throw away your confidence, which has a great reward. For you have need of endurance, so that when you have done the will of God

---

22. For the second possibility, see Michael S. Horton, "A Classical Calvinist View," in *Four Views on Eternal Security*, 37–38.

23. I reject as artificial John Owen's idea, adopted by Roger Nicole and others, that "by which he was sanctified" (*en ho hegiasthe*) refers to Christ. See Nicole, "Some Comments," 356, n. 1.

you may receive what is promised" (vv. 35–36). Perseverance to the end is necessary for final salvation. Not everyone who names the name of Christ is saved; continuance in the faith is one evidence of salvation.

"For, 'Yet a little while, and the coming one will come and will not delay; but my righteous one shall live by faith, and if he shrinks back, my soul has no pleasure in him'" (Heb. 10:37–38). The author employs the emphatic language of Habakkuk 2:3–4 (LXX) to remind his readers that their reward is as near as the Lord's impending return. Once more he offers incentive for them to persevere. God's people will continue in faith. But any who do not continue reject their covenant Lord and will reap his wrath.

The Burden of Proof Again

Here I once more accept the burden of proof. As it was in Hebrews 6, so it is in chapter 10. The description (in 10:29) of the apostates is so strong that we should interpret it as describing Christians unless there are contextual indications to the contrary. Such indications appear in verse 39: "But we are not of those who shrink back and are destroyed, but of those who have faith and preserve their souls." The writer assures his readers that he is persuaded that they believe in Christ. By changing to the first person ("we"), he includes himself with them among those who persevere in faith and are finally saved. As I did in 6:9, I take the reassuring words of 10:39 to refer to the majority of the readers. The writer is confident of the salvation and perseverance of the greater part; he fears that a minority might not be saved and as a result might turn away and be lost, and so he warns them strongly.

Objections: The Work of Scot McKnight

Though Scot McKnight and I reach different conclusions concerning the possibility of believers falling away from saving grace,

I have learned much from his article "The Warning Passages of Hebrews: A Formal Analysis and Theological Conclusions" (*Trinity Journal*, n.s. 13 [1992]: 21–59). This impressive work is worthy of summary and interaction, in part because it treats all five Hebrews warning passages. McKnight pursues a synthetic treatment of these five passages, as he investigates four components: "(1) the *subjects* or *audience* who are either committing or in danger of committing, (2) the *sin* that leads to 3) the *exhortation* which, if not followed, leads to (4) the *consequences* of that sin."[24] He adds, "in addition, to these four, another component appears twice and might be considered a component of the warning passages in spite of its absence at times. This component can be profitably labeled the *pastoral encouragement* and is found at 6:9 and 10:39."[25] Because he fails to include this component in his discussion, I regard this as a key omission to which I will return.

McKnight studies the components in a modified reverse order. First, he examines exhortations in the warning passages and correctly concludes that the writer exhorts his hearers to persevere to the end.[26] Second, he is right to contend that the consequences in the warning passages are final salvation or hellfire respectively. Since some dispute the latter conclusion, I quote McKnight's summary:

> The language of 10:26–31 is particularly clear and needs to be the decisive evidence if other images and expressions remain ambiguous. Nonetheless, when the exegete ties together "no escape" (2:2; 12:25), God's anger (3:10, 17), falling short of the rest (3:11, 18–19; 4:1, 6, 11), a condition where no sacrifice remains for someone (10:26), a fearful expectation of judgment (10:27), fire (10:27; 12:29), death without mercy (10:28), and God's judgment (10:30–31), one is forced to conclude that the author is presenting eternal damnation as a potential consequence for those to whom he gives his warnings about sin and his exhortations to persevere. . . .

24. McKnight, "The Warning Passages of Hebrews," 25, italics original.
25. Ibid., 28, italics original.
26. Ibid., 32.

The image [in 6:8] of being cursed by God, with its close association with fire, can only adequately be explained as an allusion to Gehenna or hell, an allusion to God's punishment and retributive justice (Matt 3:10; 7:19; Luke 9:45; John 15:6; Rev 20:9).[27]

Third, McKnight rightly concludes that the sin in view in the warning passages is the sin of intentional apostasy. He notes the considerable agreement on the exhortation—to persevere—and consequences—damnation—if the exhortation is not heeded. But there is not a corresponding consensus on the sin that the writer rebukes. McKnight argues based on the following terms that the author is concerned with one particular sin:

"turning away from the living God" (3:12), "fall away" (6:6), "recrucifying to themselves the Son of God and making a public display [of Him]" (6:6), "deliberately sin" (10:26), "trample the Son of God" (10:29), "regarded the blood of the covenant as common" (10:29), "treated with contempt the Spirit of grace" (10:29), "refuse the One who speaks" (12:25), "turn away from" (12:25).[28]

This is the sin of apostasy—a rejection of Christ and his sacrifice for sin. It is a conscious turning away from God, from all three Persons of the holy Trinity, and his ethical claims on our lives.[29]

The Debated Audience

Fourth, McKnight studies the most critical and debated issue in the warning passages: the audience. He relies heavily on the descriptions of the apostates in Hebrews 10—where he regards it as most important that the writer implies that they are sanctified—and in Hebrews 6:4–6—the passage he thinks most clearly

27. Ibid., 33–35.
28. Ibid., 39.
29. Ibid., 40.

depicts the audience—and concludes, "It is simply unjustified to see in these descriptions anything but what is called regeneration in systematic theology."[30]

McKnight correctly asserts that the crucial issue is the audience. Even in the light of Grudem's good work,[31] I concur with McKnight that the depiction of the readers in 6:4–6 and 10:26–29 is so strong that it is incumbent upon Calvinist interpreters to show that the writer does not teach that Christians can commit apostasy.

The Pastoral Encouragement

However, I point out a flaw in McKnight's otherwise outstanding work—that of inconsistency. Though he acknowledges an important component of the warning passages, he does not factor it in. He wrote, "Another component appears twice and might be considered a component of a warning passage in spite of its absence at times. This component can be profitably labeled the *pastoral encouragement* and is found at 6:9 and 10:39."[32] Here are the texts: "Though we speak in this way, yet in your case, beloved, we feel sure of better things—things that belong to salvation" (6:9). "But we are not of those who shrink back and are destroyed, but of those who have faith and preserve their souls" (10:39).

McKnight does not include this component in his study of the warning passages. By doing so he omits some evidence that is unfavorable to his thesis. This evidence allows Calvinist interpreters to coordinate the warnings with their view of God's preservation. A synthetic study must take into account all of the data from the warning passages. The fact that the pastoral encouragement occurs in only two of the five warning passages does not disqualify it from McKnight's list of components. This is because, according to his computation,

---

30. Ibid., 44, 48. He has chosen the wrong term (there is no reference to regeneration), but his point is clear.

31. Grudem, "Perseverance of the Saints," 152–53, 171–72, 176–79.

32. McKnight, "The Warning Passages of Hebrews," 28, italics original.

the component *audience* also appears in only two passages, and yet he includes it.[33]

Connecting the Dots

Confidence

At least five times, the writer to the Hebrews warns a group of professing Christians not to commit apostasy. The strongest such warnings appear in Hebrews 6:4–8 and 10:26–31, 35–38. The writer fears that some of them might depart from Christ. But he periodically expresses his confidence that most of them are believers who will show it by continuing in the faith. We saw this in Hebrews 6:9 and 10:39. Philip Hughes agrees:

> The confidence expressed in 6:9 and 10:39 arises from the assurance that a true work of God has taken place in their midst; but this does not exclude the possibility that some of their number are rebellious at heart and on the road to irremediable apostasy. . . . Despite all this, they, or at least some of them, had failed to such a degree to show spiritual progress that it was doubtful that they had grasped even the first principles of the faith (5:11–6:2). The author fears that they are in imminent danger of slipping away into reprobation.[34]

A Repeated Concern for Individuals

Another feature of Hebrews supports my thesis. This is the fact that though Hebrews is a covenantal, and therefore corporate, document, it also displays a significant and repeated concern for individuals. Consider the following list of texts that single out the readers as "any of you," "each one of you," "no one," and "none of you."

> Take care, brothers, lest there be in *any of you* an evil, unbelieving heart, leading you to fall away from the living God. But

33. Ibid., 29.
34. Hughes, "Hebrews 6:4–6 and the Peril of Apostasy," 144, 150.

exhort one another every day, as long as it is called "today," that *none of you* may be hardened by the deceitfulness of sin. (Heb. 3:12–13, italics added)

Therefore, while the promise of entering his rest still stands, let us fear lest *any of you* should seem to have failed to reach it. (4:1, italics added)

Let us therefore strive to enter that rest, so that *no one* may fall by the same sort of disobedience. (4:11, italics added)

And we desire *each one of you* to show the same earnestness to have the full assurance of hope until the end. (6:11, italics added)

Strive for peace with everyone, and for the holiness without which *no one* will see the Lord. See to it that *no one* fails to obtain the grace of God; that no "root of bitterness" springs up and causes trouble, and by it many become defiled; that *no one* is sexually immoral or unholy like Esau, who sold his birthright for a single meal. (12:14–16, italics added)

This emphasis on individuals fits with my view that although the writer is assured of the spiritual status of the preponderance of his audience, he has real concerns for a shaky minority in the congregation. It is individuals in this minority who are addressed in the texts above.

A Distinction

Another corroborating factor appears when the writer seems to have in mind this distinction between a faithful core and others who might be unfaithful when he chooses good and bad Old Testament examples, as Hughes points out:

The calamitous history of the Israelites of old is repeatedly set before the readers as a warning against the imitation of their evil example (2:1f.; 3:12ff.; 4:1f., 11; 10:28ff.; 12:25ff.), while at the same time they are urged to emulate the example of unwearying perseverance of the faithful core of the community (ch. 11). The principle affirmed in Romans 9:6 applies equally in the sphere of the Christian Church, to the effect, namely that all are not of the Church who are in the Church.[35]

The author's choice of Old Testament examples to set before his readers is deliberate. He urges the majority to follow the example of the heroes and heroines of faith in chapter 11 who persevered despite suffering, many times even unto death. He uses the Israelites who were at Sinai and later perished in the wilderness as a warning to the minority who are tempted to forsake Jesus.

Preservation Passages in Hebrews

The preservation texts of Hebrews 6:17–20 and 7:23–25 (examined in chapter 6) provide more evidence of the impossibility of believers committing apostasy. In the same New Testament book where the strongest warnings of apostasy occur, even after the single strongest warning in Hebrews 6, we find sweet affirmations of the saints' safety in Christ. The writer does not contradict himself. God does preserve true believers to the end; those threatened with hellfire are professors who by committing apostasy show that they possess inadequate faith.

A Pastoral Perspective

The identification of the recipients of Hebrews is crucial. If the recipients are only believers, then the Arminian position that Christians may fall from grace seems correct. I argue, however, that the readers include nonbelievers. This is not Calvinist special pleading for Hebrews. The audience of many other New Testament writings is similar—they are written to professing Christians, some of whom may be unsaved.

35. Ibid., 148.

Jesus warned of false believers who called him Lord, performed supernatural deeds in his name, and profess him up until the Last Judgment:

> Not everyone who says to me, "Lord, Lord," will enter the kingdom of heaven, but the one who does the will of my Father who is in heaven. On that day many will say to me, "Lord, Lord, did we not prophesy in your name, and cast out demons in your name, and do many mighty works in your name?" And then will I declare to them, "I never knew you; depart from me, you workers of lawlessness." (Matt. 7:21–23)

Paul urges the Corinthians to expel from the church "anyone who bears the name of brother if he is guilty of sexual immorality or greed, or is an idolater, reviler, drunkard, or swindler" (1 Cor. 5:11). Later he also, out of concern for the salvation of some at Corinth, exhorted the whole church, "Examine yourselves to see whether you are in the faith. Test yourselves. Or do you not realize this about yourselves, that Christ Jesus is in you?—unless indeed you fail to meet the test!" (2 Cor. 13:5).

In Ephesians, the apostle warns believers not to be taken in by false Christian profession: "For you may be sure of this, that everyone who is sexually immoral or impure, or who is covetous (that is, an idolater), has no inheritance in the kingdom of Christ and God. Let no one deceive you with empty words" (5:5–6).

James seeks to awaken professed Jewish believers from spiritual slumber by criticizing profession of faith that does not save, is dead, is akin to the belief of demons, and is useless (James 2:14, 17, 19, 20, 26). It is the same for Peter, who after listing eight virtues that Christians are to manifest, warns, "Whoever lacks these qualities is so nearsighted that he is blind, having forgotten that he was cleansed from his former sins" (2 Peter 1:9). Peter questions the spiritual status of professing believers who seem to lack Christian virtues.

This is not difficult for anyone active in pastoral ministry to understand. Pastors of conservative churches regard their

176

flock as mainly composed of believers, but they are not certain of the spiritual condition of every person, and sometimes in preaching and in personal work they encourage them to examine their hearts, to believe the gospel, and so forth. Many of the New Testament authors do the same, including the writer to the Hebrews. He writes to a persecuted flock to encourage them all to persevere in the faith. He is troubled by an unstable minority whom he fears might turn from Christ and whom he warns repeatedly. At the same time he encourages the greater part of his readers, whom he is convinced are saved. He reassures them, even in the midst of the two strongest warnings (in 6:9 and 10:39) and builds them up by emphasizing God's preservation of them in 6:17–20 and 7:23–25.

Warnings in the Other General Epistles and Revelation

IMPORTANT WARNINGS are found in general epistles other than Hebrews, as well as in Revelation.

- James 5:19–20: Saving His Soul from Death.
- 2 Peter 2:20–22: Unchanged Nature.
- 1 John 5:16–17: "Sin That Leads to Death."
- Revelation 3:5: "I Will Never Blot His Name out of the Book of Life."
- Revelation 22:18–19: Idolatry Reveals True Allegiance.

James 5:19–20: Saving His Soul from Death

> My brothers, if anyone among you wanders from the truth and someone brings him back, let him know that whoever brings back a sinner from his wandering will save his soul from death and will cover a multitude of sins.

These verses conclude the epistle of James. In this last chapter, James has issued a scathing warning against the

wicked rich (vv. 1–6), exhorted his readers to patient endurance (vv. 7–12), and encouraged them to prevail in prayer (vv.
13–18). Now he leaves a warning ringing in their ears: "My
brothers, if anyone among you wanders from the truth . . ."
(v. 19).

James uses the familiar Jewish form, "my brothers" to
address members of the congregation, as he frequently does (1:2,
16, 19; 2:1, 14; 3:1, 10; 4:11; 5:7, 9, 10, 12). When in this context
he shows concern for one who strays from the truth among the
brothers, he is not thinking of a community member who acci-
dentally falls into sin but of one who deliberately apostatizes.[1]
He envisions a straying from the truth—the teachings and way
of life—of Christianity. His advice? "And [if] someone brings him
back . . ." James wants believers to look after each other, to be
vigilant in case someone wanders.

In such cases, he wants believers to seek out wanderers
and to try to turn them from error to the truth. "Let him know
that whoever brings back a sinner from his wandering will save
his soul from death and will cover a multitude of sins" (v. 20).
Understanding this verse involves identifying key expressions,
including "a sinner," "save his soul from death," and "cover a
multitude of sins." We will examine these in turn.

A Sinner

What does James mean when he refers to an erring person
as "a sinner"? By adding "sinner" to "if anyone among *you*," he
speaks of one who strays, who is not living according to the truth
of the gospel. "This is the second time James has used the noun
hamartolos [a sinner]; the first was in the call to conversion in
4:8."[2] Here he does not specify whether the wanderer is a believer
or not; the important thing is that he or she is a church member
who has turned away and needs restoration.

1. Ralph P. Martin, *James*, Word Biblical Commentary (Waco, TX: Word, 1988),
218.
2. Luke Timothy Johnson, *The Letter of James*, The Anchor Bible (New York: Double-
day, 1995), 338.

Saving "His Soul from Death"

What does James mean when he speaks of saving "his soul from death"? Though sometimes in Scripture the outcome of sin is physical death (1 Cor. 11:30), the word for death is more frequently used in the Old (Deut. 30:19; Prov. 12:28) and New Testaments (Rom. 5:12; 1 Cor. 15:56) and in its only other occurrence in James (1:15) to speak of spiritual death, separation from God. James wants straying community members rescued from eternal death by those who care enough to correct them.

"Covering a Multitude of Sins"

What does James mean when he speaks of "covering a multitude of sins"? Although it is not impossible for the Greek to refer to the sins of the restorer, it is more likely in this context that they refer to the sins of the restored. Sins "being covered" means sins forgiven by God (Ps. 32:1; 85:2; Rom. 4:7). "This idea of a 'multitude of sins' . . . here serves to describe not the state of the sinner but the extent of the forgiveness."[3]

Loss of Salvation?

Does James warn readers of the possibility of losing their salvation if they wander from the truth? There is no doubt that the one who wandered was a church member, but James does not make certain his spiritual status, as Moo explains: "'Bring back' (*epistrepho*) can refer to a person's initial 'turn' from sin to God in conversion (Acts 14:15; 15:19; 26:18; 1 Thess. 1:9). Here, however, James specifically refers to one of *you*, that is, a person who has at least outwardly identified with the Christian community."[4]

He or she may be a true believer and then again, may not be. It is difficult to tell. My conclusion is that this passage in James was

3. Peter Davids, *Commentary on James*, New International Greek Testament Commentary (Grand Rapids: Eerdmans, 1982), 200.

4. Douglas J. Moo, *The Letter of James*, The Pillar New Testament Commentary (Grand Rapids: Eerdmans, 2000), 249.

not written to decide the debate between Calvinists and Arminians over eternal security. Rather, as a wise pastor writes:

> If we make this verse merely an occasion to argue whether Christians can lose their salvation, we will miss the real impact James wants to make on his readers. He is again, with passion and forcefulness, warning his readers that genuine faith includes repentance for sin and a life of obedience to Christ as Lord. What James is saying in 5:20 is simply consistent with his view throughout the letter. . . . His point is not that true believers may lose their salvation by sinning, but that sin full-grown ultimately destroys the sinner, and that genuine faith compels us to flee from sin and to help each other do the same. To the very end, James insists on the lordship of Christ as an essential part of the gospel.[5]

2 Peter 2:20–22: Unchanged Nature

> For if, after they have escaped the defilements of the world through the knowledge of our Lord and Savior Jesus Christ, they are again entangled in them and overcome, the last state has become worse for them than the first. For it would have been better for them never to have known the way of righteousness than after knowing it to turn back from the holy commandment delivered to them. What the true proverb says has happened to them: "The dog returns to its own vomit, and the sow, after washing herself, returns to wallow in the mire."

In verse 20 Peter speaks of the false teachers that he condemned in 2:1–19, not their followers (referred to in vv. 18–19), as Richard Bauckham explains:

> "They" are most naturally understood as the false teachers themselves, rather than their followers. . . . The false teach-

5. George M. Stulac, *James*, The IVP New Testament Commentary Series (Downers Grove, IL: InterVarsity, 1993), 188.

ers are in the state of definite apostasy described in vv. 20–22; their followers are doubtless in severe danger of joining them in it, and so these verses serve as a serious warning to the followers, but the author no doubt hopes that the warning will be effective in preventing them from sharing the false teachers' doom.[6]

Moral Progress

The false teachers' lives showed ethical progress. Peter's words "through the knowledge of our Lord and Savior Jesus Christ" may speak of coming to know Christ as Savior or possibly of gaining knowledge of Christ that falls short of salvation. The former meaning is more natural and is to be adopted unless there are contextual reasons not to.

Although the false teachers improve their lives through a knowledge of Christ, they later commit apostasy and revert to their evil lifestyle, which enslaves them. Jesus' end to the story of the return of the unclean spirit in Matthew 12:45[7] prompts Peter's evaluation: Their last state is worse than the first—before they knew of Christ. The descriptions "way of righteousness" and "holy commandment" stress Christianity's ethical demands. Peter bemoans that though the false teachers heard about the godly life expected of believers, they did not pursue it. The teaching did not profit them (v. 21).

Two Proverbs

Peter uses two adages (the first from Prov. 26:11, the second probably from the *Story of Ahikar*) to depict the false teachers' apostasy. He likens them to animals despised by Jews: dogs going back to sniff their filth or pigs once washed returning to the mire. In so doing he returns to an animal theme mentioned in the

---

6. Richard J. Bauckham, *Jude and 2 Peter*, Word Biblical Commentary (Waco, TX: Word, 1983), 277.

7. "Then it goes and brings with it seven other spirits more evil than itself, and they enter and dwell there, and the last state of that person is worse than the first. So also will it be with this evil generation."

preceding verses. He compares the false teachers to "irrational animals, creatures of instinct, born to be caught and destroyed" (v. 12). He blames them for leaving the straight and narrow way and pursuing the way of Balaam, the evil prophet rebuked by "a speechless donkey" (v. 16).

Most agree that 2 Peter 2:20–22 portrays the false teachers' apostasy. Does this entail the loss of salvation? Some, including Michael Green, answer affirmatively: "Apostasy would seem to be a real and awful possibility."[8]

Unchanged Nature

Others answer the question negatively, pointing to the following verses to inform their interpretation of the false teachers' knowledge of Christ in verse 20. Dick Lucas and Christopher Green hold this view:

> A *sow* was a ritually unclean animal in the Old Testament, and a *dog* was a repulsive scavenger. Coupled together by Jesus, they came to describe those who reject the gospel. The scavenging dog eating its own *vomit* and the sow *wallowing in* its own *mud* are both revolting pictures of "brute beasts, creatures of instinct" (2:12), and they vividly describe the false teachers. After an initial display of repentance and reformation, they show that nothing in their nature has changed at all, which is the last proof that these people never were Christians.[9]

I hold this view for three reasons. First, Lucas and Green correctly point to verse 22 as aiding in the interpretation of the false teachers' identity. In the proverb, the dog and pig do

8. Michael Green, *2 Peter and Jude*, Tyndale New Testament Commentaries, rev. ed. (Grand Rapids: Eerdmans, 1987), 131. See also I. Howard Marshall, *Kept by the Power of God: A Study of Perseverance and Falling Away* (1969; reprint, Minneapolis: Bethany Fellowship, 1974), 169–70.

9. R. C. Lucas and Christopher Green, *The Message of 2 Peter and Jude*, The Bible Speaks Today (Downers Grove, IL: InterVarsity, 1995), 122–23. Edwin A. Blum also takes this approach, *2 Peter*, Expositor's Bible Commentary (Grand Rapids: Zondervan, 1981), 283.

not change nature—they remain unclean animals. Similarly, though the false teachers experience outward changes, they are never regenerated.

Second, as Lucas and Green mention, Jesus refers to unbelievers as "dogs" and "pigs" in Matthew 7:6,[10] and Peter likely uses these terms in the same way in 2 Peter 2:22. Therefore, Peter's comparison of the false teachers to the same animals makes it more likely that he regards them as unbelievers than as apostate Christians. Third, we noted that Peter quotes Proverbs 26:11 in verse 22. And the "fool" of Proverbs 26:1–12 is better understood as a person never saved than as a believer who later repudiated his faith.

Peter's description of the false teachers in 2 Peter 2:20–21, then, when considered in light of verse 22, the Old Testament background of that verse's first proverb, and Jesus' saying in Matthew 7:6, leads me to regard the teachers as unregenerate persons affected for a time by Christian morality.

1 John 5:16–17: "Sin That Leads to Death"

> If anyone sees his brother committing a sin not leading to death, he shall ask, and God will give him life—to those who commit sins that do not lead to death. There is sin that leads to death; I do not say that one should pray for that. All wrongdoing is sin, but there is sin that does not lead to death.

John has just given the purpose for his first epistle ("I write these things to you who believe in the name of the Son of God that you may know that you have eternal life," 5:13—to bring assurance to his struggling readers) and has encouraged them in prevailing prayer. Now he speaks hard words. He acknowledges that "all wrongdoing is sin" and then makes a key distinction between "a sin not leading to death" and "sin that leads to death."

10. "Do not give dogs what is holy, and do not throw your pearls before pigs, lest they trample them underfoot and turn to attack you."

185

John has instructions concerning believers seeking to help others committing both types of sins. First, concerning "sin not leading to death," he says believers who see their brother committing such a sin should pray to God on his behalf and "God will give him life." Second, concerning "sin that leads to death," John teaches that no prayer is to be made for the person committing such a sin.

Although presumably John and his readers understood well what he was talking about, a survey of commentaries shows that we are unsure. What is "sin not leading to death"? John does not say "the sin" but "sin." This seems to draw attention to the act of sinning itself and not some particularly terrible sin. And though sometimes in Scripture sin leads to physical death (cf. 1 Cor. 11:30), that does not seem to be the case here. There is a consensus that spiritual death is in view.[11]

Robert Yarbrough writes wisely, "I propose that it makes the most sense to understand sin 'not unto death' as violation of God's will for which forgiveness is possible because (1) people seek it and (2) God therefore grants it."[12] John does not teach sinless perfection; rather all believers will sin and are to seek God's forgiveness (1 John 2:1; 1:8–10). "Sin not leading to death," therefore, is sin that does not lead to spiritual death for those committing it. For such sin, John enjoins the church to be vigilant and to pray for their members who are guilty of it.

"Sin That Leads to Death"

But what, then, is "sin that leads to death"? John is clear that all sin is wrong and that some sin does not lead to death: "All wrongdoing is sin, but there is sin that does not lead to death" (v. 17). He is also clear that "there is sin that leads to death" (v. 16). Moreover, he does not encourage prayer for

11. To cite one representative example, see I. Howard Marshall, *The Epistles of John*, The New International Commentary on the New Testament (Grand Rapids: Eerdmans, 1978), 247.
12. Robert W. Yarbrough, *1–3 John*, Baker Exegetical Commentary on the New Testament (Grand Rapids: Baker Academic, 2008), 308.

those who commit such sin: "I do not say that one should pray for that" (v. 16).

In order to understand "sin that leads to death," we must understand John's idea of what it means to know God in salvation. Those whom God regenerates believe in Jesus, live basically godly lives, and love other believers. In John's view, those who do not believe in Jesus, who live basically ungodly lives, and who do not love believers have not been born again; they do not know God. "Christians . . . are not chronically characterized by these fundamental deficiencies or lapses. If they are, they are not Christians, in John's outlook."[13] Again Yarbrough's words are wise: "The 'sin unto death' is simply violation of the fundamental terms of relationship with God that Jesus Christ mediates. This is sin that marks a person's confession, behavior, or affections as defective in God's sight."[14]

Fallen from Grace?

Some conclude that John here teaches that believers in Christ can commit apostasy and be unsaved: "We conclude that John attributes the possibility of 'sin which does not lead to death' to believers, but 'mortal sin' to unbelievers who are, or believers, who have become, antichristian."[15]

Respectfully, I disagree. Yarbrough gives an example of multiple murders without repentance committed by a sane woman claiming to belong to Christ and concludes that such behavior totally contradicts her claim to have been redeemed by the gospel. I agree with his conclusion: "To 'sin unto death' is to have a heart unchanged by God's love in Christ and so to persist in convictions and acts and commitments like those John and his readers know to exist among ostensibly Christian people of their acquaintance."[16]

13. Ibid., 310.
14. Ibid.
15. Stephen S. Smalley, *1, 2, 3 John*, Word Biblical Commentary (Waco, TX: Word, 1984), 299.
16. Yarbrough, *1–3 John*, 311.

Revelation 3:5: "I Will Never Blot His Name out of the Book of Life"

> The one who conquers will be clothed thus in white garments, and I will never blot his name out of the book of life. I will confess his name before my Father and before his angels.

A significant theme in Revelation is that of "the book of life" (3:5; 17:8; 20:12, 15) or "the Lamb's book of life" (13:8; 21:27). This theme first occurs in the letter to the church in Sardis, where Jesus promises the one who perseveres and conquers, "I will never blot his name out of the book of life" (3:5). Some have understood Jesus' words to imply that saved people can fall away from grace by having their names blotted out of the book of life. Grant Osborne, for example, affirms:

> Participation [in the book of life] depends on Christ's sacrificial death and the believer's faithful perseverance in Christ. Both aspects must remain intact. . . . The "book of life" itself contains both the names and deeds of all who claim allegiance to Christ, and only those who remain faithful will stay in it. The verb . . . I will blot out was often used of a name "erased" from a written record . . . and became a metaphor for removal or destruction. Here those who remain "unspotted" from the pagan surroundings are promised eternal reward in the presence of God.[17]

Names Blotted out?

Osborne interprets Jesus' saying that he will not blot people's names from the book of life as implying that some names will be blotted out and then concludes that remaining in the book of life depends on human faithfulness. But this misses the point of Revelation 3:5 as a part of one of the letters to the seven churches. Every letter promises final salvation to conquerors or overcomers. These promises are usually expressed in positive terms (2:7,

17. Grant R. Osborne, *Revelation*, Baker Exegetical Commentary on the New Testament (Grand Rapids: Baker, 2002), 180–81.

17, 26–28; 3:5, 12, 21), but three times in negative terms (2:11; 3:5, 12). It is helpful to see these promises summarized. To the one who conquers, Jesus makes the following promises (positive terms are marked with +, negative terms with –):

+ Jesus will grant the believer to eat from the tree of life in paradise, 2:7.
– The believer will not be hurt by the second death, 2:11.
+ Jesus will give the believer some of the hidden manna, 2:17.
+ Jesus will give the believer a white stone with a new name, 2:17.
+ Jesus will give the believer authority over the nations, 2:26.
+ The believer will rule the nations, 2:27.
+ Jesus will give the believer the morning star, 2:28.
+ The believer will be clothed in white garments, 3:5.
– Jesus will never blot the believer's name out of the book of life, 3:5.
+ Jesus will confess the believer's name before the Father and his angels, 3:5.
+ Jesus will make the believer a pillar in the temple, 3:12.
– The believer will never go out of the temple, 3:12.
+ Jesus will write on the believer God's name and the name of God's city, 3:12.
+ Jesus will grant the believer to sit with Jesus on his throne, 3:21.

It is imperative to see that both the positive and the negative terms serve the same purpose—to assure those who conquer of final salvation. So when Jesus says, "The one who conquers will not be hurt by the second death" (2:11), he means that the believer will certainly enjoy eternal life. In a similar vein, when Jesus promises to the one made a pillar in the temple, "Never shall he go out of it," he means that the conqueror will have a place in God's temple forever. And, therefore, when Jesus says, "I will never blot his name out of the book of life" (3:5), he means that the one who conquers will surely be found in that book.

Who is "the one who conquers"? By promising eternal blessings to the conqueror or overcomer, John is urging his persecuted readers to persevere. Only those who persevere to the end will conquer. But who are they? They are defined in 1 John: "Who is it that overcomes the world except the one who believes that Jesus is the Son of God?" (1 John 5:5). It is genuine believers in Christ who persevere so as to conquer.

Litotes

In Revelation 3:5, Jesus does not speak of names being erased from the book of life; rather by employing the figure of speech called *litotes* he emphasizes his promise. Litotes is "the negation of an antonym or contrary expression" to make an emphatic positive statement.[18] For example, when Paul says in Acts 21:39, "I am a Jew, from Tarsus in Cilicia, a citizen of no obscure city," he means that his hometown is important.

Thus never blotting out names from the book of life means assuring that the persons named will be included. This is confirmed by Jesus' very next words: "I will confess his name before my Father and before his angels." It is wrong, then, to cite Revelation 3:5 in an effort to make the strong consolation offered by the book of life passages dependent on human faithfulness.

Indeed, the main purpose of the book of life passages in Revelation is to assure those whose names are written in that book that God will protect them spiritually (3:5; 13:8; 17:8; 20:15; 21:27). Those written in the book of life from creation (17:8) will be spared the lake of fire (20:15) and will enter the New Jerusalem (21:27).

Revelation 22:18–19: Idolatry Reveals True Allegiance

I warn everyone who hears the words of the prophecy of this book: if anyone adds to them, God will add to him the plagues described in this book, and if anyone takes away from the words of the book

18. Richard N. Soulen, *Handbook of Biblical Criticism*, 2nd ed. (Atlanta: John Knox, 1976, 1981), 119.

of this prophecy, God will take away his share in the tree of life and in the holy city, which are described in this book.

This passage near the very end of Revelation contains a severe warning. For people to have the plagues described in Revelation added to them or to have their share in the tree of life and the New Jerusalem taken away amounts to the same disastrous end— everlasting hell instead of everlasting life. Though his quotation does not represent his final conclusion, George Ladd puts the matter plainly: this "seems to be a warning to believers who have access to the tree of life and the holy city that they will lose their salvation if they tamper with the wording of John's prophecy."[19] Is this correct?

Loss of Salvation?

After weighing the options with pastoral sensitivity, Grant Osborne concludes, "I would hold to the possibility of believers losing their faith. . . . Thus, the reader is warned here that distorting God's message in these prophesies is tantamount to apostasy, and the person guilty of it will become an apostate unbeliever in God's eyes."[20]

I courteously disagree. Viewing Revelation 22:18–19 in relation to two other Scripture passages illumines its message. First, Deuteronomy 4:1–3:

> And now, O Israel, listen to the statutes and the rules that I am teaching you, and do them, that you may live, and go in and take possession of the land that the LORD, the God of your fathers, is giving you. You shall not add to the word that I command you, nor take from it, that you may keep the commandments of the LORD your God that I command you. Your eyes have seen what the LORD did at Baal-peor, for the LORD your God destroyed from among you all the men who followed the Baal of Peor.

19. George Eldon Ladd, *A Commentary on the Revelation of John* (Grand Rapids: Eerdmans, 1972), 295.
20. Osborne, *Revelation*, 797.

Adding to or Subtracting from the Words of Revelation?

To "add to" or "take from" God's words (v. 2) given to Moses means to propagate or follow false teaching that contradicts God's Word, especially teaching that leads to idolatry. We know this from the reference to God's destroying the Israelites who "followed the Baal of Peor" (v. 3; see Num. 25:1–9). In a similar way, as Gregory Beale has taught me, John's prohibition against "adding to" or "taking away from" the message of Revelation "is directed against those who foster or follow such seductive teaching."[21] Thus many misunderstand John's words as prohibiting adding to or subtracting words from the book of Revelation. While that is wicked, it is not what John is talking about, as the Old Testament background makes clear. Reinforcing this conclusion is the fact that the lists of unbelievers' vices in Revelation 21:8, 27 and 22:15 all end with condemnations of deception and idolatry.[22]

The second section of Scripture that illumines the message of Revelation 22:18–19 is the letters to the seven churches (in Rev. 2–3). Some of these churches face idolatry, including those in Pergamum (2:14) and Thyatira (2:20–23).[23] Moreover, the rewards of Revelation 22:12–19 match some of the promises in the seven letters made to those who conquer. "Repaying everyone for what he has done" in 22:12 corresponds to 2:23. Partaking of the tree of life in 22:14, 19 corresponds to 2:7. The promise of entering the city of God in 22:14, 19 corresponds to 3:12.[24]

Idolatry Reveals False Profession

The promises and warning in Revelation 22:18–19 are not made to unbelievers but to the whole church community, just as the warnings of Deuteronomy were made to the whole nation of Israel. Seen against Deuteronomy 4:1–3 and Revelation 2–3,

21. G. K. Beale, *The Book of Revelation*, The New International Greek Testament Commentary (Grand Rapids: Eerdmans, 1999), 1151.
22. Ibid.
23. Ibid., 1152.
24. Ibid.

then, the warning of Revelation 22:19 does not speak of believers forfeiting their salvation because they added words to or took words away from the book of Revelation. Instead it speaks of false teachers and their followers who claim to be Christians but whose idolatrous actions show their true allegiance. This is in keeping with "the repeated characteristic highlighted in the closing portion of the book . . . of the counterfeit, double-dealing nature of people in the Christian community who will not receive the final reward."[25]

Connecting the Dots

Once more categories help summarize our findings.

Not the Point

The point of James 5:19–20 is not to settle debates over eternal security. Rather, James encourages Christians to restore wanderers, insisting, "whoever brings back a sinner from his wandering will save his soul from death and will cover a multitude of sins." James means that sin is horrible and that salvation involves taking Christ not only as Savior but also as Lord.

Unregenerate Persons Who Appeared to Be Saved

Three passages tell of unregenerate persons who appeared for a time to be Christians. Those in 2 Peter 2:20–22 were positively affected by Christian morality, but as "the dog returns to its own vomit, and the sow, after washing herself, returns to wallow in the mire," so they returned to the world's "defilements" and were "overcome" by them. They thereby demonstrated that their nature had never been changed by God's grace.

The "sin that leads to death" (in 1 John 5:16–17) is committed by professing Christians whose attitudes, emotions, and

25. Ibid., 1153.

actions showed that their hearts were unchanged. Those who commit this sin are similar to the antichrists spoken of in 2:19: "They went out from us, but they were not of us; for if they had been of us, they would have continued with us. But they went out, that it might become plain that they all are not of us." The church is not to pray for those who show that they do not know the Lord by persisting in flagrant sin, refusing to repent, and therefore reap God's wrath.

Revelation 22:18–19 is commonly misinterpreted. It does not speak of believers in Christ forfeiting their salvation because they added words to or took words away from the book of Revelation. Instead it speaks of false teachers and their followers who claim to be Christians but whose idolatry contradicts their profession.

These passages do not warn believers that they can lose eternal life; rather, they speak of those who were never believers.

A Strong Affirmation of Preservation

When viewed alongside the other promises to the overcomers in the letters to the seven churches (in Rev. 2–3), Revelation 3:5 does not deny preservation but affirms it. Using litotes—a strong positive made through denial of a negative—never blotting out names from the book of life means underscoring that the persons named will be included in it. Those who conquer (true believers) will never ever be removed from God's book of life; they will surely be included.

12

Connecting the Dots

WE BEGAN with the question: Why give attention to preservation and apostasy? To this we gave four answers. Now, after devoting ten chapters to biblical passages on preservation and warnings, we return with greater insight to the same four answers. Now, however, the last answer is first:

- The Bible Often Speaks of Preservation and Apostasy.
- God Uses Preservation to Assure His Children.
- God Teaches His Children the Need to Persevere to the End.
- God Warns His Children of the Danger of Apostasy.

The Bible Often Speaks of Preservation and Apostasy

We explored eighteen preservation passages in the Gospels, Paul, and the general epistles. And we examined twenty-four warning texts in the Gospels, Acts, Paul, Hebrews, the other general epistles, and Revelation. Surely preservation and apostasy are major biblical themes! But what have we learned about the significance of preservation and apostasy, their connections, and implications for life?

God Uses Preservation to Assure His Children

The Bible's case for preservation is even more powerful than we have shown. This becomes clear when we systematize our findings.

God Bases Our Preservation on the Roles of the Persons of the Trinity

Preservation is the work of God the Father, Son, and Holy Spirit. As we investigate the roles of each of the three Persons, we repeatedly encounter references to the other two Persons.

The Father. Viewed against its Old Testament background, Philippians 1:6 teaches that the Almighty Creator of everything, the Redeemer of Israel, is trustworthy to finish the work of salvation that he began in the church at Philippi. Because he is distinguished from "Jesus Christ," he is none other than God the Father. He preserves Christians' salvation until "the day of Jesus Christ."

Peter blesses "the God and Father of our Lord Jesus Christ" who in "his great mercy, . . . has caused us to be born again to a living hope . . . to an inheritance that is . . . kept in heaven for you" (1 Peter 1:3–4). The Father's mercy caused him to give us new life that results in a heavenly inheritance that we will not miss because it is "kept" for us. How can we be sure? Because it is "by God's power" that Christians "are being guarded through faith for a salvation ready to be revealed in the last time" (v. 5). The Father is the Protector of our salvation and will not let us fail.

The Son. The Son also has an important role in our preservation. He "will never cast out" those who come to him in faith (John 6:37). He will lose none of the elect but will "raise" them "up on the last day" to enjoy eternal life (v. 39).

In contrast to the Levitical priests whose deaths prevented their "continuing in office," Jesus "holds his priesthood permanently, because he continues forever." He is, then, "able to save to the uttermost those who draw near to God through him" (Heb. 7:23–25). Jesus, our High Priest, rose from the dead, lives forever, and saves believers forever.

Sin and Satan are enemies too great for every believer; on our own, each of us would fall. But the unique Son of God, "protects him, and the evil one does not touch him" (1 John 5:18). Because the mighty Son keeps us, Satan and sin do not defeat us.

The Holy Spirit. The Spirit too plays an important role. Ephesians 1 teaches preservation from a Trinitarian perspective. The Father seals believers' union with Christ with "the promised Holy Spirit" (Eph. 1:13). The Father thus permanently secures our bond to the Son by giving us the Spirit as a seal. Paul strengthens this idea by adding the image of the Spirit as guarantee. We now receive the Spirit as God's pledge of our full deliverance (v. 14). Later Paul adds the goal of God's sealing us when he says by "the Holy Spirit of God" we "were sealed for the day of redemption" (Eph. 4:30).

God Bases Our Preservation on His Attributes

We are kept because of who God is. Scripture reveals that he keeps us by his love, power, justice, and faithfulness.

Love. Paul affirms that nothing will ever sever God's people from his love: "For I am sure that neither death nor life, nor angels nor rulers, nor things present nor things to come, nor powers, nor height nor depth, nor anything else in all creation, will be able to separate us from the love of God in Christ Jesus our Lord" (Rom. 8:38–39).

Power. Jesus explains that his sheep "will never perish" because "no one will snatch them out of my hand . . . no one is able to snatch them out of the Father's hand" (John 10:28–29). The almighty Father and Son have a firm grasp on the sheep, and thus the sheep are safe. Peter praises "the God and Father" by whose "power" we "are being guarded through faith for a salvation ready to be revealed in the last time" (1 Peter 1:3, 5).

Justice. Paul writes, "Who shall bring any charge against God's elect? It is God who justifies" (Rom. 8:33). God the Judge, the supreme standard of justice, has declared us righteous, and no one will overturn his verdict. His justice guarantees our justification.

Faithfulness. Paul tells why he is confident that Jesus will sustain the Corinthians blameless until his return: "God is faithful, by whom you were called" (1 Cor. 1:8–9). Paul prays for the Thessalonians' final sanctification and extols God's faithfulness: "He who calls you is faithful; he will surely do it" (1 Thess. 5:24).

God Bases Our Preservation on Christ's Saving Events

We are kept not only because of who God is but also because of what Christ has done for us.

Death. "There is therefore now no condemnation for those who are in Christ Jesus" (Rom. 8:1). Why is this so? Paul explains: "By sending his own Son in the likeness of sinful flesh and for sin, he condemned sin in the flesh, in order that the righteous requirement of the law might be fulfilled in us" (vv. 3–4). In his sacrificial death, our Substitute took the penalty that our sins deserved so that his righteousness might be credited to our spiritual bank accounts.

Resurrection. Scripture bases our eternal security on Christ's resurrection: "For if while we were enemies we were reconciled to God by the death of his Son, much more, now that we are reconciled, shall we be saved *by his life*" (Rom. 5:10, italics added). Since God did the harder thing—he reconciled his enemies by Christ's death and resurrection—he will do the easier—he will keep them saved by that same death and resurrection.

Hebrews testifies that Christ "holds his priesthood permanently, because he continues forever," and "he is able to save to the uttermost those who draw near to God through him, since he always lives" (7:16, 24–25).

Intercession. Scripture bases our eternal security on Christ's intercession. When Peter denied Jesus, he did not fall from grace because, Jesus said, "I have prayed for you that your faith may not fail" (Luke 22:32). He prayed for his disciples' spiritual safety in his high-priestly prayer (John 17:11, 15, 24). Similarly, Jesus, our High Priest, preserves us by presently making intercession for us in heaven (Rom. 8:34; Heb. 7:23–25).

Second Coming. Scripture bases our eternal security on Christ's second coming. He will "never cast out" any believer or "lose" him but "will raise him up on the last day" (John 6:37, 39–40). That is why Peter urges, "Set your hope fully on the grace that will be brought to you at the revelation of Jesus Christ" (1 Peter 1:13).

Jesus performed a unique work to save us, and that excellent work keeps us saved.

God's Promises, Therefore, Are Trustworthy

Because Scripture bases our preservation on the Trinity's roles, God's qualities, and Christ's saving events, its promises are sure. Jesus categorically states that his sheep "will never perish" (John 10:28). Paul boldly proclaims that there is "no condemnation" for God's people (Rom. 8:1). He states that nothing "in all creation, will be able to separate us from the love of God in Christ Jesus our Lord" (Rom. 8:39). The Truth himself guaranteed his promise with an oath, "so that by two unchangeable things, in which it is impossible for God to lie, we who have fled for refuge might have strong encouragement" (Heb. 6:18).

As a Result, We Have Assurance and Give Our Lives to Him

God's preservation of his saints has massive implications for faith and life. He does not threaten to put us out of his family in order to keep us in line. Instead he assures us that he will always belong to us, and we will always belong to him! Consequently, preservation lays an unshakable foundation under our lives. We are God's people, and by his grace we are safe. So, then, let us enjoy this confidence of final salvation every day of our lives.

Does he preserve us so that we might lead careless lives? To ask the question is to answer it. If we abuse his grace, we should be ashamed of ourselves and repent. God's preservation is a great motivation to give our all to him who loves us and keeps us. What kind of people ought we to be in love and gratitude to him, in godly lives, in zeal for the lost! In Paul's words, "You are not your own, for you were bought with a price. So glorify God in your body" (1 Cor. 6:19–20).

God Teaches His Children the Need to Persevere to the End

Perseverance and Assurance Are Important Too

For years I have studied four biblical teachings and their interrelation. Due to space constraints I only treat two of them in this volume: preservation and apostasy. But assurance and perseverance are also important. Assurance is confidence of final salvation. To summarize biblical teaching, assurance is based on three things: chiefly on God's promises in Christ to save and keep us (the eighteen preservation passages), also the Holy Spirit's witness in our hearts (Rom. 5:5; 8:16), and God's work in our lives (Gal. 5:22–24; Heb. 12:14). God's work in our lives viewed from the standpoint of human beings' responsibility is our perseverance.

Perseverance is believers' continuing to the end in faith, love, and holiness. If we would be finally saved, we must not only make an initial profession of faith but keep on believing the gospel.

200

We must keep on loving God and other Christians. We must not continue living as before salvation but must live a holy life, which includes daily confession of sin (1 John 1:8–10).

We have focused on preservation and apostasy. But we must consider perseverance and assurance to round out the picture. Though we cannot devote chapters to these topics, for the sake of completeness we must see how they relate to preservation and apostasy.

There Is Dynamic Interplay between Preservation and Perseverance

God's Sovereignty and Our Responsibility. Preservation is God's work of keeping us, and perseverance is our work of keeping on. As such, their relation is a subset of the bigger relation between divine sovereignty and human responsibility. Scripture teaches that God is the sovereign Lord, God almighty, who is in control of his creatures and their actions (Ps. 33:10–11; Isa. 14:26–27; Rom. 11:36; Eph. 1:11). The Bible also teaches that we are responsible covenant partners with God (Josh. 24:15; Ezek. 18:20, 31–32; Rom. 14:23; 1 Peter 1:15–16). Though we lack the freedom that God has, every day we make genuine choices. For example, it matters whether or not we believe in Christ (John 3:17–18) and whether or not we share the gospel (1 Cor. 9:22). God's sovereignty and our responsibility are taught frequently in Scripture; so we have to affirm them both as true. But understanding how they fit together is very difficult and beyond the scope of this volume.[1]

Because the relation between preservation and perseverance is a subset of the relation between divine sovereignty and human responsibility, we cannot fully understand it either. That is one reason why we struggle to explain every story we hear of people falling away from the faith—we do not have all of the answers. But Scripture tells us what God wants us to know, and so we have some important answers.

1. See chapter 8, "Free Will," in my *Election and Free Will* (Phillipsburg, NJ: P&R Publishing, 2007).

201

God's Preservation Is the Cause of Our Perseverance. The connection between preservation and perseverance works in two ways. First, because God preserves us, we persevere. Because he keeps us saved, we keep on in the Christian life. This is evident in many passages. I will cite a few examples.

Paul repeatedly corrects the Corinthians and presses home their need to persevere in many areas (1 Cor. 1:11–13; 3:1–4; 4:8, 14; 5:1–2; 6:1–8; 10:14, 20–22; 11:17–22, 30; 15:12). Yet, he is confident that "the Lord Jesus Christ will sustain" them "to the end, guiltless in the day of our Lord Jesus Christ" (1:8). Why? Because "God is faithful, by whom" they "were called into the fellowship of his Son" (v. 9). Paul's confidence in God's faithful preservation undergirds his frequently urging the Corinthians to persevere. Amazingly, Paul's emphasis on preservation (1:8–9) precedes his numerous corrections. His confidence in divine preservation does not hinder his admonitions. And the Corinthians' need for instruction does not cause Paul to doubt whether the true believers among them (see 5:11; 2 Cor. 13:5) finally will be saved.

It is the same with the church in Thessalonica. After Paul reminds a healthy congregation of its need to persevere in love (1 Thess. 4:9–12) and holiness (4:1–8; 5:6, 15), he assures them that God will finally and perfectly sanctify them (5:23). He states why he is sure of this: "He who calls you is faithful; he will surely do it" (v. 24). God's faithful preservation assures their entire sanctification at Christ's return. But for Paul this is compatible with many exhortations to godliness. And the exhortations do not call into question God's preservation of them.

This same point is made by saying that perseverance is one of the means God uses to preserve us.[2] This is what Paul means when he tells the Philippians to "work out your own salvation with fear and trembling, for it is God who works in you, both to will and to work for his good pleasure" (Phil. 2:12–13). God commands the Philippians to persevere (to "work out [their] salvation") and

2. This is a major insight of Thomas Schreiner and Ardel Caneday, *The Race Set before Us: A Biblical Theology of Perseverance and Assurance* (Downers Grove, IL: Inter-Varsity, 2001).

does so because he preserves them (works in them to give them incentive and energy to obey his commands).

Paul exemplifies the fact that God uses perseverance to preserve his saints: "For this [to present disciples mature in Christ] I toil, struggling with all his energy that he powerfully works within me" (Col. 1:29). The apostle's labor and struggle (perseverance) is used by God who energizes him and works mightily in him (preservation).

Perseverance Is Also One of the Fruits of Preservation. First, looked at from God's vantage point, his preservation causes our perseverance; he uses perseverance to preserve his people. Second, then, looked at from the human vantage point, perseverance is one of the fruits of preservation. We keep on because God keeps us, and as a result our keeping on is evidence of his keeping us.

This too is seen in many passages. Jesus taught this when he repeated, "You will recognize them by their fruits" (Matt. 7:16, 20). The false prophets' appearance and impressive words are insufficient to save them because they are not saved (and kept) by God—"inwardly [they] are ravenous wolves" (v. 15). Calling him "Lord" and performing mighty deeds in his name is not enough. "Lawlessness" reveals the truth that Jesus "never knew" them with saving knowledge (vv. 21–23). True salvation, whether of prophets or disciples, shows up, as does the lack thereof. God's grace saves, keeps, and bears fruit.

Fruitfulness, therefore, is evidence of salvation and preservation, and fruitlessness is evidence of the opposite. So, "every branch that does not bear fruit" is cut off, discarded, "thrown into the fire, and burned" (John 15:2, 6). Fruitlessness reveals no eternal life, because God's salvation is real and shows up in fruit (Rom. 8:13; Gal. 6:7–8). This is the problem in passage after passage in Paul's condemnation of the false teachers in 1 and 2 Timothy and Titus. In a word, "They profess to know God, but they deny him by their works" (Titus 1:16). If professed Christians do not persevere, this is a very bad sign. It may point to the fact that God has not saved and preserved them.

God Warns His Children of the Danger of Apostasy

If preservation is biblical and believers cannot lose salvation, why does God include warnings in his Word?

Biblical Warnings Have Many Purposes, One of Which Concerns Apostasy

Reflecting on the twenty-four warning passages that we studied helps us to see God's reasons for issuing them.

To Help the Church Distinguish True Believers from False. By a large margin, the greatest number of warnings mark the difference between those who truly believe and those who do not. Jesus' principle sums up many passages: "You will recognize them by their fruits" (Matt. 7:16, 20, 21–23; Luke 8:4–15; John 15:1–8; Acts 8:13, 20–24). Closely related to it is Romans 8:13, which sharply distinguishes the lifestyles of the finally lost and saved.

Many passages expose inadequate faith, among them 1 Timothy 1:3–7, 18–20; 2 Timothy 2:11–13. Other passages warn against rejecting the gospel, including Matthew 10:33; 1 Timothy 4:1–5; and 2 Timothy 2:17–19. Still others expose unregenerate persons who appear to be saved (see 1 Tim. 5:8, 11–12; 2 Peter 2:20–22; 1 John 5:16–17; and Rev. 22:18–19).

To Show That God Hates Sin. Acts 5:5, 10 and James 5:19–20 serve chiefly to show God's attitude toward sin.

To Speak of Redemptive History and Not Individuals' Salvation. Paul treats God's dealings with Jews and Gentiles in faith and unbelief in Romans 11:20–22.

To Warn of Disqualification from Office. First Corinthians 9:27 warns of Paul's possible disqualification from apostolic office.

To Warn of Temporal Judgment. First Corinthians 11:32 warns of God's punishments in time on sinning believers, rather than in eternity.

To Underscore the Necessity of Perseverance. Many passages teach that professed Christians must continue to the end to be saved, including some warning texts: Colossians 1:23; Hebrews 6:4–8; 10:26–31, 35–38.

To Underline Preservation. Somewhat ironically, Matthew 24:24, 1 Corinthians 11:32, and Revelation 3:5 teach preservation.

We see, then, that God issues specific warnings in a variety of contexts. But the chief lesson from studying the warnings is that God's main concern is to distinguish true from false faith. Michael Horton's strong words are hard to hear but are vital: "The visible church is filled with hypocrites who outwardly have shown signs of faith and repentance but have never been truly united to Christ through faith alone."[3] Concerned Christians must pray for and lovingly challenge those who rely on a profession of faith but whose lives call that profession into question. Our study also underscores the need for more careful presentations of the gospel and better discipleship. And pastors need to be reminded that a well-rounded ministry of the Word involves at times sounding the alarm that to depart from Christ is to commit spiritual suicide.

Scripture Itself Correlates Preservation, Perseverance, Assurance, and Apostasy

Though the Bible does not contain a complete systematic theology of preservation, perseverance, assurance, and apostasy, it does bring some of these themes together.

3. Michael S. Horton, "A Classical Calvinist View," in *Four Views on Eternal Security*, ed. J. Matthew Pinson (Grand Rapids: Zondervan, 2002), 40.

Preservation and Apostasy Are Taught in the Same Biblical Books. It is striking that Luke, John, Romans, 1 Corinthians, Hebrews, and 1 John all appear in our study of both preservation and apostasy. What are we to make of this? Unless we are prepared to find contradictions in Scripture, which I am not, then the biblical writers are able to integrate preservation and apostasy. Because of their strong affirmations of eternal security, I argue that they do not intend their warnings to jeopardize the truth of preservation. Instead, along the lines of our findings above, they employ the warnings primarily to separate true from false believers.

In fact, one passage—1 John 2:19—does this very thing: "They went out from us, but they were not of us; for if they had been of us, they would have continued with us" (1 John 2:19). The apostates had been a part of the church but did not really belong to it—they were not believers. If they had been, they would have remained in the church. Here John correlates perseverance and apostasy. True believers do not apostatize; they persevere. Those who commit apostasy show by that act that they were not true believers: "But they went out, that it might become plain that they all are not of us" (v. 19).

All Four Doctrines Are Combined in One Extended Passage. There is an extended passage that correlates preservation, perseverance, assurance, and apostasy—Hebrews 5:11–6:20. The writer first rebukes his readers for their spiritual immaturity (5:11–14) and reminds them of their need to persevere (6:1–3). He then issues a stern warning of apostasy to those with much exposure to the things of God (vv. 4–6). His agricultural illustration distinguishes true, fruitful believers from false, fruitless ones (vv. 7–8). Next he assures the majority of his readers that they are saved—"Yet in your case, beloved, we feel sure of better things—things that belong to salvation" (v. 9)—and that their fruit evidences it (v. 10). Then he urges his hearers to perseverance to bolster their assurance (vv. 11–12). Last, he gives a strong preservation passage (vv. 13–20), assuring his readers in eight ways.[4]

4. See page 88 of this book.

Why does the writer put the four doctrines together in this manner? Because he wants us to understand them in interrelation. His extensive section on preservation makes it clear that true Christians cannot lose God's grace. But in his mind that truth is compatible with exhortations to persevere and even a warning against apostasy. Why? Churches are composed of believers and unbelievers. All need to be encouraged to go on with God. Unbelievers in the church need strong words to awaken them from spiritual slumber. Believers need to be urged to strengthen their assurance by relying on God's promises of preservation and walking close to him. And church leaders need to continue to give such exhortations, even if they lack God's knowledge of the true spiritual status of every member of their flock.

In the end the Bible has much to say about preservation and apostasy because God is very gracious to us. He wants those within churches who do not know Christ to come to know him; so he warns them of the danger of forsaking the gospel. He loves his people and wants to nurture their relationship with him; so through words of preservation and promptings to persevere he strengthens and assures them.

Three stanzas of John Newton's famous hymn "Amazing Grace" capture well these biblical truths.

Thro' many dangers, toils, and snares,
I have already come;
'Tis grace has brought me safe thus far,
And grace will lead me home.

The Lord has promised good to me,
His Word my hope secures;
He will my shield and portion be,
As long as life endures.

And when this flesh and heart shall fail,
And mortal life shall cease,
I shall possess within the veil
A life of joy and peace.[5]

5. Words: John Newton 1779. Music: Traditional American melody.

Questions for Study and Reflection

Chapter 1—Setting the Stage

1. Have you heard stories similar to Slade's?

2. Why do dedicated Christians, like Slade and his pastor, disagree concerning eternal security?

3. Have you known a Christian who committed suicide? What effect did it have on others?

4. Do you agree with his pastor's counsel to Craig? Have you observed "once saved, always saved" being abused?

5. My student former Paul tells one sad and one glorious story about professed Christians who fell away. Do these stories raise questions in your mind?

6. Were you aware of how much the Bible has to say about preservation and apostasy?

Chapter 2—Preservation and Apostasy in the Old Testament

1. God's preservation of Old Testament Israel as a nation is based on his covenant with, choice of, and love for the nation. How do these three factors fit together?

2. Israel's apostasy is evident in the wilderness rebellion. Did the Israelites who died in the desert suffer God's temporal punishment, eternal punishment, or both?

3. How did God demonstrate his love for Israel after the Babylonian captivity?

4. How do God's dealings with Jacob show God's preservation of individuals?

5. How does Esau's life demonstrate the apostasy of an individual Israelite?

6. In New Testament terms, was King Saul ever born again? Why do you answer as you do?

Chapter 3—Preservation in the Gospels

1. Though Peter denies Christ three times (in Luke 22:57–60), his faith does not completely fail. Why?

2. In what ways do the Father and Son work together to keep believers according to John 6:35–44?

3. Should we qualify Jesus' promise, "They will never perish" (John 10:28)?

4. How do the Father and Son preserve the sheep according to John 10:28–30?

5. Describe the ways in which Jesus' intercession for his own in John 17 preserves them.

6. Did Judas lose his salvation (John 17:12)? Explain your answer.

Chapter 4—Preservation in Paul, Part 1

1. Explain how Paul uses the Jewish argument from harder to easier to teach preservation in Romans 5:9–10.

2. Put together what Paul says in Romans 8:1 with his teaching in verses 3–4.

3. How does the apostle argue for eternal security in Romans 8:29–30?

4. Explain how we know for sure that almighty God is on our side (Rom. 8:31–32).

5. The Son of God will judge all humankind. Should we fear condemnation (Rom. 8:34)?

6. Show the comprehensiveness of Paul's language in Romans 8:38–39.

Chapter 5—Preservation in Paul, Part 2

1. Explain how God's faithfulness undergirds the Corinthians' final salvation (1 Cor. 1:8–9).

2. Ironically, God's visiting the sinning Corinthians with weakness, illness, and even death proves their preservation (1 Cor. 11:30–32). Explain.

3. What is the Holy Spirit's role in preservation according to Ephesians 1:13–14; 4:30?

4. How does the background in Genesis and Isaiah illumine Philippians 1:6?

5. Sanctification is initial, progressive, and final. Which aspect does Paul highlight in 1 Thessalonians 5:23? How does this testify to our preservation?

6. Where does Paul place his confidence that the Thessalonians will persevere (v. 24)?

Chapter 6—Preservation in the General Epistles

1. Why does God, who is Truth, swear an oath to guarantee his truthfulness (Heb. 6:17–18)?

2. Explain how the mixing of maritime and religious metaphors by the writer of Hebrews assures our final salvation (Heb. 6:19–20).

3. How does Jesus' resurrection guarantee our preservation (Heb. 7:24–25)?

4. Peter speaks of a "kept" inheritance and "guarded" people (1 Peter 1:4–5). Explain how both show preservation.

5. Explain how John's words about first-century antichrists (1 John 2:19) assume eternal security.

6. Ultimately, why are believers not destroyed by sin and Satan (1 John 5:18)?

Chapter 7—Warnings in the Gospels and Acts

1. What does Jesus mean when he tells the miracle-workers, "I never knew you" (Matt. 7:23)?

2. Jesus separates true disciples from false ones in Matthew 10:32–33. Explain how.

3. Which of the four types of soil (Luke 8:5–8) represents Christians? How do you know?

4. What do the fruitless branches of John 15:2, 6 stand for?

5. Are Ananias and Sapphira (Acts 5:5, 10) good examples of believers who lost salvation?

6. Evaluate Simon the sorcerer's faith (Acts 8:13, 20–24) based on the context.

Chapter 8—Warnings in Paul, Part 1

1. Explain how the two bold truths of Romans 8:13 are compatible with eternal security.

2. How do Romans 8:1–4, 28–39 influence your understanding of 8:13?

3. When Romans 11:22 warns of branches being "cut off," does it threaten individual believers with the loss of salvation? Explain your answer.

4. Paul fears disqualification in 1 Corinthians 9:27. Is he referring to forfeiture of his salvation?

5. How can we reconcile Paul's insistence that believers persevere in faith to the end to be saved (Col. 1:23) with preservation?

6. Do you find the writer's labeling Colossians 1:21–23 inconclusive for the debate about preservation unsettling? Explain.

Chapter 9—Warnings in Paul, Part 2

1. How does 1 Timothy 1:5–7 shed light on Hymenaeus's and Alexander's shipwrecked faith in 1:19–20?

2. Are those who "depart from the faith" (1 Tim. 4:1) lapsed believers? Explain.

3. Should we understand the one who is "worse than an unbeliever" (1 Tim. 5:8) as being formerly saved?

4. Explain why Paul condemns promiscuous young widows for wanting to remarry (1 Tim. 5:11–12) before he encourages young widows to remarry (v. 14).

5. Explain the distinction between church members denying Christ and being unfaithful to him (2 Tim. 2:12–13). How does this distinction uphold preservation?

6. Evaluate the author's appealing to earlier passages, especially 1 Timothy 1:3–7, when interpreting later ones in 1 and 2 Timothy.

Chapter 10—Warnings in Hebrews

1. Why should we not regard the warnings of Hebrews 6 and 10 as hypothetical?

2. Explain how Hebrews 5:11–6:3 sheds light on the warning passage in 6:4–8.

3. Explain how the blessings of 6:4–5 are different ways of speaking of affirming the gospel.

4. How does the writer to the Hebrews indicate that the potential apostates of 6:4–6 are not saved?

5. Do the preservation passages of Hebrews 6:17–20 and 7:23–25 contradict the warnings of 6:4–6 and 10:26–29? Explain.

6. How does considering a pastor's perspective help us understand the warnings of Hebrews?

Chapter 11—Warnings in the Other General Epistles and Revelation

1. Was James 5:19–20 written to decide the debate between Calvinists and Arminians over eternal security? Explain your answer.

2. Show from the context that those who "escaped the defilements of the world through the knowledge of our Lord and Savior Jesus Christ" (2 Peter 2:20) were never saved.

3. Explain how committing "sin that leads to death" (1 John 5:16) reveals an unregenerate heart.

4. Does Jesus' promising the spiritual conqueror that he "will never blot his name out of the book of life" (Rev. 3:5) imply that some Christians' names will be blotted out?

5. Is the common understanding that Revelation 22:18–19 speaks of adding words to or taking them away from the last book in the Bible correct? Explain.

214

6. Identify the spiritual condition of violators of the prohibitions of Revelation 22:18–19.

Chapter 12—Connecting the Dots

1. Discuss at least one way in which each Person of the Trinity keeps us saved.

2. What qualities of God stand behind our preservation?

3. Explain how Jesus' saving deeds guarantee our final salvation.

4. How does God use warnings in his children's lives?

5. Why does the Bible say so much about inadequate faith?

6. Elaborate on how God uses the warnings of apostasy in the life of a congregation.

Select Resources on Preservation and Apostasy

Bateman, Herbert W., IV, ed. *Four Views on the Warning Passages in Hebrews*. Grand Rapids: Kregel, 2007.

Pinson, J. Matthew, ed. *Four Views on Eternal Security*. Grand Rapids: Zondervan, 2002.

Arminian Sources

Marshall, I. Howard. *Kept by the Power of God: A Study of Perseverance and Falling Away*. Minneapolis, MN: Bethany Fellowship, 1969; reprint, 1974.

Oropeza, B. J. *Paul and Apostasy*. WUNT 2.115. Tubingen: Mohr Siebeck, 2000.

Osborne, Grant. "Exegetical Notes on Calvinist Texts," in *Grace Unlimited*, ed. Clark H. Pinnock. Minneapolis: Bethany House, 1975.

_____. "Soteriology in the Epistle to the Hebrews," in *Grace Unlimited*, ed. Clark H. Pinnock. Minneapolis: Bethany House, 1975.

Pinnock, Clark H., ed. *Grace Unlimited*. Minneapolis: Bethany House, 1975.

———. *The Grace of God, the Will of Man: A Case for Arminianism*. Grand Rapids: Zondervan, 1989.

Shank, Robert. *Life in the Son: A Study of the Doctrine of Perseverance.* 2nd ed. Springfield, MO: Westcott, 1960, 1961.

Walls, Jerry L., and Joseph R. Dongell. *Why I Am Not a Calvinist.* Downers Grove, IL: InterVarsity, 2004.

Calvinist Sources

Berkouwer, G. C. *Faith and Perseverance*, trans. Robert D. Knudsen. Studies in Dogmatics. Grand Rapids: Eerdmans, 1958.

Carson, Donald. *The Difficult Doctrine of the Love of God.* Wheaton, IL: Crossway, 2000.

———. *Divine Sovereignty and Human Responsibility: Biblical Perspectives in Tension.* Grand Rapids: Baker, 1994.

———. *How Long, O Lord?: Reflections on Suffering and Evil.* Grand Rapids: Baker, 1990.

Peterson, Robert A. *Election and Free Will.* Explorations in Biblical Theology. Phillipsburg, NJ: P&R Publishing, 2007.

Peterson, Robert A., and Michael D. Williams. *Why I Am Not an Arminian.* Downers Grove, IL: InterVarsity, 2004.

Schreiner, Thomas R., and Ardel B. Caneday, *The Race Set before Us: A Biblical Theology of Perseverance and Assurance.* Downers Grove, IL: InterVarsity, 2001.

Schreiner, Thomas R., and Bruce A. Ware, eds. *Still Sovereign: Contemporary Perspectives on Election, Foreknowledge, and Grace.* Grand Rapids: Baker, 1995, 2000.

Volf, Judith M. Gundry. *Paul and Perseverance: Staying In and Falling Away.* Louisville: Westminister/John Knox. 1990.

Index of Scripture

Genesis
1–2—79
2:2—79
12—12
15—12
17—12
17:4—12
17:5–6—12
17:6–8—12
17:7—12
22:17—86
25:21–26—22
25:31–33—20
25:34—23
26:7—20
27—23
27:19—20
27:24—20
27:30–40—23
27:35—20
27:41—23
28:15—20
31:20—20
31:31—20
33:3—20
33:8—20
35:9–15—20
41:42—76

Exodus
34:6–7—13

Numbers
11–14—16
14:21–24—18n3
16—16
20—16
23:19—82
25—16
25:1–9—192

Deuteronomy
4:1–3—191–92
4:2—192
4:3—192
7:6–8—13
17:2–3—166
28—22
28:26—22
28:30—22
28:41—17
30:19—181
32:35–36—168

Joshua
24:14–15—22
24:15—201

1 Samuel
9:1–2—24
9:15–17—24
10:1—24
10:6—24

10:10—24
11—24
11:6—24
11:15—24
12:22—14
13:1–7—24
13:13–14—24
13:14—20
15–16—24
16:13—24
16:14—24
18:11—25
18:12—24
18:17—25
18:21—25
18:25—25
18:29—24
19:1—25
19:10—25
19:11—25
19:15—25
19:23—24
20:31—25
20:33—25
22:18—25
23:15—25
23:25–26—25
24:2—25
24:3–15—25
24:11—25
26:2—25
26:7–12—25
26:21—25
28—25

2 Samuel
11—20
12:9—20
12:13—20

1 Kings
19:10—15
19:18—15

2 Kings
15:29—17
24:14–15—17–18

Ezra
2:1–2—18

Psalms
32:1—181
32:1–2—21
33:10–11—201
44:22—66
51—21
51:1—21
51:4—21
51:12—21
78—16
78:32—16
78:36–37—16
78:38—16–17
78:40—16
78:54–55—16–17
78:68—16–17
78:70—16–17
85:2—181
94:16–18—19
103:10–11—14
125:1—19
125:1–2—19
125:2—19

Proverbs
12:28—181
26:1–12—185
26:11—183, 185

Isaiah
1:27–28—18
5:1–7—109
14:26–27—201
42:5–6—79
43:1—79
45:17—19
54:10—19

Jeremiah
31:3—14

Ezekiel
18:20—201
18:31–32—201
34:10—37

Daniel
6:17—76

Hosea
2:14—14
2:19–20—14

Micah
4–5—18

Habakkuk
2:3–4—169

Malachi
3:16–17—15

Matthew
3:10—171
7:6—185
7:15—102, 203
7:16—103, 117, 203–4
7:16–19—102

7:17–18—102
7:19—102, 171
7:20—103, 117, 203–4
7:21—103
7:21–23—9, 101–3, 117, 176, 203–4
7:22—103
7:23—103, 117, 212
10:1–5—104
10:5–8—149
10:5–15—103
10:16–20—149
10:16–25—104
10:17–42—104
10:18–20—104
10:26—149
10:28—104, 149
10:32—104
10:32–33—104, 149–50, 212
10:33—9, 101, 103, 117, 204
12:33–37—71
12:45—183
13:20—108
13:23—108, 118
24:9—108
24:9–13—105
24:21—108
24:22—105
24:22–24—105
24:23—105
24:24—9, 101, 105, 117, 205
24:29—108
26:39—106
27:66—76

Luke
8:4–15—117, 204
8:5–8—107, 212
8:5–15—9, 101, 106–7

221

8:12—107
8:13—107
8:14—108
8:15—108, 117
9:45—171
22:22—46
22:28–30—28
22:31—28
22:31–34—9, 27, 49
22:32—28, 30, 49, 199
22:34—29
22:54–55—29
22:57—29
22:57–60—210
22:58—29
22:59—29
22:60—29
22:62—29

John
1:3–4—38
1:12—63
3:17–18—201
3:19–21—109
3:36—109
5:21—38
5:24—109
6—36
6:35—9, 27, 32–33, 38
6:35–44—210
6:37—33–36, 49, 196, 199
6:37–40—9, 27, 32, 49
6:37–54—33
6:39—3, 34–36, 49, 196
6:39–40—199
6:40—34–35
6:44—9, 27, 32, 34–35, 49
6:64—41, 45–46
6:70–71—45
8:42–44—109

8:44—47
10—44
10:1—41
10:7–18—98
10:8—41
10:12—41
10:25—37
10:25–30—9, 27, 37, 49
10:26—37
10:28—2, 4, 38–40, 49, 199, 210
10:28–29—41, 98, 197
10:28–30—41, 48, 210
10:29—33, 39, 50
10:30—40, 50
11:25—38
12:3–5—45
12:4–6—110
12:6—45–46
12:7—45
12:31—47
13:2—46–47
13:10–11—45
13:19—46
13:26—46
13:27—46–47, 110
13:28–29—110
13:30—110
14:6—38
14:23–24—109
14:30—47
15—109
15:1–8—9, 101, 109–10, 118, 204
15:2—109–10, 203, 212
15:2–3—110
15:3—110
15:5—110
15:6—36, 110, 171, 203, 212
15:7—110
15:8—110, 118
15:9—111

15:10—111
15:12–13—111
15:12–14—111
15:16—111
15:19—111
16:11—47
17—42, 48, 50, 210
17:1–5—42
17:2—33
17:3—43
17:4—42
17:6—33, 43
17:6–8—43
17:6–19—42
17:9—42
17:9–10—33–34, 42
17:9–12—9, 27, 42, 49
17:11—42–44, 48, 50, 199
17:11–12—31–32, 42
17:12—43–44, 46, 48, 50, 210
17:14—47
17:15—9, 27, 31–32,
    42, 47–50, 199
17:17—42
17:18—42
17:19—42
17:20–26—42
17:21—42
17:22—42
17:23—42
17:24—9, 27, 31–33,
    42, 47–50, 199
17:26—43
21:15–17—30

Acts
2:23—46, 62
4:27–28—46
4:32—112
4:33–34—112

4:34–35—112
4:36–37—112
5:1–11—111–12
5:3–4—113
5:5—9, 101, 111, 113,
    117, 204, 212
5:7–8—113
5:9—113
5:10—9, 101, 111, 113, 117, 204,
    212
8:9–11—115
8:10—114
8:11—114
8:12—114
8:12–13—116
8:13—9, 101, 114, 118, 204, 212
8:14–17—115
8:18–19—115
8:20–21—115
8:20ff.—116
8:20–23—115
8:20–24—9, 101, 114, 118, 204,
    212
8:21–22—115
8:23—116
8:24—116
12—30
14:15—181
15:19—181
16:11–40—78
21:39—190
26:5—62
26:18—181

Romans
1:18—54n
2:5—54n
2:8—54n
2:28–29—19
3:5—54n

223

3:25—59
3:25–26—51
4:6—21
4:7—181
4:25—55n3
5:1—52–53
5:1–5—53
5:1–11—53, 55
5:2—52–53
5:2–5—53
5:3–4—52
5:5—52–54, 200
5:6—53
5:6–8—52–53
5:7—52
5:8—53
5:9—54–55, 55n3
5:9–10—9, 51, 53–54, 68, 82, 125, 134, 210
5:10—54–55, 55n3, 198
5:11—53
5:12—181
5:12–21—51, 56
5:16—56, 60
5:18—51–52, 56, 60
5:18–19—56
5:19—71
6—56
6:1–11—57
6:1–7:25—56
6:3—57
6:3–5—148
7—56
7:6—56
7:25—56–57
8—57, 64, 126, 161
8:1—56–60, 68, 198–99, 210
8:1–4—9, 51, 56, 68, 82, 121–22, 125, 134, 213
8:1–4a—59

8:1–13—56
8:2—57
8:2–4—119–20
8:3—58, 60
8:3–4—198, 210
8:3b—59
8:4—58–60
8:4bff.—59
8:4b–17—58
8:5–8—120
8:6—120
8:7–8—120
8:9—120
8:10–11—120
8:12–13—120
8:13—9, 119, 119n, 120–22, 134, 203–4, 212, 213
8:14—121–22, 134
8:16—200
8:17—65
8:18—61
8:22—61
8:23—61
8:26—61
8:26–27—66
8:28—61
8:28–39—9, 51, 60, 82, 121–22, 125, 134, 213
8:29—62–63
8:29–30—33, 61–64, 211
8:29–39—68
8:30—61, 63
8:31—64
8:31–32—61, 64, 211
8:32—64
8:33—65, 198
8:33–34—61, 65
8:34—31–32, 49, 60, 65–66, 199, 211
8:34b—60

8:35—66
8:35–39—61, 66
8:36—66
8:37—66
8:38–39—3, 67, 197, 211
8:39—67, 199
9:6—19
9:22—54n
10:9—102–3
11—123
11:1—123
11:2—62
11:5—123
11:7–10—123
11:11—123
11:12–16—123
11:17—125
11:17–18—124
11:17–24—122–23
11:19—125
11:19–22—124
11:20–22—9, 119, 122, 134, 204
11:22—124, 213
11:23—125
11:24—125
11:36—201
12:19—54n
14:23—201

1 Corinthians
1—72
1:1–3—70
1:1–7—70
1:4—9, 69, 82, 134
1:4–9—69
1:8—70, 202
1:8–9—9, 69, 82, 134, 198, 202, 211
1:9—71, 202
1:11–13—202

3—71
3:1–4—202
3:21–23—65
4:8—202
4:14—202
5—71
5:1–2—202
5:11—176, 202
6—71
6:1–8—202
6:9–11—45
6:19–20—200
7—71
7:14—168
8:1—129
9—128, 130, 134
9:1–22—129
9:2—76
9:4–6—130
9:5—129
9:12—129
9:14—130
9:15—129
9:16—126
9:18—126, 129
9:19—129
9:19–22—126
9:22—129, 201
9:22–23—126
9:24—127
9:24–27—126, 128–29
9:25—127
9:26–27—127
9:27—9, 119, 126–30, 134, 204, 213
10—71
10:14—202
10:20–22—202
11—71
11:17–22—202

11:27—73
11:27–32—9, 134
11:27–33—69, 72, 82
11:28—73
11:29—73
11:29–34—73
11:30—73, 181, 186, 202
11:30–32—211
11:31—73
11:32—73, 113, 205
11:34—73
12–14—71
15—71
15:12—202
15:20—79
15:45—79
15:47—79
15:56—181

2 Corinthians
1:21—76
1:21–22—76–77
1:22—76–77
5:3—133
5:21—59
13:3—128
13:5—3, 128, 176, 202
13:6—128

Galatians
3:4—133
3:13—59
3:24—63
5:5—71
5:22–24—200
6:7–8—119n, 134n, 203

Ephesians
1—197
1:4—62

1:4–5—76
1:7—76
1:11—76, 201
1:13—76, 197
1:13–14—9, 69, 75, 77, 82, 134, 211
1:14—197
2:3—54n
2:8—153
3:2—133
4:21—133
4:26—77
4:29—77
4:30—9, 69, 75, 77–78, 82, 134, 197, 211
4:31—77
5:5–6—6, 176
5:6—54n

Philippians
1:1–5—78
1:6—9, 69, 78, 80, 82, 134, 196, 211
2:12–13—202
2:13—80

Colossians
1:12–14—131
1:15–17—130
1:18—79
1:18–20—130
1:19–20—130–31
1:20—131
1:21—131
1:21–22—131
1:21–23—9, 119, 130–33, 213
1:22—131
1:23—4–5, 132, 135, 205, 213
1:29—203
2:5—133

2:7—4
3:4—63
3:6—54n

1 Thessalonians
1:9—181
1:10—54n
2:16—54n
3:11–13—80
4:1–8—202
4:3–6—81
4:9–12—202
5:6—202
5:9—54n
5:15—202
5:23—202, 211
5:23–24—9, 69, 80, 82, 134
5:24—81, 198, 202, 211

2 Thessalonians
2:14—63

1 Timothy—138, 144, 150, 153
1:3—138, 153
1:3–7—138–39, 141–43, 154–55,
    204, 213
1:5—138
1:5–7—139, 213
1:6–7—153
1:8–11—138
1:18—138
1:18–19—139
1:18–20—9, 137, 139, 154, 204
1:19—138
1:19–20—138–39, 141, 213
1:20—140, 151
3:15—140–41
3:16—140–41
4:1—9, 137, 140–42, 213
4:1–2—143, 154

4:1–5—140, 143, 154–55, 204
4:2—142
4:3—142
4:3–5—142
5:1–2—144
5:3—144–45
5:3–16—144
5:4—145–46
5:4–7—145
5:6—145, 148, 155
5:7—145
5:8—9, 137, 144–45, 155, 204,
    213
5:9–10—147
5:11—147
5:11–12—9, 137, 146–47, 155,
    204, 213
5:11–15—145
5:12—148, 155
5:14—147, 213
5:15—147
5:17–25—144
6:1–2—144
6:9–10—154n
6:20–21—155n

2 Timothy—150–51, 153
1:8–9—63
1:9—62
2:1–7—149
2:1–10—148
2:8—148
2:8–10—149
2:8–14—151
2:9—148
2:10—148
2:11—148
2:11–13—9, 137, 148, 154, 204
2:12—149–50, 154
2:12–13—213

2:13—150, 154
2:14—151
2:15—151
2:16—151
2:16–19—151
2:17—151
2:17–18—155
2:17–19—9, 137, 151, 154, 154n, 204
2:18—152
2:19—152

Titus
1:15—155
1:16—155, 203

Hebrews—91
1:1–2—27
1:3—39
1:5–2:5—159n6
2:1f.—174
2:1–4—157
2:2—170
2:16—86
3:1–4:13—159n6
3:7–4:13—157
3:10—170
3:11—170
3:12—171
3:12–13—174
3:12ff.—174
3:17—170
3:18–19—170
4:1—170, 174
4:1f.—174
4:6—170
4:11—170, 174
5:6—160
5:10—160
5:11—165

5:11–14—206
5:11–6:2—173
5:11–6:3—159, 214
5:11–6:12—9, 157, 159, 164
5:11–6:20—206
5:12—160
5:14—160
6—2, 165, 214
6:1–3—206
6:3—160
6:4—161–62
6:4–5—161–62, 167, 214
6:4–6—6–7, 158n2, 158n3, 159n4, 159n5, 160–61, 162n14, 163–64, 166n, 171–72, 173n34, 206, 214
6:4–8—160, 164, 173, 205, 214
6:4–12—86, 159n6
6:6—162–63, 171
6:7–8—163, 206
6:8—164, 171
6:9—164, 169–70, 172–73, 177, 206
6:9–12—164
6:10—164, 206
6:11—159, 174
6:11–12—164, 206
6:12—164
6:12b—86
6:13—88
6:13–15—86
6:13–20—87, 206
6:14—88
6:16—86
6:17—86, 88
6:17–18—86, 211
6:17–20—9, 85, 175, 177
6:18—88–89, 199
6:19—87–89
6:19–20—88, 98–99, 212

6:20—88
7:1—160
7:11–14—89
7:11–22—89
7:15–22—90
7:16—89, 199
7:23—90
7:23–24—90
7:23–25—9, 31–32, 49, 65, 85, 88, 91, 175, 177, 197, 199, 214
7:24—90
7:24–25—99, 199, 212
7:25—90
7:26—91
7:27—91
9:6—175
9:13—168
10—2, 165, 214
10:11—91
10:14—91, 98
10:19–25—165
10:19–39—9, 157, 159, 165
10:22—165
10:23—165
10:24—165
10:25—165
10:26—166, 170–71
10:26–29—7, 172, 214
10:26–31—166, 168, 170, 173, 205
10:26–39—159n6
10:27—159, 166, 170
10:28—166, 170
10:28–29—158
10:28ff.—174
10:29—167–69, 171
10:30–31—168, 170
10:31—159, 168
10:32–34—168
10:34—168

10:35–36—169
10:35–38—173, 205
10:37–38—169
10:39—159, 169–70, 172–73, 177
11—20–21, 25, 175
11:12—86
11:20—23
11:21—20
11:32—21
12:1–29—157
12:14—5, 200
12:14–16—174
12:15—23
12:15–17—23
12:16—23
12:25—170–71
12:25ff.—174
12:25–29—159n6
12:29—170

James
1:2—180
1:15—181
1:16—180
1:19—180
2:1—180
2:14—176, 180
2:17—176
2:19—176
2:20—176
2:26—176
3:1—180
3:10—180
4:8—180
4:11—180
5:1–2—180
5:7—180
5:7–12—180
5:9—180
5:10—180

5:12—180
5:13–18—180
5:19—180
5:19–20—9, 179, 193, 204, 214
5:20—180, 182

1 Peter
1:2—62
1:3—92, 94, 198
1:3–4—196
1:3–5—9, 85, 92
1:4—99
1:4–5—93, 212
1:5—93, 99, 196, 198
1:6—92
1:6–9—93
1:13—199
1:15–16—201
1:20—62
4:12—92
5:1—63
5:8—97

2 Peter
1:9—176
2:1–19—182
2:12—184
2:16—184
2:18–19—182
2:20—182, 184, 214
2:20–21—185
2:20–22—9, 179, 182–84, 193,
    204
2:21—183
2:22—184–85
3:17—62

1 John
1:3—72
1:8–10—186, 201

2:1—186
2:18–19—9, 85, 94
2:19—95–97, 99, 194, 206, 212
2:26–27—97
3:8—98
4:1–3—95
4:1–6—97
4:4—47
5:1—98
5:5—190
5:13—3, 97, 185
5:16—186–87, 214
5:16–17—9, 179, 185, 193, 204
5:17—186
5:18—9, 85, 97–99, 197, 212
5:19—98

Jude
1—98
3—153

Revelation
2–3—192, 194
2:7—188–89, 192
2:11—189
2:14—192
2:17—189
2:20–23—192
2:23—192
2:26—189
2:26–28—189
2:27—189
2:28—189
3:5—9, 179, 188–90, 194, 205, 214
3:12—189, 192
3:21—189
7:2–8—76
9:4—76
13:8—62, 188, 190
17:8—62, 188, 190

20:9—171
20:12—188
20:15—188, 190
21:8—192
21:27—188, 190, 192
22:12—192

22:12–19—192
22:14—192
22:15—192
22:18–19—9, 179, 190–92, 194,
    204, 214–15
22:19—192–93

Index of Subjects and Names

abiding in Christ, 19, 109–11
Abraham, 12, 86–87, 123–24
acknowledging Christ. *See* faith
    (trust in Christ)
Adam, 51, 56
adoption (as sons of
    God), 63, 72, 121
Alexander, 137–39, 151, 154, 213
Ananias, 111–14, 117, 212
anchor for the soul. *See*
    Jesus Christ
antichrist(s), 94–96, 194, 212
apostasy, 2–3, 11–12, 40–41,
    95–96, 141, 145, 148, 150,
    175, 180, 195, 200–201, 209
  irremediable, 160, 162–65,
    166–68, 171–72, 173,
    183–85, 187
  in the Old Testament:
    corporate, 14, 15–18;
    individual, 21–25, 210
  warnings of, 6–9, 22, 100,
    105, 157–58, 191,
    204–7, 214, 215
apostleship, 127–28
Arminianism, 91, 115, 133, 135,
    160, 162–63, 175, 182, 214
Ashby, Stephen M., 167

assurance, 1–2, 3–4, 6, 19, 40,
    49–50, 60, 66, 68, 80, 86–87,
    89, 97, 99, 110, 134, 150,
    159, 164–65, 168, 174, 185,
    189–90, 196–203, 205–7, 212

Barnabas, 112
Barrett, C. K., 127
Bauckham, Richard J., 182–83
Beale, Gregory, 192
Blum, Edwin A., 184n9
book of life, 188–90, 194, 214
Bruce, F. F., 114
burden of proof, 162, 169

calling,
  as effective to salva-
    tion, 33, 60, 62–64
  by the Father to the Son, 34–35,
    61, 63, 69, 71–72, 202
Calvinism, 133, 135, 161, 163,
    172, 175, 182, 214
Caneday, Ardel B., 36, 46, 132
captivity of Israel,
  Assyrian, 17–18
  Babylonian, 15, 17–18, 210
Carson, D. A., 41, 96–97,
    104, 106, 108
chiasm, 53

church, the, 74, 95, 96–97, 112,
    126, 130, 141, 144–45,
    150–51, 167, 175, 186, 192,
    194, 204, 205, 206, 207
Cockerill, Gareth L.,
    160–61, 162, 167
coming to Jesus. *See* faith
    (trust in Christ)
condemnation,
    none for believers, 54, 56–60,
        65–66, 68, 72, 73–74, 110,
        113
    of unbelievers, 59, 66, 74, 110,
        148, 155, 198, 199, 211
confessing faith in Christ. *See*
    faith (trust in Christ)
conquers, the one who, 188–90,
    192, 194, 214
conscience, 138–40, 142–43,
    153–54
covenant,
    Abrahamic, 12–16, 18–19,
        89–90, 124, 209
    new, 68, 90–91, 151, 158,
        165–68
creation, new, 79–80, 130

David, 14, 17, 19–21, 24–25
dead, spiritually, 57, 109,
    145, 148, 155, 176
death, saving someone's soul
    from, 179–81, 193
demons, teachings of,
    140–43, 154
denial,
    by Christ, 101, 103–4, 117, 137,
        148–51, 154
    of Christ, 27, 29–31, 101, 103–4,
        137, 148–51, 154, 213

departing from the faith. *See*
    faith (what is believed)
destruction. *See* hell
devil. *See* Satan
discipline,
    by God. *See* judgment: temporal
    self-, 126–29, 134
disqualification from service,
    126–30, 134, 204, 213
doctrine, 82, 206–7
    false, 138, 139–40, 142–43,
        153, 154
drawing. *See* calling

election,
    of Israel, 13, 14
    people given to Jesus, 34
    to salvation, 34
Elijah, 15, 123
Esau, 21, 22–23, 25, 174, 210
eternal life, 3, 32, 35–36, 49, 57,
    97, 108–10, 120, 122, 131,
    149, 163, 185, 189, 196
    as gift from Jesus, 2, 33–34,
        37–41, 43–44, 50
    as imperishable wreath, 126–27
examination, *See* self-examination
    (to see if one is saved)

faith (trust in Christ),
    and acknowledging Christ, 5,
        35, 49, 138, 153, 158, 160,
        166–67
    and being worse than an
        unbeliever, 144–46, 155
    false, 113, 117, 139, 205
    inadequate, 5, 107–8, 116, 153,
        175, 204, 215

profession of, 32, 114, 150,
153–54, 160, 166–68, 176,
200, 205
faith (what is believed),
departing from, 2, 6–7, 139,
141, 143, 146–48, 154, 155,
157, 164, 168, 213
as the gospel, 3–5, 41,
99, 141, 152, 157
and spreading the gospel, 30
false teachers, 95–97, 132, 138,
139–40, 141–43, 150, 151–52,
153, 154–55, 182–85, 192–93,
194, 203
Fanning, Buist M., 86,
158n3, 161
Fee, Gordon D., 142
foreknowledge, 33, 41, 60, 62–64
fruitfulness, 12, 102–3, 108,
109–11, 117–18, 163–64,
203, 206
fruitlessness, 106–8, 109–11, 116,
117–18, 163–64, 203, 206,
212

Gentiles, 92, 123–26, 134, 204
given to Jesus. See election
glorification, 33, 42, 50, 60,
62–64, 68, 109–10, 200
glory of heaven. See heaven
God,
faithfulness of, 15, 69, 71–72,
80–81, 86–87, 150–51, 165,
198, 202, 211
grace of, 5, 8, 13–14, 20, 22–23,
40, 52, 56, 63, 64, 68, 69–70,
72, 112, 114, 150, 152, 157,
160, 174, 193, 207
justice of, 61, 65–66, 68, 198

love of: for Israel, 12, 14–15,
19, 210; for the elect, 3–4,
52–56, 61, 62, 66–67, 68,
197, 199
mercy of, 7, 13–14, 21, 105
power of, 4, 64–65, 68, 92–94,
99, 106, 112, 114, 123, 196,
197–98
sovereignty of, 46, 61, 62–64,
68, 201
wrath of, 6, 51, 53–55, 57, 59,
105, 166, 194
gospel, the. See faith
(what is believed)
Green, Christopher, 184–85
Green, Joel, 31
Green, Michael, 184
Grudem, Wayne, 93–94, 167, 172

Harris, Murray J., 132n19
heaven,
as glory, 33, 47–50
hope of, 87, 89, 92, 98, 196
reserved for Christians, 33, 44,
48–50, 92–94, 99
hell, 39, 54, 54n1, 57, 102, 104,
116, 120, 171, 191
Hiebert, D. E., 96
Hodge, Charles, 125–26
holy place, the most, 87–88
Holy Spirit, the,
bringing victory, 120–21
intercession of, 66
law of, 56–57
living according to,
119–20, 122, 134
as seal of redemption,
75, 76–78, 197
sharing in, 6, 160–61
as Spirit of life, 56–57, 119

hope. *See* heaven
Horton, Michael S., 205
House, Paul, 20
Hughes, Philip E., 91, 158,
    161–62, 173–75
Hymenaeus, 137–39, 151–52,
    154–55, 213
hypocrites, 144, 205

idolatry, 5, 14, 19, 45, 71, 166,
    176, 192–94
immaturity, spiritual, 160, 206
immorality, 5, 23, 45, 71, 146,
    148, 155, 174, 176
imperishable wreath.
    See eternal life
inheritance, believers', 5, 64–65,
    75, 77, 92–94, 99, 164, 176,
    196, 212
intercession of Jesus Christ,
    29–32, 49, 60, 65–66, 89–91,
    98–99, 199, 210
Isaac, 12, 22–23
Israel,
    in the Old Testament, 11–22,
    24–25, 37, 79–80, 109,
    123–25, 168, 209–10
    as olive tree, 123–25
Israelites, 11, 13–15, 18–20, 22,
    33, 123, 166, 174–75, 192,
    209–10

Jacob, 12, 20–23, 25, 79, 210
Jesus Christ,
    as anchor for the soul, 85, 87,
    88–89, 98–100
    ascension of, 43, 47, 140–41
    death of, 25, 31, 48, 51, 53, 55,
    55n3, 58–60, 64–65, 68, 79,
    131, 148–49, 198–99, 165

as forerunner, 85, 88, 98
as High Priest, 30, 49–50, 85,
    87–88, 89–90, 98, 165,
    196–97, 199
incarnation of, 37–39,
    58, 60, 140–41
resurrection of, 25, 31, 43,
    47–48, 55, 55n3, 60, 65,
    68, 79, 92, 94, 112, 131,
    148–49, 198–99, 212
as second Adam, 51, 56, 79
Johnson, Dennis, 113, 115
Joshua, 12, 22
joy, 8, 21, 46, 52–53, 55,
    107–8, 168
Judas, 32, 44–48, 50, 110–11, 210
judgment, 72–74, 159,
    163–66, 170
    corporate, 122, 125
    of Israel, 209
    last, the, 71, 103, 117, 129,
    131, 150, 154, 176
    temporal, 73–75, 113, 117, 205
justification, 33, 45, 51–56,
    59–60, 62–65, 68, 70–72, 198
    as justice. *See* God: justice of
    and the law fulfilled by
    Christ, 56–59, 68, 198

Keener, Craig S., 36, 40–41
Kruse, Colin G., 95

Ladd, George Eldon, 191
Lane, William L., 87
law. *See* justification
legalism, 138, 140, 154
litotes, 190, 194
Lucas, R. C., 184–85
Luke, 31, 107, 112–14, 116, 118
lying to the Holy Spirit, 111–13

Marshall, I. Howard, 25n8, 32, 36, 48, 75, 105, 128–29, 132, 141

McKnight, Scot, 157, 159, 169–72

Melchizedek, 85, 88–90, 159

miracles, 102, 114, 116, 161, 163

money, 45, 112, 115

Moo, Douglas J., 58–59, 133, 181

Morris, Leon, 41, 81–82, 106

Mounce, William D., 143–44, 147

new covenant. See covenant, new

new creation. See creation, new

Nicole, Roger, 158, 168n23

oath (taken by God), 13, 85–88, 90, 98, 199, 211

Oberholtzer, Thomas Kem, 159, 159n6

O'Brien, Peter T., 79, 132

Oden, Thomas C., 138

olive tree, the. See Israel

Osborne, Grant R., 124–25, 162, 188, 191

overcomer, the. See conquers, the one who

Owen, John, 168n23

Paul,
  on preservation, 51, 54–57, 60–68, 69–72, 74–83, 85, 98–99, 121–22, 134, 210–11
  warnings of, 45, 119–20, 124–26, 134, 137, 141, 147, 151, 154, 204

peace with God. See reconciliation

perish (God's people will never), 2, 37–38, 40–41, 49–50, 197, 199, 210

persecution, 61, 66, 89, 94, 105, 108, 165, 168, 177, 190

perseverance, 4, 7–8, 30–31, 36–37, 40–41, 86, 89, 91, 96–97, 99, 105, 108, 125–26, 131–33, 135, 148–51, 164–65, 168–71, 175, 177, 188, 190, 200–203, 205–7, 213

Peter. See Simon Peter

Philetus, 151–52, 155

prayer of Jesus Christ. See intercession of Jesus Christ

predestination, 33, 60, 62, 62n11, 63–64. See also election

preservation, 2–4, 9, 32, 51, 54, 56, 60, 63–64, 66–68, 69, 82–83, 85–86, 88–89, 93–94, 99–100, 106, 121–22, 125, 150, 157–58, 166, 166n18, 169, 172, 175, 177, 194, 195, 197–98, 199–207, 213–15
  by the Father, 40, 43–44, 47–50, 75, 77–78, 196–97, 210
  by the Holy Spirit, 77–78, 197, 211
  by Jesus, 30–31, 34–36, 40, 44, 48–50, 70, 72, 75, 77, 91, 98, 196–97, 198–99, 210, 212
  in the Old Testament:
    corporate, 11–15, 17, 18, 19, 25, 209; individual, 18–21, 25, 210
  in Paul. See Paul
  promises of, 18, 20, 25, 36, 50, 55, 88, 93, 98, 188–90, 192, 194, 199–200, 207, 210, 214

profession of faith. See faith (trust in Christ)

proverbs, 182, 183–85

punishment, eternal. See hell

reconciliation, 51–55, 68, 130–31, 198

regeneration, 92, 97, 172, 185, 187

reigning with Christ, 148–50, 154

responsibility, human, 46, 146, 152, 200, 201

resurrection of the dead,
  having already occurred, 151–52, 155
  of believers, 34–36, 131

salvation, loss of, 2, 21, 24, 38, 50, 100, 101, 103–4, 117, 121, 124–26, 128, 130, 132–34, 152, 163, 181–82, 184, 191, 204, 210, 212–13

Sapphira, 111–14, 117, 212

Satan, 27–29, 46–48, 64, 98–99, 111, 113, 137, 140, 142, 144, 147, 197, 212
  as devil, 46–47, 97–99, 106–7, 109

Saul (king of Israel), 21–25, 210

Schreiner, Thomas R., 36, 46, 63, 92–93, 120–21, 132

seal of redemption. See Holy Spirit

second Adam. See Jesus Christ

second coming of Christ, 70, 72, 78, 79, 80–81, 94, 105, 165, 169, 198, 199, 202

self-examination (to see if one is saved), 3, 72–73, 128, 176, 177

shipwreck (of ones faith), 137–39, 213

Simon Peter, 27–32, 49, 92–94, 99, 111–13, 115–16, 118, 176, 182–83, 185, 196, 198–99, 210, 212

Simon of Samaria (Simon Magnus), 114–15, 115n13, 116, 118, 212

sin that leads to death, 185–87, 193, 214

sons of God. See adoption

sovereignty. See God

Stott, John R. W., 95, 97–98

suffering,
  of Christ, 59, 149
  of Christians, 52, 61, 92, 104, 149, 168

Thiselton, Anthony C., 71, 128

Towner, Philip H., 139, 143, 146–47, 152

trials, 61, 92, 93, 168

Trinity, 75–76, 167, 171
  and preservation, 77–78, 196–97, 199, 215

unbelief, 37, 122–26, 204

unity (of God's people), 112

unregenerate, 116, 184–85, 193–94, 204, 214

Verbrugge, Verlyn D., 158–59

Volf, Judith M. Gundry, 55–56, 60, 74, 78, 130

Wallace, Daniel B., 38, 96

Waltke, Bruce, 18

wandering from the truth, 179–82, 193

Westcott, Frederick Brooke, 132

widows, 144–48, 155, 213
wilderness wanderings,
    16–17
Witherington, Ben, III, 113,
    115–16

world (as foe of God), 46–47, 48,
    73–74, 98, 190
wrath of God. *See* God

Yarbrough, Robert W., 186–87